The East India Company, 1600–1858

A Short History with Documents

PASSAGES: KEY MOMENTS IN HISTORY

The East India Company, 1600–1858

A Short History with Documents

Ian Barrow

Hackett Publishing Company, Inc.
Indianapolis/Cambridge

22 21 20 19   2 3 4 5 6 7

For further information, please address
    Hackett Publishing Company, Inc.
    P.O. Box 44937
    Indianapolis, Indiana 46244-0937

    www.hackettpublishing.com

Cover design by Rick Todhunter
Interior design by Laura Clark
Maps by Beehive Cartography
Composition by Aptara, Inc.

Library of Congress Cataloging-in-Publication Data

Names: Barrow, Ian J., author.
Title: The East India Company, 1600/1858 : a short history with
    documents / Ian Barrow.
Description: Indianapolis : Hackett Publishing Company, Inc., [2017] |
    Series: Passages: Key moments in history | Includes bibliographical
    references and index.
Identifiers: LCCN 2016047052 | ISBN 9781624665967 (pbk.) |
    ISBN 9781624665974 (cloth)
Subjects: LCSH: East India Company—History. | East India Company—
    History—Sources. | British—India—History—Sources.
Classification: LCC DS465 .B38 2017 | DDC 382.0941/05—dc23
LC record available at https://lccn.loc.gov/2016047052

The paper used in this publication meets the minimum requirements of
American National Standard for Information Sciences—Permanence of
Paper for Printed Library Materials, ANSI Z39.48–1984.

∞

CONTENTS

ACKNOWLEDGMENTS

It has taken more than two years to research and write this book. My greatest debt goes to my wife, Dana, for her patience as I (endlessly) chatted about the seventeenth and eighteenth and nineteenth centuries, for her encouragement whenever I ran out of steam, and, most importantly, for her love. Along the way friends and colleagues have offered generous support and invaluable advice by reading the manuscript, discussing the ideas behind the book, or sharing their enthusiasm for the project. A heartfelt thank you to Andrew Amstutz, Febe Armanios, Michelle Baird, Hayden Bellenoit, Vivek Bhandari, Dan Brayton, Nat Caldwell, Maggie Clinton, Boğaç Ergene, Philip Gould, Rebekah Irwin, Maya Joshi, Adam Lougee, Joyce Mao, Sonali Mishra, Paul Monod, Cynthia Packert, Sumathi Ramaswamy, Mark Rogers, Awadhendra Sharan, and Kurt Suchomel. While writing the book I had my students in mind and I often shared drafts with my classes. The suggestions they offered were invariably thoughtful. Three anonymous reviewers provided detailed and helpful comments and I thank them for the considerable time they spent reading the manuscript and drafting their responses. Much of the writing was conducted while I was on sabbatical and I am grateful to Middlebury College for giving me that time. The book was first imagined in a conversation with Rick Todhunter on a cold winter's afternoon in Vermont. Ever since that serendipitous meeting, he has been an exemplary editor while his colleague Liz Wilson has expertly shepherded the book through production.

This book is dedicated to my mother, Yvonne. When I was a little boy she very often took me to visit castles, country estates, and museums spread across England and Wales. They were glorious trips, and since then she has never stopped sharing her delight in seeing and learning about the past. I could not have written this book without her love, inspiration, and encouragement.

CHRONOLOGY

GLOSSARY

The definitions below provide a quick aid to readers, but they are not comprehensive.

Awadh: A state in northern India, ruled by a Shia dynasty (1722–1856).

Banyan: A servant to the Company's British employees in India; also a merchant; also a long garment.

Batta: A Company soldier's additional pay; also a discount applied to coins after they had been in circulation for two and three years.

Begum: A wife or mother to a Muslim ruler.

Bhadralok: Socially respectable and usually wealthy upper-caste Bengalis.

Bills of exchange: Financial instruments allowing British Company servants, and others, to repatriate wealth from Asia or move money within Asia.

Board of Control: Established by the 1784 India Act to ensure British government oversight over the Company.

British India: The term used to describe territories in India under direct Company control.

Calico: Common name for cotton cloth.

Canton System: Chinese regulations established in 1760 requiring, among other stipulations, that all foreign trade be conducted through Canton and with a small group of specified Chinese merchants.

Cartaz: A license sold to merchants by the Portuguese in exchange for safe travel in the Indian Ocean.

Chairman: The title given to the head of the Company after the union of the two East India companies in 1709.

Committee: The title given to one of the twenty-four men who ran the Company. Collectively they sat as a Court of Committees. After

the union of the two rival English companies in 1709, the title
was changed to director.

Country trade: Intra-Asian trade; often a source of considerable wealth
for the Company's servants.

Currency: The Company minted its own coins. For most of its
existence it circulated a variety of silver rupees of varying weight,
size, and silver content. In Madras it also circulated gold coins.
Small transactions were made with copper coins or cowry shells.
The Company also developed an imaginary currency, called the
current rupee, that was only used for accounting purposes.

Director: The title given to one of the twenty-four men who governed
the Company after its union with its rival in 1709. Collectively
they sat as a Court of Directors.

Diwani: The right, given by the Mughal emperor, to collect the revenue
from a province.

East Indiamen: The name given to the Company's ships sailing to and
from Asia.

East Indies: A broad term for what is today South and East Asia.

Factor: A Company merchant; higher than a writer.

Factory: A Company settlement where trade was conducted.

Governor: The title given to the head of the Company before the union
of the two East India companies in 1709; he was aided by a
deputy; after the union the governor became the chairman; also,
in the eighteenth and nineteenth centuries, the title given to the
man responsible for the running of a presidency.

Governor General: A post created by the 1773 Regulating Act to
ensure that the governors of Madras and Bombay reported to the
governor of Bengal, now called the governor general.

Investment: The goods the Company bought in India.

Jagir: The right to collect revenue from specified land. A holder of such
a right, a "jagirdar," was not a landlord, and the ruler who gave the
jagir could, in theory, withdraw it at any time.

Maharaja or Raja: King, also given as a title to prominent men in India.

Mercantilism: An economic theory that holds that a country can increase its wealth by maintaining a positive balance of trade and reducing consumption of unnecessary foreign goods and products. Even though the Company exported silver and imported spices and cotton cloth, by the second half of the eighteenth century it was characterized as a mercantilist venture because it had a monopoly of trade to and from Asia.

Middling sort: Term used to describe the middle social orders, such as merchants, before industrialization and the rise of the middle class in Britain.

Mughal Empire: A powerful and wealthy Muslim dynasty that, at its height, controlled most of South Asia and much of Afghanistan. It was at its most powerful between its founding in 1526 and the death of Aurangzeb in 1707, although it lasted until 1858.

Nabob: A corruption of "nawab"; a term used to describe wealthy Company employees.

Nawab: Title of a ruler, often nominally subordinate to the Mughal emperor.

Nizam: Title of the ruler of the state of Hyderabad, nominally subordinate to the Mughal emperor.

Peshwa: Often described as the "prime minister" to the Maratha king, although by the late eighteenth century the peshwa had developed considerable independence.

Presidency: An administrative area of the Company. In the seventeenth century, Surat and Bantam were presidencies with subordinate factories under their control. They were superseded by Bengal, Madras, and Bombay in the eighteenth and nineteenth centuries. A presidency was run by a president or, by the eighteenth century, a governor.

Princely India: The term used to describe Indian states that were under indirect, not direct, rule by the Company.

Proprietor: Stockholder of the Company. On regular occasions throughout the year proprietors met as a Court of Proprietors or General Court.

Raj: Meaning "rule," the Raj is often used to refer to the 1858–1947 era of British rule in India.

Resident: The Company's powerful ambassador to an important princely state.

Rohillas: Muslim rulers, of Afghan heritage, who in the second half of the eighteenth century ruled a small state to the west of Awadh.

Safavid empire: A Shia Muslim dynasty that ruled Persia (Iran) from 1501 to 1736. The Safavids were contemporaries of and rivals to the Mughals and the Ottomans.

Sati: A woman who dies on her husband's funeral pyre; also the practice of dying on a husband's funeral pyre.

Spice Islands: Islands in eastern Indonesia where spices, especially cloves, nutmeg, and mace were grown.

Straits Settlements: The administrative term for the Company's territories on the Malay peninsula; specifically, Singapore, Malacca, and Penang.

Thug: A member of an early nineteenth-century gang that strangled and robbed travelers in India.

Viceroy: The title given to the governor general after the transfer of the Company's responsibilities to the British Crown in 1858.

VOC: The Dutch East India Company: Verenigde Oost-Indische Compagnie or United East India Company (1602–1799).

Wazir: Title given to a high minister in the Mughal Empire; the ruler of Awadh was often called the nawab wazir.

Writer: A junior employee of the Company; below a factor.

Zamindar: Revenue collectors in Bengal. After the Permanent Settlement (1793) zamindars became landholders.

LIST OF MAPS

LIST OF ILLUSTRATIONS

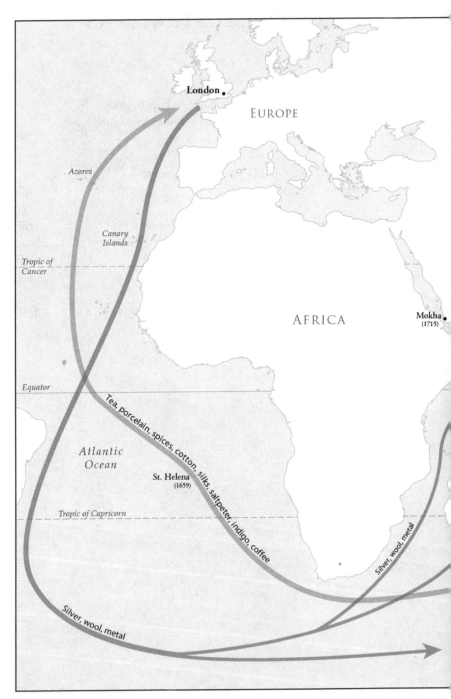

London

EUROPE

Azores

Canary
Islands

Tropic of
Cancer

AFRICA

Mokha
(1715)

Equator

Tea, porcelain, spices, cotton, silks, saltpeter, indigo, coffee

Atlantic
Ocean

St. Helena
(1659)

Tropic of Capricorn

Silver, wool, metal

Silver, wool, metal

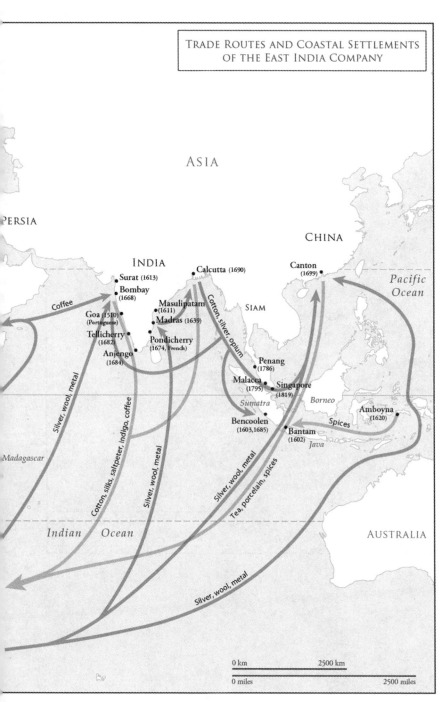

TRADE ROUTES AND COASTAL SETTLEMENTS OF THE EAST INDIA COMPANY

ASIA

PERSIA

CHINA

Pacific Ocean

INDIA

Surat (1613)
Bombay (1668)

Calcutta (1690)

Canton (1699)

Coffee

Goa (1510) (Portuguese)

Masulipatam (1611)

SIAM

Madras (1639)

Tellicherry (1682)

Pondicherry (1674, French)

Anjengo (1684)

Cotton, silver, opium

Penang (1786)

Malacca (1795)

Singapore (1819)

Silver, wool, metal

Sumatra

Borneo

Amboyna (1620)

Cotton, silks, saltpeter, indigo, coffee

Bencoolen (1603,1685)

Spices

Madagascar

Silver, wool, metal

Bantam (1602)

Java

Indian Ocean

Silver, wool, metal

Tea, porcelain, spices

AUSTRALIA

Silver, wool, metal

0 km   2500 km

0 miles   2500 miles

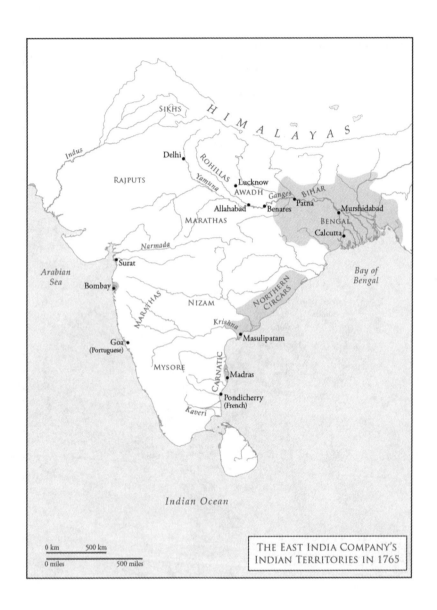

SIKHS

H I M A L A Y A S

Indus

Delhi

RAJPUTS

ROHILLAS

Yamuna

Lucknow
AWADH

Ganges

BIHAR

Patna

Allahabad

Benares

Murshidabad

MARATHAS

BENGAL

Calcutta

Narmada

*Arabian
Sea*

Surat

Bombay

MARATHAS

NIZAM

NORTHERN
CIRCARS

*Bay of
Bengal*

Krishna

Goa
(Portuguese)

Masulipatam

MYSORE

CARNATIC

Madras

Kaveri

Pondicherry
(French)

Indian Ocean

0 km   500 km

0 miles   500 miles

THE EAST INDIA COMPANY'S
INDIAN TERRITORIES IN 1765

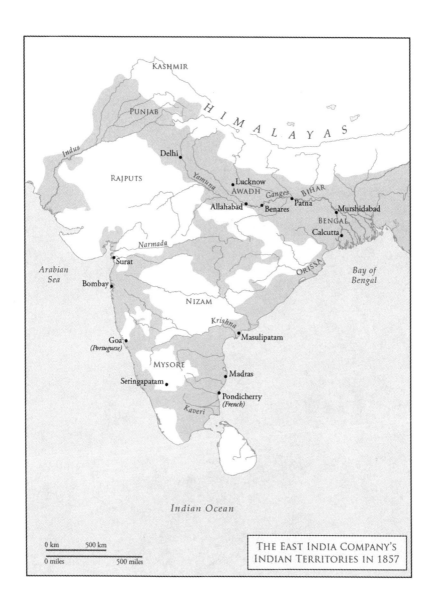

KASHMIR

PUNJAB

H I M A L A Y A S

Indus

Delhi

RAJPUTS

Yamuna

Lucknow
AWADH
Ganges
BIHAR

Allahabad
Benares
Patna

Murshidabad

BENGAL
Calcutta

Narmada

Surat

*Arabian
Sea*

Bombay

ORISSA

*Bay of
Bengal*

NIZAM

Krishna

Masulipatam

Goa
(Portuguese)

MYSORE

Seringapatam

Madras

Pondicherry
(French)

Kaveri

Indian Ocean

0 km   500 km

0 miles   500 miles

THE EAST INDIA COMPANY'S
INDIAN TERRITORIES IN 1857

INTRODUCTION

At about ten o'clock in the morning of August 5, 1775, an elderly man, thought to be seventy years old, was carried in a palanquin to a scaffold on the outskirts of Calcutta. A crowd of between eight and ten thousand had assembled at the execution ground and all eyes were on the passenger, Maharaja Nandakumar Bahadur (d. 1775). Nandakumar had once been a man of great power and wealth, rising to become the principal deputy to the ruler of Bengal, a province in eastern India. But by August 1775 his luck had run out. Just seven weeks earlier an all-white jury had convicted him of forgery, and a panel of British judges had sentenced him to "be hanged by the neck." The sheriff responsible for the execution, Alexander Mackrabie, tells us that when Nandakumar arrived at the scaffold he showed no signs of fear. He looked for friends in the crowd and instructed the sheriff that he wanted no one but his Brahmin attendants to touch his dead body. When told that he could choose the precise moment of his death by giving a signal to the executioner, Nandakumar suggested he would make that signal with his hands. Mackrabie replied that signaling in that fashion would not be possible since his hands would have to be tied, and so they agreed that he would move his foot. Nandakumar then mounted the scaffold with difficulty, "but he showed not the least reluctance, scrambling rather forward to get up. He stood erect on the stage, while I examined his countenance as steadfastly as I could till the cloth covered it, to see if I could observe the smallest symptom of fear or alarm, but there was not a trace of it. My own spirits sank and I stept into my palanquin; but before I was seated he had given the signal, and the stage was removed. . . . The body was taken down after hanging the usual time, and delivered to the Brahmins for burning."[1]

Nandakumar, known to the British as Nuncomar, had misjudged his ability to manipulate the new British governors of Bengal. He also

---

1. Sir James Fitzjames Stephen, *The Story of Nuncomar and the Impeachment of Sir Elijah Impey* (London: Macmillan and Co., 1885), 243–44. See also H. E. Busteed, *Echoes from Old Calcutta* (Calcutta: Thacker, Spink and Co., 1888), 89–90. The back of the indictment read: "guilty Sus. per coll. an abbreviation for the Latin 'suspendatur per collum', let him be hanged by the neck." J. Ghosal, comp., *Celebrated Trials in India* (Bhowanipore: Manomohan Press, 1902), 77.

tragically underestimated their ruthlessness. As a result of successful wars against Indian forces in 1757 and 1764, the East India Company made the ruler of Bengal its puppet and took control of the province. A subsequent reform of the Company's Bengal administration resulted in a divided governing council. Nandakumar saw the dysfunction among the British and believed that the time had come to increase his political influence by discrediting the governor general, Warren Hastings (1732–1818), with whom he had never been close. He therefore chose to ally himself with the three new members of the Bengal Council, who had arrived in Calcutta from London in 1774 and who constituted a majority and were hostile to Hastings.

In March 1775 Nandakumar publicly accused Hastings of corruption, alleging that he had accepted extremely large sums of money in exchange for specific political favors. Nandakumar no doubt hoped that these claims would force the governor general's resignation or, at the least, diminish him further as a force within the council. However, just two months later an old and nearly forgotten case of forgery against Nandakumar was suddenly, and somewhat mysteriously, revived and placed before the Supreme Court. No one had ever been executed by the Company for forgery, but the chief justice and the governor general were good friends, and it was widely assumed that Nandakumar paid the ultimate price for challenging the power of the British. As Nandakumar's lawyer later said, the effect of the execution was to spread "general terror and dismay" among Indians in Bengal.[2]

Nandakumar's execution came at a time of great change for the East India Company. Just twenty years earlier the Company was primarily a trading organization, and its concerns were those of the merchant—ensuring the safe passage of its ships, auctioning its goods for a handsome profit, and maintaining good relations with the king and Parliament of Britain, who gave it its charter, and with local Asian rulers, who permitted it to trade.

---

2. *The Parliamentary Register; or, History of the Proceedings and Debates of the House of Commons. Volume II* (London: J. Debrett, 1781), 496. More information on Nandakumar's trial can be found in Lucy S. Sutherland, "New Evidence on the Nandakuma Trial," *The English Historical Review* 72, no. 284 (1957): 438–65; Nicholas B. Dirks, *The Scandal of Empire: India and the Creation of Imperial Britain* (Cambridge: Harvard University Press, 2006), 225–30; H. Beveridge, *The Trial of Maharaja Nanda Kumar, A Narrative of Judicial Murder* (Calcutta: Thacker, Spink and Co., 1886); Keshub Chandra Acharya, *The Defence of Nunda Kumar: A Reply to Sir James Stephen's Book* (Calcutta: Wooma Chura Chacravarti, 1886).

By the 1770s it controlled extensive territories and was establishing the foundation for a colonial state. Based in London and run by twenty-four directors, working on behalf of several hundred investors, the Company exerted ever-tighter control over the lives of its new Asian subjects. At first this control was meant to yield previously undreamed of profits, but eventually it came to see Asian civilizations as inferior. In its final decades, the Company's leadership believed they had a moral duty to rule Indians, introduce Western science and technology, establish English as the language of administration, and allow Christian missionaries to proselytize. Despite the moralizing tone it adopted, the Company's rule was based on threat and violence: those who rebelled against its domination or who refused to pay the high land rents that became the source of most of its income were met by force and many, like Nandakumar, were hanged.

The English East India Company can be said to have been one of the most powerful companies ever founded. In existence for 258 years, it ran a complex, highly integrated, and truly global trading network. It governed territories that far exceeded, in extent and population, the British Isles and protected its seaborne trade and vast territories with a navy and one of the world's largest armies. It minted coins in its name, established law courts and prisons, sponsored scientific expeditions, prosecuted wars and signed treaties, and accounted for about 14 percent of all imports to Britain during much of the eighteenth century. It supplied the tea for Boston's tea party, the saltpeter for Britain's gunpowder industry, and the opium for China's principal nineteenth-century addiction. For most of its history it was a form of monopoly, with exclusive rights to trade and, eventually, rule in Southern and Eastern Asia. What it brought back to London was astonishingly varied, from wealth that helped underwrite Britain's European wars to the Chinese porcelain and silks that inspired the eighteenth-century Chinoiserie craze, to new words, such as "loot" and "cash" and "thug," that are now so much a part of the English language. What it took from London were woolen goods it could barely sell, Spanish silver that always opened doors, and a fiercely competitive mentality. Over time, the Company developed a pronounced and aggressive nationalism that laid the foundation for Britain's Eastern empire. A study of the Company, then, is a study of the rise of the early modern world.

The Company was born at a time when England had no empire. Queen Elizabeth was on the throne and, only a dozen years before, had narrowly escaped a Spanish invasion. The union of England and

Scotland was more than a century away. England was a poor country in 1600, especially when compared to the magnificence of the Mughal Empire that dominated northern India. The emperor, Akbar (1542–1605), had consolidated and added to conquests made by his father and grandfather and had created a wealthy and cosmopolitan empire, known for its artistic patronage and ability to extract enormous land revenues to sustain an expanding and ravenous military establishment. The Mughals were, in many ways, the equal to the Ottomans and Safavids to its west and the Ming to its northeast.[3] Whereas England's population in 1600 was not much more than 4 million, India's was about 116 million.[4] Looking ahead, no one would have predicted that in a little more than two hundred years the Company, coming from a relatively sparsely inhabited island on the margins of the centers of world power, would rise to control the very lands once ruled by one of the great empires of the time.

There are many surprising aspects to the rise and success of the Company. As we explore the history of the Company, it is important to remember that the Company's relationship with the English and, later, British, state is not so straightforward as we might at first imagine. This is especially true when we consider the question of how much sovereignty the Company exercised. During its early years the Company was able to govern its settlements as if it were a government with many of the attributes of a sovereign state. For example, it could sign treaties with Asian states, build forts, and imprison and even execute criminals. It was understood that ultimate sovereignty lay with the English Crown, but the Company functioned as if it had sovereign rights over its scattered settlements and inhabitants. As one leading Company historian explains:

> During the greater part of its history as an active commercial enterprise, the East India Company was a state within a state. . . . it is not surprising to discover that the Company's organisational structure and bureaucratic apparatus share

---

3. John F. Richards, *The Mughal Empire* (Cambridge: Cambridge University Press, 1998), 1.

4. In 1801, England's population had climbed to about 10.5 million, while India's had reached more than 158 million. Paul Kléber Monod, *Imperial Island: A History of Britain and Its Empire, 1660–1837* (Chichester: Wiley-Blackwell, 2009), 33, 242; Sumit Guha, *Health and Population in South Asia, from Earliest Times to the Present* (New Delhi: Permanent Black, 2001), 34, 58.

many of the attributes of a great department of state. All this happened long before the Battle of Plassey and the revolution of 1757.[5]

Paradoxically, as the Company conquered territory after 1757, its sovereign powers were gradually stripped away. The British government began to exert greater control over the decisions that the Company made and at the same time began to reduce its monopoly privileges. After 1833 the Company ceased operating as a trading company and focused only on its role as state. Real power, however, lay not with the Company's directors, but with an arm of the British government known as the Board of Control. As we will read, historians have debated how the Company gained territory and control over millions of Asians, established a colonial form of rule, and, at the same time lost its trading and sovereign privileges.

Another surprising development is that the Company's trade was very controversial at home. Its numerous critics argued that the Company did not act in the national interest. It exported silver, considered the basis for the country's wealth, and imported "frivolous" goods, such as pepper and cloves. Later in the seventeenth century the Company was attacked for importing cotton cloth from India and silks from Persia to the detriment of the wool industry, once the pride of the nation. By the beginning of the nineteenth century, the Company was again criticized but this time for restricting, at least for a while, the export of British-manufactured cotton cloth to India.

For most of its existence the Company was also accused of undermining national trade because it was a monopoly. It was argued, for instance, that as a monopoly it could deliberately limit the supply of goods and thereby increase the cost to the English consumer. The Company countered these claims with some ingenious arguments, including the assertion that it could not be a monopoly because it created a trade where none existed before. Opponents resented the fact that a very small number of men controlled the trade and the management restricted participation. They wondered how this could benefit the nation and repeatedly asked the king and Parliament to give more English merchants a chance to conduct business in Asia.

---

5. K. N. Chaudhuri, *The Trading World of Asia and the East India Company, 1600–1760* (Cambridge: Cambridge University Press, 1978), 20.

Any assessment of the importance of the Company must address not only how the Company changed but also whether the Company was itself an agent of change. In what ways did the Company help to cause people to act and behave differently? We can see the Company's impact in two broad areas: the economy and governance.

During the seventeenth and eighteenth centuries, Asians and Arabs, not the Company, conducted most of the regional trade in the Indian Ocean. However, the Company's increasing interest in cotton textiles meant that it, along with the Dutch and other European companies, spurred economic growth, especially on the northwestern and south-eastern coasts of India. The silver they imported was quickly absorbed into the interior economies and helped sustain India's imperial and royal states. The influx of silver eventually caused inflation, but the diffusion of silver allowed states to demand that land revenues be paid in cash to the nobility, who would, in turn, use the silver to raise troops for the emperor's army.

In England, the sale of cheap Indian cotton cloth had a profound effect by the end of the seventeenth century. Rich and poor alike began to wear less wool. As we will see in Chapter One, this development was deeply resented by those whose livelihoods depended on the sale of woolen products, but the trend away from wool was permanent. At the same time, the Company began to ship Chinese tea to England, again revolutionizing consumption patterns. The combination of cheap West Indian sugar and cheap tea laid the foundation for broad economic and industrial change. Finally, the Company's monopoly over the production and sale of Patna and Benares opium, considered the "finest" in the world, meant that it was a vital link in the shipment of the drug to China. Chinese officials' exasperation at their inability to stop opium from being smuggled into the country, coupled with British traders' frustrations with the constraints and restrictions the Chinese placed on their trade, eventually led to war.

The second half of the Company's existence was increasingly focused on governance. As we will discover in Chapters Two and Three, the Company itself changed dramatically in the decades after the 1750s, but it also introduced a form of bureaucratic state that would have a lasting effect in both India and Britain. In India, the Company developed a colonial administration that was hierarchical, racist, and, toward the end, suffused with a Christian evangelical perspective. Their British employees came to believe that they had conquered India because they were part of a superior civilization and that they now had a moral obligation to govern peoples who were incapable of ruling themselves in any way other than in a despotic and violent manner. Ironically, the Company's governing system was unrepresentative and brutal. Control was only possible because administrators could rely upon a large army to suppress opposition. Although in 1830 there were only 895 British civil servants responsible for, among other tasks, collecting the all-important revenue, they were backed by 36,409 European Company soldiers; 20,000 British Crown troops, paid for by the Company; and 187,067 Indian soldiers.[6] The repressive state the Company established was inherited by the British government in 1858 and continued, in modified form, until at least the time of India and Pakistan's independence in 1947.

The Company's impact on the state in Britain was less than it was in India. Nonetheless, it was important. In the early nineteenth century the Company's London headquarters in Leadenhall Street was run along lines that would have been recognizable to British civil servants. The Company generated a vast archive—between 1814 and 1829, for instance, it received a total of 12,414 folio volumes of letters just from India—that was not unlike the records produced by the state.[7] Nevertheless, the Company did introduce an innovation that was adopted by the British state. In the early 1850s the Company decided to formally abandon its long-standing and once-lucrative practice of awarding jobs to young men based on patronage. Instead, it introduced competitive civil service examinations that would become the norm for entry into modern bureaucracies.

The Company also affected the British state in less direct ways. Its Indian territories offset the loss of the American colonies by offering employment to large numbers of British, notably Scots and Irish, and by providing a market for goods manufactured in Britain. The wars it fought in India, especially against Tipu Sultan (1750–99) in 1799, gave officers experience that would prove helpful in campaigns against Napoleonic France. The Company also regularly gave, sometimes under duress, large sums of money to both the king and Parliament, who were often strapped for cash.

A final important question concerns the extent to which the Company contributed to the underdevelopment or even the immiseration of its

---

6. H. V. Bowen, *The Business of Empire: The East India Company and Imperial Britain, 1756–1833* (Cambridge: Cambridge University Press, 2008), 262–64.

7. Figures from Bowen, *Business*, 169.

territories in India and elsewhere in Asia. For the early Company, there is no simple answer to this question. On the one hand, the silver it shipped to India and the settlements it established, such as at Madras on the southeast coast of India, unquestionably developed the export-oriented textile industry in the seventeenth and eighteenth centuries. Many of these settlements became vibrant economic hubs that attracted diverse economic and social communities. However, the Company operated in a brutally competitive arena. To create a trade it had to act violently. The Portuguese and the Dutch vigorously opposed the Company's efforts to buy and sell goods, and the Company fought other Europeans to expand and defend its settlements and networks of trade. It also conducted wars against Asian states and enforced contracts with weavers and others that were anything but fair. From the beginning, the Company's commerce was created, sustained, and expanded through force.

The case against the Company is clearer once it conquered territory in the mid-eighteenth century. The Company seized monopolies over lucrative commodities such as opium and salt, encouraged or permitted crippling land revenue assessments, discouraged investment in industrial manufacturing, and transformed its territories into captive markets for British-manufactured goods. By the second half of the eighteenth century the outlines of a colonial economy had been drawn. The state's attention was focused almost exclusively on ensuring predictable and high land revenues. It did so by pursuing a twin strategy of enacting conservative social policies, in order not to provoke peasant revolts, and stationing its army at strategic locations, in order to swiftly counter any uprising. This oppressive environment, coupled with the total exclusion of Indians from any position of responsibility within the colonial administration, meant that the Company did indeed stifle economic growth and deliberately sought to exclude republican and democratic ideas that had roiled the American colonies and were altering the political landscape in Europe and even in Britain.

The Company changed dramatically from the seventeenth to the nineteenth centuries, but it also had deep and long-lasting effects in Asia and Britain. A study of the Company gives us a window into regional and global economic systems and how they were transformed over time. It provides a glimpse into the politics of empire and shows us how colonial elites lived the good life at the expense of conquered populations. It introduces us to religious divisions and social hierarchies and allows us to see how race became an all-important category by the nineteenth century.

This book has three chapters, each focusing on a century and corresponding, roughly, to the phases of the Company's trade and rule. We will begin in 1600, at the Company's founding, and ask the following questions: Why and how did the Company establish a trade to Asia; why did it change its focus away from spices to cotton textiles; and why was it under constant attack in England, so much so that it nearly disappeared as a company by the end of the century? In the second chapter, we will ask why it began to conquer territory beyond the small settlements it had established in the seventeenth century and why, despite acquiring vast new resources, it was so financially insecure that it had to ask for help from the British government in order to remain solvent. We will also look closely at the kind of state the Company created and see how "colonialism" changed over time. One late eighteenth-century development that helped to fund the colonial state, and one that we will examine in detail, was the sale of Indian opium and Chinese tea. Then, in the third chapter, we will discuss why the Company was so successful militarily, why it changed its long-standing relationship to religion and proselytization, and why it wanted to introduce a new kind of governance. Finally, we will turn to the Company's abrupt end and examine the popular rebellion that spread throughout northern India in 1857–58 and nearly overthrew British rule. The British government shut down the Company, took over its responsibilities, and continued to govern India until 1947.

CHAPTER ONE
The Seventeenth Century

Organization and Settlements

Toward the end of the sixteenth century, a group of English merchants based in London realized that there was an opportunity to make money in the spice trade. The Dutch were in the process of achieving independence from Spain, and their new freedoms gave them the power to send a number of ships to what is today eastern Indonesia, the heart of what was loosely called the East Indies. The voyages were successes and suggested that long journeys around the Cape of Good Hope in southern Africa were more economical than slow overland routes through the Middle East, then known as the Levant. The English already had a Levant Company, which bought spices, silks, and other goods from their contacts in the Middle East, but there was concern among the London merchants that the Dutch would corner the spice market. They therefore pledged money to establish a new company to rival Dutch efforts and asked Queen Elizabeth for a charter granting them the privilege of exclusive trade to the East Indies. A charter was issued to the Governor and Company of Merchants of London trading into the East Indies on December 31, 1600.

Over the next 258 years the Company acquired a number of names. As we will see, in 1698 a rival company was formed called the English Company trading to the East Indies. Informally it was known as either the English Company or the New Company to distinguish it from the London Company or the Old Company. When the two companies merged in 1709 they became the United Company of Merchants of England trading to the East Indies. The title was too long for anything but the most formal document, and so it was usually called the East India Company. In official correspondence it was also called the Honorable East India Company or even just the Honorable Company, and, by the turn of the nineteenth century, it was sometimes personified as John Company or the Company Bahadur. For convenience I will refer to it as the Company and the short-lived rival as the New Company.

The Company was a joint-stock company, which distinguished it from a regulated company, the other common way of organizing a business venture, in two important ways. In a joint-stock company anybody—merchants, gentry, aristocrats, even foreigners—could contribute to the capital and in return receive profits in the form of dividends. At first dividends were usually paid as a share in the goods, such as pepper, but they were sometimes paid as cash. As the Company became more established investors could also sell their share of the stock, the value of which might rise or fall. Moreover, investors in a joint-stock did not conduct any trade. Instead, an elected board managed their pooled capital. The board hired traders, set policies, and managed the accounts. Historians have often pointed to these arrangements as signs that the modern corporation was emerging at this time.[1] A joint-stock structure became a popular form of investment throughout the seventeenth century, especially when the risks were high. For example, joint-stock companies operated in the Americas (the Governor and Company of Adventurers of England trading into Hudson's Bay, founded in 1670) and in Africa (the Royal African Company of England, founded in 1672). In all of these cases it was extremely expensive to organize a voyage; buy bullion or domestic goods for sale overseas; employ agents to buy or exchange goods in foreign locations, hire seamen to bring them home, and establish warehouses to store merchandise until the ships arrived. A joint-stock company spread the risk and, of course, the profits among many investors.

Regulated companies, such as the reformed Governor and Company of Merchants of the Levant (founded in 1592), were associations of independent merchants who nevertheless saw the advantages to having common rules of trade and warehouses. Unlike joint-stock companies, members of regulated companies traded on their own behalf. Any profit was theirs to enjoy immediately. Similarly, any loss was their misfortune. Moreover, membership was generally restricted to merchants, which on the one hand made it more exclusive but on the other hand limited investment.

Both joint-stock and regulated companies sought royal charters. The main advantage was that a royal charter gave them a monopoly of trade. The Company's charter gave it "the whole entire and only Trade and Traffick"

---

1. For example, see Nick Robins, *The Corporation That Changed the World: How the East India Company Shaped the Modern Multinational* (London: Pluto Press, 2006), 22–24; Philip Lawson, *The East India Company: A History* (London: Longman, 1987), 20–21.

to all the islands, ports, havens, cities, towns, and places "beyond the Cape of Bona Esperanza to the Streights of Magellan."[2] It stipulated that the Company was to be run by twenty-four men to be called committees. A governor and his deputy presided over the committees. The investors or subscribers who elected the administration every year were termed the General Court, and in 1600 they numbered slightly more than two hundred men. Most of the early subscribers were merchants, some also involved in the Levant Company, but others were gentry and aristocrats. Later in the century foreigners, especially the Dutch, invested in the Company. By the eighteenth century large numbers of women were also investing. In the Company's first charter the queen gave its first four voyages an exemption from paying export duties and gave it the privilege of exporting silver provided a proportion was coined at the mint. The charter could be renewed after fifteen years.

The internal organization was further spelled out a few years later in *The Lawes or Standing Orders of the East India Company*. Published in 1621 it noted that the governor and his deputy were responsible for convening the General Court of Adventurers; overseeing the election of officers, which was to take place every year on June 24; and arranging for the reading and replying to letters from the East Indies. Committees were expected to work in pairs, probably to provide a check and balance:

> They shall perform the Orders of Courts for setting out of Ships, selling of goods, buying of Provisions, Victuals, Stores and Marchandize: wherein especiall care is to be had, that no one man alone is to be intrusted with the making of those provisions, but Two at least appointed unto it by the Court.[3]

Over time their correspondence grew to become one of the great archives of the world. It is now housed in the British Library and is one of the principal ways scholars learn about the Company and the world in which it operated.

Below the elected officers, the Company employed a wide range of people, some with very specific tasks. The *Standing Orders* tells us about

---

2. *Charters Granted to the East India Company, from 1601, also the Treaties and Grants Made with, or Obtained from the Princes and Powers in India, from the Year 1756 to 1772* (London?: 1773?), 12, 19.

3. *The Lawes or Standing Orders of the East India Company* (1621), 10

the duties of the secretary and his assistant, the remembrancer, as well as the husband, who was in charge of provisioning the ships. We learn about the clarke of the stores and the purveyors of timber and plancke, who oversaw the loading of the ships with sufficient food and equipment to last through the long journey east. The list of jobs is long and fascinating and includes a beadle to summon investors to meetings; a "chirurgion general," or doctor; and keepers of anchors. The Company also licensed a pub, or taphouse, at its docks that sold little more than beer, bread, porridge, eggs, and cheese. In the seventeenth century, people generally did not drink water, preferring beer and cider, and although tolerance for alcohol must have been high, the Company was still concerned about drunkenness and absenteeism. The taphouse keeper was ordered to "not suffer any of the Companies Workemen to come within Roomes of the Taphouse, to drinke, rest, or hide themselves in the time of worke . . . neither shall they deliver more than two pence in Beere to one man every day at breakfast, and betwitxt Meales."[4]

The initial investors in the Company expected a relatively quick return, and so the first twelve voyages were financed independently. When the ships came home after a voyage that took, on average, sixteen months, the proceeds were distributed and new capital was raised for the next voyage. During this period profits were high, averaging 155 percent. Beginning in 1613 and lasting until 1623, the Company began to use its capital for more than one voyage. This was the beginning of its joint-stock ventures, with the second and third joint-stocks operating between 1617 and 1632 and between 1631 and 1642. The first joint-stock gave a profit of 87 percent but the subsequent two were less successful, producing profits of only 12 percent and 35 percent. There were also separate voyages to Persia that returned 60 percent profits.[5] Thereafter voyages were financed by temporary joint-stocks until 1657, when the joint-stock became permanent. The great advantages to a permanent joint-stock were that it provided capital for long-term investment in forts and warehouses that were not easily or quickly liquidated and that it made it easier to finance and plan multiple voyages over many years. It also avoided the messy accounting that arose when the Company sent out more than one separately financed voyage.

---

4. Ibid., 32.

5. K. N. Chaudhuri, *The English East India Company: The Study of an Early Joint-Stock Company 1600–1640* (London: Frank Cass & Co LTD, 1965), 22.

The first voyage left England in 1601 in search of spice markets. The fleet comprised four ships and was led by James Lancaster (1554/5–1618) on the *Red Dragon*. It first sailed to Sumatra and then to Bantam (Banten) in Java, where Lancaster established a "factory," or warehouse. A description of the voyage tells us that, even on this first expedition, trade was often violent. At sea the English captured a Portuguese ship full of valuable cotton textiles and on shore the English felt the need to protect themselves from the local population, who were "reckoned among the greatest pickers and theeves of the world." Lancaster was obviously worried about robbers and so had received permission from the local king to kill "whosoever he tooke about his house in the night . . . so, after foure or five were thus slaine, we lived in reasonable peace and quiet."[6] Lancaster returned to England in 1603 with pepper, glutting the market. It was the first indication that the Company would have to be careful to control the flow of its commodities and would have to learn the best way to space out its auctions.[7]

When Lancaster entered the Indian Ocean trade, he found that it was already crowded. Chinese, Indians, and Arabs were prominent traders, but the high seas and many of the important ports were still dominated by the Portuguese. Their power had been established in the sixteenth century through naval superiority and was enforced by means of the *cartaz* system. Non-Portuguese ships, especially those traveling between the west coast of India and the Red Sea, were compelled to buy a license, or *cartaz*, and were then forced to sail via Portuguese-controlled ports and pay customs duties. They were also to avoid carrying spices and weapons and were to travel in convoys that were protected by Portuguese ships.[8] Failure to comply could result in the ship's confiscation or sinking. The system has been called "a vast protection racket" because the Portuguese were protecting Indian Ocean merchants from Portuguese violence.[9]

Portuguese power was widespread but it was never absolute. The Portuguese had neither the navy nor the manpower to enforce their

6. *The Voyages of Sir James Lancaster to Brazil and the East Indies, 1591–1603* (Nendeln: Kraus Reprint Limited, 1967), 115.

7. For a full discussion of the Company's pepper trade, including sales, see Chaudhuri, *English*, 140–67.

8. Om Prakash, *European Commercial Enterprise in Pre-Colonial India* (Cambridge: Cambridge University Press, 1998), 46, 64.

9. Michael Pearson, *The Indian Ocean* (London: Routledge, 2006), 121.

authority at all times and in all places and, as the seventeenth century progressed, they began to cede control over oceanic trade to the Dutch. After dominating the Asia to Europe pepper trade in the sixteenth century, the Portuguese share of the trade declined to 20 percent by the 1620s.[10] At the beginning of the century they had close to fifty forts, but by the end they had only nine scattered around the ocean.[11] Their most significant losses to the Dutch were Malacca in 1641, Colombo in 1656, and Cochin in 1663. The Portuguese-Dutch rivalry was particularly strong, but the English also aggressively opposed the Portuguese until an agreement in 1635 brought hostilities to an end.

Historians have debated the rapid decline of the Portuguese in Asia during the seventeenth century. Attention has focused on the introduction of better-financed, well-equipped, highly motivated, and belligerent Dutch and, to a lesser extent, English companies. Scholars have also pointed to other causes, including a switch in Portuguese attention away from Asia and toward protecting Brazil and its highly lucrative sugar plantations. The Portuguese were also hampered by shortages of personnel to defend its sprawling Asian and South American territories, systemic corruption (although the Dutch and the English companies were also corrupt), and the strength and shifting political alliances of regional Asian states.[12]

The Portuguese and then the Dutch and English participated aggressively in the spice and pepper trade, but much of that trade remained within the Indian Ocean basin. It has been estimated that, despite European efforts to dominate it, only 10 percent of the spice production went to Europe.[13] Intra-Asian trade, or the "country trade" as it was later called, was lucrative and sometimes as rewarding as Asia-Europe trade. Indeed, the Company came to recognize, as a result of its second voyage, that the country trade was key to making a profit in London.

The second voyage was delayed in part because of an outbreak of plague in England in 1603. The committees mentioned this calamity in the first letter they ever wrote to their factors: "Notwithstanding since

10. Prakash, *European*, 49.

11. Pearson, *Indian Ocean*, 137.

12. Ibid., 131–43; for further analysis, see Sanjay Subrahmanyam, *The Portuguese Empire in Asia, 1500–1700: A Political and Economic History* (London: Longman, 1993), 144–80.

13. Pearson, *Indian Ocean*, 138.

[the death of Queen Elizabeth and the accession of King James], as tymes have their chandges and as God doth many tymes humble His people lest they should forget themselves in prosperitie, yt hath pleased Him to chastice this kingdomes with greate sicknes and mortalitie in divers places thereof, espetiallie in the cittie of London."[14] The "pestilence," as the plague was sometimes called, finally abated, allowing Henry Middleton (d. 1613) and his crew to set sail in 1604. They sailed to Bantam and further east to the Moluccas (Maluku Islands), where they bought pepper, cloves, and nutmeg. The survival rate among the crew was very low. Men "fell sick with the scurvy, calenture (fever), bloody flux (dysentery), and the worms." It turned out that the fleet's doctor was incompetent, "being as unwilling as ignorant in anything that might help them—a great oversight . . . and no doubt will be better looked to hereafter."[15] It quickly became apparent that the easiest way for the Company to buy these commodities was by offering cotton cloth. Prized textiles were made in India, especially in Gujarat, then known as Cambay or Cambaia, and so in 1608 the Company sent ships to Surat to buy cotton goods. The first difficulty facing the Company was that the Portuguese dominated the export market from the west coast of India and, because of the power of their fleets, were able to influence the city's governor. The second difficulty was that the Company needed permission from the Mughal emperor to establish a secure trading presence at Surat and other inland towns. At this time the Mughals were the dominant power in northern India and would, over the course of the seventeenth century, extend their control south to cover almost the entire peninsula. Their empire shrank considerably during the eighteenth century, giving rise to a variety of powerful Muslim, Hindu, and Sikh "successor states." However, even as its power diminished, the Mughal emperors retained some of the aura and legitimacy of their seventeenth-century ancestors.

In 1612 Thomas Best (1570–1639), commanding the tenth voyage, consisting of the *Dragon* and *Hosiander*, traveled to Surat and fought a more powerful Portuguese fleet that had sailed from Goa in order to drive the English away. Best was able to inflict considerable damage before a lack of ammunition forced him to travel on to Indonesia. His

---

14. Cited in William Foster, *The East India House: Its History and Associations* (London: John Lane, 1924), 57.

15. Bolton Corney, ed., *The Voyage of Sir Henry Middleton to Bantam and the Maluco Islands* (London: Hakluyt Society, 1855), 6–7.

success led to the establishment of a factory at Surat in 1613, prompting the governor of the company, Sir Thomas Smythe (ca. 1588–1625), to remark that Best had

> performed worthie service, both for the honour of this kingdome and English nation and for the setling of a beneficiall trade in Cambaia . . . a service of very greate moment and consequence, in the prosecutinge whereof he had many oppositions, assaults, and sundrie attempts made by the Portugalls . . . in all which yt pleased God soe to blesse his endevours as that he repeld them.[16]

Two years later Nicholas Downton (d. 1615) held off and damaged another Portuguese fleet near Surat. In a letter reporting the news of what was interpreted as a victory, a Company employee described how the Portuguese swarmed around one of the Company ships, the *Hope*, and "came running aboard with great resolution . . . but their courages were soon quailed." Many Portuguese ships were burned and they were forced to withdraw.[17] The victory was so remarkable that it was the only time the Mughal emperor Jahangir (1569–1627) referred to the English in his memoirs.[18] Best and Downton's victories persuaded the Mughal authorities in Surat that the English were powerful newcomers and should be accommodated. The Company was therefore allowed to establish a factory, although the emperor did not condescend to enter into a treaty with the Company.

In the early seventeenth century a Company's factory meant an establishment—a few "factors," or traders, and some buildings to house them and the Company's goods. By the 1610s the two main factories were Bantam in western Java, dealing principally in pepper, and Surat in western India, dealing mainly in textiles but also in indigo and saltpeter.

---

16. Cited in William Foster, ed. *The Voyage of Thomas Best to the East Indies, 1612–14* (Farnham: Ashgate, 2010), ix.

17. Thomas Elkington to John Oxwicke, January 23, 1614, in Frederic Charles Danvers, ed., *Letters Received by the East India Company* (Amsterdam: N. Israel, 1968), II.1613–15, 303.

18. Jahangir, *The Jahangirnama: Memoirs of Jahangir, Emperor of India*, ed., trans., and annotated by Wheeler M. Thackston (New York: Freer Gallery of Art, Oxford University Press, 1999), 165.

The men in charge of the factories were at first called chiefs but, after 1618, they were called presidents. This title would, in turn, give a name to the collection of subordinate factories that reported to either Bantam or Surat. Over time the northern area of operations, or presidency, included Ahmedabad, Ajmer, Agra, Burhanpur, and Persia, while the southern presidency was responsible for trade in Java, Sumatra, the Spice Island further east, and Masulipatnam on the east coast of India.[19] The Company also attempted to establish trade at towns in what are today Japan, Thailand, and Malaysia but abandoned these efforts by the early 1620s for financial reasons.[20]

From the time that it established its factories at Bantam and Surat, the Company faced tension between wanting to project a peaceful face and recognizing that sometimes its trade networks could be formed and protected only through the use of force. Wars, however, were expensive, were full of danger, and might easily backfire. Sir Thomas Roe (1581–1644), the Company's ambassador to the Mughal court between 1615 and 1619, warned the Company that a land war in Asia could be its undoing. "A warr and trafique are incompatible," he wrote and:

> It is the beggering of the Portugall, notwithstanding his many rich residences and territoryes. . . . It hath been also the error of the Dutch, who seeke Plantation heere by the Sword. . . . Lett this bee received as a rule that, if you will Profitt, seek it at Sea, and in quiett trade; for without controversy it is an error to affect Garrisons and Land warrs in India.[21]

Better, he believed, to pursue peaceful trade on land and, if necessary, fight at sea: "At sea you may take and leave; your Designes are not Published."[22] The seemingly contradictory impulses of trading peacefully and acting aggressively in the name of protecting trade would continue into the early nineteenth century.

---

19. Chaudhuri, *English*, 60.

20. H. V. Bowen, "Uncertain Beginnings: The East India Company, 1600–1709," in *Monsoon Traders: The Maritime World of the East India Company*, ed. H. V. Bowen, John McAleer, and Robert J. Blyth (London: Scala Publishers Ltd, 2011), 42.

21. William Foster, ed., *The Embassy of Sir Thomas Roe to Court of the Great Mogul, 1615–19* (London: Hakluyt Society, 1899), II.344–45.

22. Ibid.

The voyages to the presidencies were inherently risky. Ships could run aground, be captured, or be destroyed by fire or storm. In the sixteenth century the Portuguese suffered a 10 percent loss on its shipping and crew (of the 171,000 people who traveled to Asia, an estimated 17,000 were lost).[23] The Company's ships, known as East Indiamen, were generally better constructed than Portuguese galleons and so the percentage lost was lower. Over the course of its existence as a trading venture, from 1600 to 1833, the year it was stripped of its trading privileges, the Company embarked on 4,600 voyages, losing 5 percent, or 231, of its ships. These numbers were sufficiently tolerable for the Company to stop insuring its cargoes after 1650.[24]

The pressures placed on the ships were extreme. Shipworms attacked hulls, while cyclone winds could snap masts. When a ship returned to England it usually needed extensive repairs. Sheathing a ship in copper extended its life considerably, but that practice did not become common until the end of the eighteenth century. Until then, most East Indiamen remained seaworthy for three or four round trip voyages before they were sold for their wood or for local shipping needs.

At first the Company built its own ships and dockyards at Deptford and Blackwall in England, but after 1639 it almost always hired ships, some of which were later built in Bombay. Many of the owners were also investors in the Company and became a powerful clique, or "interest," especially toward the end of the eighteenth century. The ships they built ranged in size from one hundred to twelve hundred tons. The largest ships were built at the beginning of the sixteenth century and at the end of the eighteenth century for the tea trade, but for most of the Company's existence the average size was between five hundred and eight hundred tons.[25] For protection a three-decked East Indiaman usually carried thirty-six cannon, while a two-decked ship had thirty.[26]

The captain was generally paid £10 a month and his crew £5 a year, which was not high.[27] However, the Company gave the captain and his

23. Pearson, *Indian Ocean*, 138.

24. Anthony Farrington, *Trading Places: The East India Company and Asia 1600–1834* (London: British Library, 2002), 29.

25. Bowen, *Monsoon*, 51.

26. Jean Sutton, *Lords of the East: The East India Company and Its Ships (1600–1874)* (London: Conway Maritime Press, 2000), 46.

27. Chaudhuri, *English*, 105.

officers designated space on the ship, called privilege tonnage, to take or bring back goods to sell privately. At first the space given to mariners was limited to a chest measuring 4 by 1.5 by 1.5 feet, but by 1715 captains were allowed three hundred pounds of goods for every one hundred tons carried on behalf of the Company.[28] While the Company focused its efforts on buying goods that would appeal broadly, captains tended to buy exquisite or even commissioned items, such as porcelain featuring a family's crest, that they could sell at high prices. In addition, they could bring back raw silk, musk, and carpets, but they were forbidden from transporting indigo, cotton textiles, diamonds, and spices, since this would compete directly with the Company. Privilege tonnage could also be sold to factors who wanted to repatriate their wealth. Factors were also not paid particularly highly and so, together with the ships' officers, they participated extensively in the trade. They would invest in goods in one part of Asia and sell in another.

The Company was at first uneasy about this sort of private trade. Its charter gave it the sole right to trade to the East Indies, and its own *Standing Orders* announced, "The Trade for the *East Indies* shall be unlawfull to all men, otherwise then in the generall or joynt Stocke, which shall be mannaged by the Governour, Deputy and Committees . . . in the behalfe of all the Adventurers."[29] It found, however, that it could not stop intra-Asian private trade; therefore, it permitted it after 1662 so long as it did not compete with the Company's business or involve goods, such as pepper and cotton textiles, over which the Company had a monopoly, although even some of those restrictions were eased in 1679.[30] Until it was once again restricted in the 1780s as part of an effort to root out corruption, the country trade became the surest way for the Company's employees to amass a fortune in the seventeenth and eighteenth centuries. As we will see in the next chapter, getting that fortune back to England was not easy. In the late seventeenth century one way was to buy Company bills of exchange. Between 1675 and 1683 about £100,000 was remitted every year.[31] This arrangement benefited the Company because

---

28. Emily Erikson, *Between Monopoly and Free Trade: The English East India Company, 1600–1757* (Princeton: Princeton University Press, 2014), 58.

29. *Standing Orders*, 64.

30. Erikson, *Between Monopoly and Free Trade*, 59.

31. Ibid., 60.

it made a profit on bills and received silver in its factories abroad that it could use to purchase goods.

The journey out to Surat or Bantam was long and somewhat circuitous. Ships were loaded in the autumn and set sail in the winter, usually in December and January but sometimes a little later. Ships traveled in convoys for safety and, for much of the seventeenth and eighteenth centuries, were escorted partway into the Atlantic Ocean and back by Royal Navy ships. After leaving the southern coast of England, the convoys would travel past the Madeira, Canary, and Cape Verde islands, but beyond these islands the ships could not sail along the African coast because of countervailing trade winds and ocean currents. These winds and currents carried ships out into the southern Atlantic toward the coast of Brazil and then south, where the powerful "roaring forties" carried them directly east to the Cape of Good Hope. Once in the Indian Ocean the East Indiamen had to time their voyages to the monsoon seasons. The expectation was that they would arrive at their destination in the early summer. They would begin their return in the late autumn or early winter, often stopping at St. Helena, which became a Company possession in 1659, and then continuing north in order to arrive back in England in the early summer.[32] The journey could last as long as eight months each way, and if a ship missed the favorable monsoon winds, delaying its return, it would participate in the Company's intra-Asian trade until its eventual journey home. Delays were costly, because the Company gained its profits from its auctions in London, and so the Company did its best to keep its outgoing and incoming fleets on a tight schedule.

Once the ships returned to England the cargo had to be sold. Some merchandise, such as saltpeter, a key ingredient in gunpowder, was often sold directly to the government or to a single purchaser. However, by the middle of the seventeenth century the most common way to dispose of goods was by candle auction, which was held four times a year to avoid glutting the market. These auctions differed slightly from typical outcry auctions in that each auction was timed. The Company auctioneers would light a candle, which was sometimes one inch high, and the lot would be sold to the highest bidder once the candle had fizzled out. This approach encouraged potential buyers to bid high quickly because no one

---

32. For schedules of voyages, see H. V. Bowen, *The Business of Empire: The East India Company and Imperial Britain, 1756–1833* (Cambridge: Cambridge University Press, 2008), 154.

knew exactly when the flame would die. Such an approach was taken on April 24, 1635, for instance: "Silence prevailing, the Governor caused a candle to be set up for the sale of their fifty-five chests of sugar at 4*l*. 10*s*. per hundred . . . at the going out of the candle the sugar is assigned to Mr. Thomas Culling at 5*l*. 9*s*. per hundred."[33] The Company would sometimes delay selling a portion of its stock if it believed that the going price was too low or there was too little interest at that time.

The prominence of Surat began to decline in the 1630s, partly as a result of a famine that decimated western India. An eyewitness provided a vivid account of the stricken city in 1631, writing,

> When wee came into the cytty of Suratt, we hardly could see anie livinge persons, where hertofore was thousands; and ther is so great a stanch of dead persons that the sound people that came into the towne were with the smell infected, and att the corners of the streets the dead laye 20 together. . . . In these parts ther may not bee anie trade expected this three yeares.[34]

The textile and indigo trade at Surat did recover, but the disruption in trade began a gradual process that saw the Company turn its attention south to the new settlement at Bombay, but especially to the eastern, or Coromandel, coast of India and, finally, to Bengal.

The Portuguese had given the island of Bombay to the English king Charles II (1630–85) in 1661 as part of the political settlement leading to his marriage with the Portuguese princess, Catherine of Braganza (1638–1705). Unwilling to spend the funds to manage it, Charles allowed the Company in 1668 to take over its operation. The settlement, including a town and a fort, called Bombay Castle, grew slowly, especially in comparison to Madras or, later, Calcutta. However, by the mid-1680s Bombay's importance increased as tensions with Mughal grandees in Surat rose. The Company's trade was under pressure from the Dutch, Portuguese, and unlicensed English traders, known as interlopers, and so the Company decided to pursue aggressive policies that included seizing

---

33. Ethel Bruce Sainsbury, *A Calendar of the Court Minutes of the East India Company, 1635–1639* (Oxford: Clarendon Press, 1907), 48. The letters "*l*" and "*s*" stand for "pounds sterling" and "shillings."

34. Cited in Holden Furber, *Rival Empires of Trade in the Orient, 1600–1800* (Minneapolis: University of Minnesota Press, 1976), 66–67.

ships off India's western coast. At the same time, the Company hoped to extract better trade privileges from the Mughals. The Mughals were not pleased with these developments since they interfered with their own profits from trade. The Company also knew that Surat was not necessarily the safest location for its headquarters since the Mughal's great regional enemy, the Marathas, had sacked the city in 1664 and 1670. For all these reasons the Company decided in 1687 to transfer its presidency headquarters from Mughal-dominated Surat to Bombay.

Even as Bombay rose in prominence, it developed a reputation for being an unhealthy and dissolute place for the Company's European servants. John Ovington (1653–1731), a chaplain, traveled to the island in 1690 and commented on how quickly Europeans died. His ship was delayed for three months during the monsoon, and during that time fifteen crewmembers and twenty out of twenty-four passengers died. Ovington was asked to stay, but he politely declined, knowing that the common expression in Bombay was "Two Mussouns (monsoons) are the Age of a Man."[35] He believed that events in nature followed from a community's moral standing, and in Bombay "the evil Practices of the *English* forwarded their Miseries, and contributed to fill the Air with those pestilential Vapours that seized their Vitals, and speeded their hasty passage to the other World."

The Company's trade on India's southeastern, or Coromandel, coast was first established at Masulipatam (Machilipatnam) in 1611. The port was part of Golconda, an independent Muslim kingdom that succumbed to Mughal pressure in 1687 after years of conflict.[36] The Golconda-Mughal wars encouraged the Company to transfer the base of its operations on the Coromandel from Masulipatam to a settlement further south, outside of the conflict zone. Madras (Chennai) became a Company settlement in 1639 and, as Masulipatam declined, it quickly became a center for the export of textiles. Its population grew quickly, so that by 1700 about 100,000 people lived in the city. The Company built Fort St. George for protection and divided the burgeoning population into "black" and "white" towns. Because Madras does not have a natural harbor, ships anchored off the coast in what was known as the "roads."

---

35. J. Ovington, *A Voyage to Surat in the Year 1689* (London: Oxford University Press, 1929), 87.

36. John Richards, *The Mughal Empire* (Cambridge: Cambridge University Press, 1993), 222.

Catamarans would then come from land to transport goods and people to and from the ships. Charles Lockyer (dates unknown) traveled to the town at the turn of the eighteenth century and came away with a good impression: "The Prospect it gives at Sea is most delightful; nor appears it less magnificent by Land: The great Variety of fine Buildings, that gracefully over-look its Walls, affording an inexpressible Satisfaction to a curious eye."[37] Once inside the fort Lockyer noticed that the streets were made of deep sand, with only the sides paved with brick. The principal buildings included a town hall, church, hospital, and the governor's lodgings. A mayor and six aldermen were responsible for resolving disputes over debts and other everyday matters of law. They met twice a week at the town hall and almost always settled disputes only among Indians since Europeans were able to complain straight to the governor. If Indians were unhappy with the decision, they could "appeal to a higher Court; where for much Money, they have little Law, with a great deal of Formality."[38] If a serious crime had been committed, the criminal would be brought before a judge and jury.

The administration at Madras was hierarchical. Lockyer tells us that the governor was supported by six ranked councilors. Below them were six senior merchants, two junior merchants, five factors, and ten writers. All were given an annual salary in pounds, ranging from £300 for the governor to £5 for a writer. Below the writers, but paid more, were two ministers, one surgeon, and two "essay masters" (presumably for the mint), and one judge. The administration was rounded out with an attorney general, a scavenger, and a "secretary for extraordinary services," all paid a gratuity in the local currency of pagodas.[39] This structure was replicated in other presidencies and settlements and would not change until reforms were introduced in the 1770s.

The trade from Madras began to eclipse Surat by the 1670s and was itself passed by Calcutta (Kolkata), in Bengal, around the turn of the century. The Company had been trading in Bengal since the early 1650s and found that Bengal muslin and raw silk sold well in Europe. Following a brief war with the Mughals, the Company was given permission to build a factory at a spot on the eastern bank of the Houghly (Hugli) River.

---

37. Charles Lockyer, *An Account of the Trade in India* (Cornhill: Samuel Crouch, 1711), 4.

38. Ibid., 6.

39. Ibid., 13–14.

Alexander Hamilton (b. before 1688, d. after 1732) visited Calcutta and its Fort William during his extensive travels as a captain between 1688 and 1723 and was disappointed with the city's location.[40] Hamilton claimed that its founder, Job Charnock (ca. 1630–93), chose the place because of a large shady tree,

> Tho' he could not have chosen a more unhealthful Place on all the River; for three Miles to the North-eastward, is a Salt-water Lake that overflows in *September* and *October*, and then prodigious Numbers of Fish resort thither, but in *November* and *December* when the Floods are dissipated, those Fishes are left dry, and with their Putrification affect the Air with thick stinking Vapours (that) cause a yearly Mortality.[41]

Despite its location, life for the wealthy in the city was "very agreeable," since food and clothing were cheap and readily available. At that time factors and writers lived in the fort and had already developed regular habits. Business was conducted in the morning, followed by lunch. The afternoon was spent resting and the evening was filled with various forms of recreation such as fishing, hunting, or even just going out on the water in pleasure boats or to gardens in palanquins. Late evening was spent visiting friends. These habits lasted until at least the end of the eighteenth century. We know this from a number of firsthand accounts of life in the city, including a fascinating novel, *Hartly House, Calcutta*, published anonymously in 1789, although now thought to have been written by a woman. The novel is clearly based on direct knowledge of social life in the city and echoes Hamilton's observations, although by the end of the century other pastimes had been introduced, such as horse racing and a very popular amateur theater in which all the actors were men. One constant was the amount of alcohol drunk by the Company's European servants. The novelist notes that a woman typically drank at least a bottle of wine a day while a man drank four times as much.[42]

At the same time as the Company's trade from Madras and Bengal was growing, the Company embarked on a war with the Mughal Empire.

---

40. This Hamilton should not be confused with the later American.

41. Alexander Hamilton, *A New Account of the East Indies* (London: Argonaut Press, 1930), II.5.

42. Anonymous, *Hartly House, Calcutta* (London: Pluto Press, 1989), 135.

The war, now sometimes called the First Anglo-Mughal War (1686–90), offers a glimpse into the ever more belligerent state of the Company and the role of a powerful individual in controlling the Company's policies in India.[43] The decision to attack the Mughals was driven by Josiah (or Josia) Child (1630/1–99) and so some termed it Child's War. Child had made his money in the 1650s by working for and supplying provisions to the Royal Navy. Described as "sordidly avaricious" by a contemporary, he first bought Company shares in 1671 and, by rapidly increasing his investment over the next decade, maneuvered himself into the Company's administration, rising to deputy governor (1684–86, 1688–90) and governor (1681–83, 1686–88). His prominence was such that he was one of very few men who controlled large blocks of Company shares of stock. For example, in 1691 only eight men owned more than £10,000 worth of stock, but together they controlled more than 25 percent of the stock. Child's enormous £51,150 block gave him a 7 percent share of the stock.[44] His voting power was matched by his ambition, and he dominated the Company during the 1680s.

The war was launched to force the Mughals to treat the Company as a sovereign power and thereby grant it trading privileges and a fortified settlement in Bengal. A settlement in Bengal was also seen as a way to protect the Company from the Dutch and from interlopers who, as Child wrote to Madras, had prompted the Company to leave its "peaceable way." As a result, "we look upon the Mogoll's Governours but as instruments which we hope to compell by fair means or foul to use us better hereafter."[45] The war was fought on both coasts of India (and was even extended to Siam and the Persian Gulf) but did not go well on either front. In the west the Company attacked the Mughals at sea but found itself besieged at Bombay. The man in charge in Bombay was John Child (1637/38–90; no relation to Josiah). He was generally maligned at the time for rash decisions that put the Company's trade and standing in peril. For example, he decided in 1689 to broaden the war against the Mughals by confiscating

43. For an overview of the war, see Part One of Margaret R. Hunt and Philip J. Stern, eds., *The English East India Company at the Height of Mughal Expansion: A Soldier's Diary of the 1689 Siege of Bombay with Related Documents* (Boston: Bedford/St. Martin's, 2016).

44. Andrea Finkelstein, *Harmony and Balance: An Intellectual History of Seventeenth-Century English Economic Thought* (Ann Arbor: University of Michigan Press, 2000), 132.

45. K. N. Chaudhuri, *The Trading World of Asia and the English East India Company 1660–1760* (Cambridge: Cambridge University Press, 1978), 117, 579.

a convoy of ships carrying grain to Sidi Yakut Khan (d. 1707), a regional leader. Although Sidi Yakut was an ally of the Mughals he had not, up until then, ordered his troops to attack the Company. However, Child's move created an unnecessary crisis: according to Alexander Hamilton, who was in Bombay for part of the war, Child told one of the Company's captains, who had objected to the seizure of the grain, that should Sidi Yakut "dare to come with his Forces on *Bombay*, he [meaning Child] would blow him off again with the Wind of his Bum."[46] Sidi Yakut did indeed land a force at Bombay and began a siege of the fort that lasted nearly a year and a half. In the east of India, a harebrained scheme to attack Chittagong floundered from the very beginning. Peace finally came in February 1690, when the Mughal emperor, Aurangzeb (1618–1707), issued a *farman*, or imperial order, that allowed the English to resume their trading, but at a cost. As the losers, the Company had to comply with certain conditions, such as paying a fine and returning seized goods.

Although the ensuing peace with Aurangzeb laid the foundation for the establishment of Calcutta, there was vehement opposition in England to the war and its seemingly disastrous consequences. One critic published an eight-page pamphlet complaining that Josiah Child had single-handedly caused the stock price to fall by embarking on "fatal and destructive" policies. According to the author, the war had been a particularly poor decision since it had ruined the good name of the English: "Thus has the *English* Nation been made to *stink in the Nostrils* of that People; when before, from the time that we first set footing on that Golden Shoar, we were the most beloved and esteemed of all *Europeans*."[47]

Trade: Spices, Pepper, Textiles

Over the course of the seventeenth and eighteenth centuries, the Company altered its patterns of trade. During the first phase, which lasted until the 1640s, the Company concentrated most of its attention on the spice and, especially, the pepper trade. It found, however, that Dutch

---

46. Hamilton, *New Account*, I.124.

47. Anonymous, *Some Remarks upon the Present State of the East-India Company's Affairs: With Reasons for the speedy Establishing a New Company, to Regain That almost Lost Trade, Which Is Computed to Be in Value and Profit One Full Sixth Part of the Trade of the Whole Kingdom* (London: 1690), 1, 7.

control over the Spice Islands, combined with the need to pay for spices with Indian textiles, encouraged a shift in focus to the Indian textile markets. Textiles remained the Company's principal commodity until the second half of the eighteenth century, when it found greater profits in the sale of Indian opium to China and Chinese tea to Europe. We will concentrate on the spice, pepper, and textile trade in this section and discuss the shift to tea and opium in the next chapter.

By the time the Company was founded, the English had learned to use and enjoy spices. Spices gave flavor to dishes, preserved meats, masked unpleasant smells when collected in a pomander, and even soothed toothaches. Both the Dutch and the English companies were particularly interested in purchasing cloves, nutmeg, mace, and pepper. The great difficulty for the Company was that cloves, nutmeg, and mace could be found only in and around the Banda group of islands and the Moluccas, a region that was increasingly under the control of the Dutch. Pepper was widely grown in Southeast Asia as well as on the southwestern coast of India.

The Dutch established their dominance over the spice trade very quickly. Their United East India Company, Verenigde Oost-Indische Compagnie, or VOC, was founded in 1602 with strong financial backing. While the English Company raised £68,373, the VOC accumulated £550,000 to fund its first voyages. This comparative strength continued for the rest of the century. On average, the VOC sent seven ships to Asia for every three sent by the Company.[48] The VOC's ships were powerful vessels and they were able, over the course of about sixty years, to displace and marginalize the Portuguese. At the heart of the VOC's Asian network was Batavia, an impressive canal-lined and fortified city on the island of Java. Founded in 1619, Batavia was the capital of an elaborate, centralized commercial and political system. The Dutch used silver from the Americas and, until 1668, Japan to purchase Indian textiles to trade for spices and pepper in Southeast Asia. They differed from the English in that almost all goods were transported first to Batavia and then on to the Netherlands. The Company did not have a similar commercial hub but instead developed several presidencies.

The Dutch desire to monopolize the spice and pepper trade pushed the VOC to control the source of those commodities. In the case of pepper, the VOC's reach was limited, largely because pepper vines grew in many parts of Asia. In the case of cloves, nutmeg, and mace, however,

---

48. Furber, *Rival Empires*, 38, 78.

the VOC was able to exert more control. An early VOC director general, Jan Pieterszoon Coen (1587–1629), established a brutal regime over the Spice Islands, which involved the forced destruction of unneeded clove trees, the enslavement of the island's population, and the public execution of those who resisted.[49] The violence enabled the VOC to dominate the flow of spices to Europe to such an extent that one Company factor in the Moluccas, writing about the Dutch in 1618, complained, "[These] butter-boxes are groanne soe insolent that yf . . . they be suffred by a whit longer, they will make claime to the whole Indies, so that no man shall trade but themselves or by their leave."[50] The Company tried to seize the upper hand by fighting the Dutch in Java, but their efforts were unsuccessful.

Conflict between the Dutch and English companies was temporarily resolved in 1619 with an agreement that gave the Company one third of the spice trade and one half of the pepper trade in exchange for contributing one third toward the cost of VOC fortifications. It quickly became apparent, however, that the Dutch were unwilling to share and the English were unwilling to pay. Tensions mounted in the subsequent years, resulting in an incident on a small Spice Island that clouded relations between the Dutch and English companies for much of the rest of the century.

In early 1623 the Dutch governor of Amboyna (Ambon) accused the English traders, Japanese mercenaries, and a Portuguese slave overseer of plotting a coup. According to the English version of events, the Dutch governor used torture to extract false confessions. Tactics included tying men to a doorframe and wrapping a cloth around each face.

> That done, they poured the Water softly upon his Head until the Cloath was full up to the Mouth and Nostrils . . . so that he could not draw breath, but he must withal suck in the water: Which being still continued to be poured in softly, forced all his inward parts, to come out of his Nose, Ears, and Eyes, and . . . at length took away his breath, and brought him to a swoun or fainting.[51]

---

49. Ibid., 45.

50. Cited in Shankar Raman, *Framing "India": The Colonial Imaginary in Early Modern Culture* (Stanford: Stanford University Press, 2002), 196.

51. *A True Relation of the Unjust, Cruell, and Barbarous Proceedings against the English at Amboyna in the East Indies: By the Neatherlandish Governour and Councel There* (London?: 1624), 9.

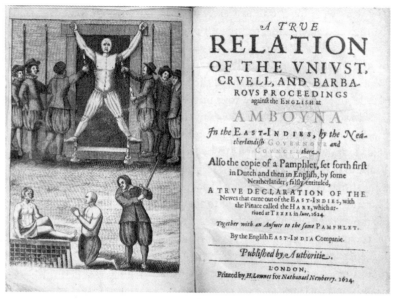

Fig. 1. Frontispiece and Title Page, *A True Relation of the Unjust, Cruell, and Barbarous Proceedings against the English at Amboyna* (1624). Middlebury College Special Collections and Archives, Middlebury, Vermont.

When waterboarding was insufficient they lit candles under the men's armpits and feet. In the end ten Englishmen were executed.[52]

The Amboyna Massacre, as it became known in England, was partially resolved in 1654, when the Dutch paid £85,000 in compensation,[53] but the tragedy was too good a massacre to be forgotten by propagandists. It was the subject of a pamphlet war between the Company and VOC and was used as a means of generating hostility toward the Dutch during the three Anglo-Dutch naval wars (1652–54, 1665–67, and 1672–74).[54]

---

52. For more information on the events and consequences, see D. K. Bassett, "The 'Amboyna Massacre' of 1623," *Journal of Southeast Asian History* 1, no. 2 (1960): 1–19; Karen Chancey, "The Amboyna Massacre in English Politics, 1624–1632," *Albion* 30, no. 4 (1998): 583–98.

53. Catherine Pickett, *Bibliography of the East India Company: Books, Pamphlets and Other Materials Printed Between 1600 and 1785* (London: British Library, 2011), 17.

54. See, for example, *A Remonstrance of the Directors of the Netherlands East India Company . . . And the Reply of the English East India Company* (London: John Dawson for the East India Company, 1632).

The wars were fought almost exclusively in European waters over trade, fishing, and navigation rights, although the hostility between the two companies was a factor.[55] The massacre was even the subject of a play by the celebrated poet and playwright John Dryden (1631–1700).[56] Written in 1673, at the height of the last Anglo-Dutch war, much of the play focuses on an invented love interest as the trigger for the more historically accurate events. In the play, the Dutch governor's son, Harman Junior, falls in love with the leading English merchant's fiancée-turned-wife, Ysabinda, who happens to be from Amboyna. After failing to win Ysabinda's heart, the governor's son ties her to a tree and rapes her. The Englishman, Gabriel Towerson, discovers her bound and proceeds to kill Harman but is then denounced to the governor for robbery, murder, and plotting a coup. In the play's final act Towerson and his fellow Englishmen are tortured and tried by the governor. To an English seventeenth-century audience it would have been clear that the rivals' fight over Ysabinda mirrored the larger struggle over corporate and national access to the Spice Islands and their products.

Because of the VOC's strength, the Company found that it had better access to and greater profits from pepper than from the other spices. Pepper imports peaked at 3,000,000 pounds in 1626 but then began to trend down so that by 1640 the Company shipped only about 600,000 pounds.[57] As with any wholesaler, the Company had to monitor purchase and sale prices closely since in order to make a profit it had to auction goods at between two to three and a half times their cost.[58] Beginning in 1628 the Company established its pepper headquarters at Bantam to the east of Batavia. The factors at Bantam also oversaw the shipment of cloves, many of which were bought at Makassar, having been smuggled out of the Dutch-controlled Spice Islands. The Dutch finally forced the Company to leave Bantam in 1682, compelling the Company to conduct its diminishing pepper trade from Bencoolen (Bengkulu) in southern Sumatra.

---

55. J. R. Jones, *The Anglo-Dutch Wars of the Seventeenth Century* (London: Longman, 1996).

56. John Dryden, *Amboyna: A Tragedy* (London: Henry Herringman, 1673).

57. Chaudhuri, *English*, 148.

58. Ibid., 201.

When profits from the sale of pepper and cloves declined in the 1630s, the Company turned its focus to textiles. To buy textiles, whether for auction in London or for barter in Asia, the Company had to provide large quantities of silver bullion. The problem the Company faced was that it could not sell English goods, whether wool or metals, such as tin, copper, and iron, in nearly sufficient quantities to buy textiles. However, silver was accepted and, as a result, the Company, like the VOC, established what has been called a triangular trade. First it acquired Spanish silver from European bullion markets in London, Amsterdam, and Cadiz. The silver had been mined in Mexico and Peru and the Company bought bars and coins, usually in the form of reales, sometimes called pieces of eight or, in the eighteenth century, Spanish dollars.[59] Not all silver coin was equal, however. Asians preferred coins minted in Seville and Mexico City to those minted to a lesser standard in Potosi and Lima.[60] Huge quantities of silver were transported to Europe, especially after the Potosi mines were opened in 1545. For example, in the period 1521–44 the world's average annual output of silver was 90,200 kilograms. Eighty years later the figure had jumped to 422,900 kilograms, the difference coming mostly from the Americas.[61] It was this silver that funded the purchase of textiles, which, when brought back to London, closed the triangle. The export of bullion was so important to the Company that it has been calculated that, between 1660 and 1720, 79.4 percent of Company imports to Asia were in the form of bullion. European goods accounted for the remainder.[62] As we will see in the next section, the export from England of so much silver was controversial.

The Company's fortunes were at a relative low between the 1620s and 1657, which included the turbulent years of the English Civil Wars (1642–51). Oliver Cromwell (1599–1658) confirmed the Company's charter, which was reconfirmed by Charles II during the early years of the Restoration, and the Company then entered a period of growth that would last until 1684. Thereafter the Company would not see imports rise to 1680s levels until the 1740s.[63]

59. Sutton, *Lords of the East*, 7.

60. Chaudhuri, *Trading*, 170.

61. Raman, *Framing "India,"* 223.

62. Pearson, *Ocean*, 151.

63. Chaudhuri, *Trading*, 15.

During the last three decades of the seventeenth century the Company decreased its imports of pepper only slightly, from 90,996 pounds in 1668–70 to 80,719 pounds between 1698 and 1700, but it began to increase its imports of textiles to England. As a result, the value of the pepper trade decreased. Table 1 shows the invoice value to the Company for pepper, textiles, and tea between 1668 and 1740.

Table 1. Invoice values for pepper, textiles, and tea
in triennial increments, 1668–1740[64]

1668–70:	pepper 25.25%
	textiles 56.61%
	tea 0.03%
	Other products include silk, coffee, indigo, and saltpeter
1698–1700:	pepper 7.02%
	textiles 73.98%
	tea 1.13%
1738–40	pepper 3.37%
	textiles 69.58%
	tea 10.22% (and trending up to 25% by 1758–60)

As we might expect, the decline in the value of pepper is reflected in a decline in the percentage of goods exported to England from Bencoolen and other settlements in Southeast Asia. In the period 1668–70, Southeast Asia accounted for 23.29 percent of goods, but in 1698–1700 the share had dropped to 0.56 percent and then remained steady, so that in 1738–40 it was 0.75 percent. Bombay and Madras also saw an erosion of their trade, which reflects the Company's shift toward Bengal as the center for its textile trade. During the period between 1668 and 1740 the percentage of goods exported to Europe from Bombay and Madras declined from 36.07 percent and 27.81 percent, respectively, to just 6.06 percent and 12.31 percent, respectively. Over the same period Bengal saw its share increase from 12.33 percent to 65.92 percent. The first forty

---

64. Source: Prakash, *European*, 120.

years of the eighteenth century also saw the China trade increase from 2.06 percent to 12.28 percent.[65]

It is clear from these statistics that the cotton textile trade became the Company's bread and butter by the second half of the seventeenth century and that the trade increasingly focused on Bengal. One of the important consequences of the shift to cotton is that it underpinned the Company's eighteenth-century transformation into a land-based state. Because of cotton's importance we must examine it in more detail.

A common name for cotton cloth during the seventeenth and early eighteenth centuries was calico. The word "stuffs" was also used, although it could mean any kind of fabric, whether made of cotton, silk, or wool. There was an enormous variety of calico available, as many as eighty-five kinds,[66] and each region of India produced its own signature textiles. For example, Surat was known for its *baftas*, undecorated cloth that was often dyed red or blue.[67] The Coromandel Coast produced pintadoes, a painted cloth, and the famous chintzes, which were cotton fabrics, often featuring elaborate floral motifs, printed in red, indigo, green, and yellow.[68] Clothing, especially dresses, made of chintz became all the rage by the turn of the eighteenth century. This period was also the height of the chinoiserie craze and so the Company, responding to its customers' desires for Chinese exotica, ordered chintzes that combined Chinese, Indian, and European patterns. Because it was relatively inexpensive, at least in small quantities, servants and the middling sort were the first to wear chintz, but by the 1690s royalty and the aristocracy had also adopted it.[69] Large chintzes that were used as curtains and bedspreads were called palampores and remained popular well into the eighteenth century. The Bengal region was famous for its fine, light muslin.

Cotton textiles became popular because, unlike wool, they could be dyed and printed in vivid colors that did not run when washed. Although cotton clothing did not last as long as wool clothing, it was relatively

65. Source: Ibid., 121.

66. Chaudhuri, *Trading*, 501–5.

67. John Guy, *Woven Cargoes: Indian Textiles in the East* (New York: Thames and Hudson Inc, 1998), 50.

68. John R. Jenson, ed., *Journal and Letter Book of Nicholas Buckeridge, 1651–1654* (Minneapolis: University of Minnesota Press, 1973), 9.

69. Rosemary Crill, *Chintz: Indian Textiles for the West* (London: V&A Publishing, 2008), 15–16.

cheap and demand ballooned toward the end of the seventeenth century. The statistics are impressive. In 1613 the Company only imported 5,000 piece goods, but the number rose to more than 250,000 in 1664 and then 1,400,000 by 1694.[70] To put it another way, between 1670 and 1760 the Company imported on average three yards of cloth per person per year.[71] It has been estimated that between 1700 and 1725 the Company and the VOC together exported 22 percent of south Indian cotton production, although the value of those purchases was even higher since the companies tended to buy better than average textiles.[72]

The effects of this burgeoning trade were felt in both India and England. In India the influx of silver prompted or accelerated change at the local, regional, and imperial levels. At the local level, large numbers of weavers and merchants (who gave weavers advances and acted as the Company's intermediaries) migrated to Company settlements, such as Madras, contributing to their growth and prosperity. Rising demand for cotton at the ports stimulated internal trade since vast quantities had to be transported considerable distances from the cotton fields inland. More broadly, the circulation of silver inland helped the Mughal Empire and other Indian states maintain agricultural and military economies that were based on cash payments.

In England, in addition to spurring changes in fashion, the cotton trade threatened a long-standing domestic industry. For many centuries wool had been a source of English wealth, and the wool industry remained politically powerful. Wool was so important to the nation that the lord speaker of the House of Lords used (and still uses) a woolsack as his seat. The Company was required to export wool, which was mostly heavy broadcloth that could be used to line saddles and tents. However, the danger to the industry began to grow in the 1660s as more and more Europeans began to wear and use cotton, prompting the backers of wool, both inside and outside of Parliament, to organize.

---

70. Amelia Peck, "'India Chints' and 'China Taffaty': East India Company Textiles for the North American Market," in *Interwoven Globe: The Worldwide Textile Trade, 1500–1800*, ed. Amelia Peck (New York: Metropolitan Museum of Art, 2013), 283; Beverly Lemire, *Fashion's Favourite: The Cotton Trade and the Consumer in Britain, 1660–1800* (Oxford: Oxford University Press, 1991), 15.

71. Girogio Riello, *Cotton: The Fabric That Made the Modern World* (Cambridge: Cambridge University Press, 2013), 113.

72. Prasannan Parthasarathi, *The Transition to a Colonial Economy: Weavers, Merchants and Kings in South India, 1720–1800* (Cambridge: Cambridge University Press, 001), 73.

Between 1666 and 1680 several laws were passed to try to force the English to use wool. These laws stipulated that the dead could only be buried in wool: "No corpse of any person," one law stated, "shall be buried in any shirt, shift, sheet or shroud . . . made or mingled with flax, hemp, silk, gold, or silver, or in any other than what is made of sheep's wool only."[73] In addition, there were attempts to force the English to wear wool for six months of the year, require students and professors to wear woolen gowns all year round, and force female servants to wear felt hats.[74] These measures were defeated in Parliament, but import duties on cotton were increased to 35 percent by 1700 in the hope that this would discourage the use of imported textiles.[75]

The debates in Parliament had a cumulative effect. They eroded the Company's reputation and, as we shall see in the next section, helped create the conditions for the establishment of a new company. Many of the debates centered on the effects of the Company's imports on domestic industries; in a session in the House of Lords in 1695, John Pollexfen (1636–1715), a member of Parliament and a critic of the Company, testified that the Company exported £500,000 of bullion and imported goods worth £400,000 that would otherwise have been made in England. He went on to state that the cost of making cloth in India was one-twentieth the cost in England and, were it not for the Nine Years' War against France (1689–97), which hindered imports, everyone in England would now be dressed in calicos. He then famously announced, "Companies have bodies, but it is said they have no souls; if no souls, no consciences."[76]

Despite these protestations, stipulations that the dead must be buried only in wool, and increased cotton duties, the Company continued to import calicos for the domestic market. In response, Parliament changed its approach in 1701 and instead of forcing the use of wool, it banned the wearing of certain kinds of cotton: "All wrought silks, Bengalls, and stuffs mixed with silk or herba, of the manufacture of Persia, China or East Indies and all calicos painted, dyed, printed or stained there . . . shall not be worn or otherwise used within this kingdom of England."[77] The wool

---

73. Cited in Lemire, *Fashion's Favourite*, footnote 77, 24.

74. Lemire, *Fashion's Favourite*, 25.

75. Riello, *Cotton*, 119.

76. *The Manuscripts of the House of Lords, 1695–1697*, new series (London: His Majesty's Stationery Office, 1903), II.11.

77. Lemire, *Fashion's Favourite*, 31.

industry might have been cheered by this development, but any advantage it had won quickly disappeared. Cotton piece goods were smuggled into the country in large quantities, so that it remained possible to buy chintzes and palampores. Daniel Defoe (1660?–1731), now famous for his novel *Robinson Crusoe*, was then best known as a prolific commentator on current affairs. He was no friend of the Company, and in January 1708, at the height of the calico controversy, he bemoaned the popularity of cotton and silk cloth, which even the queen wore on occasion:

> Nor was this all, but it crept into our Houses, our Closets, and Bed Chambers, Curtains, Cushions, Chairs, and at last Beds themselves were nothing but Callicoes or Indian Stuffs, and in short almost every Thing that used to be made of Wool or Silk . . . was supply'd by the Indian Trade.[78]

Smuggling was certainly a problem, but the 1701 law had a loophole: the Company was still allowed to sell unfinished and white cotton cloth to be dyed and printed in England. This loophole stimulated a new domestic printing industry. By 1711 more than one million yards of calico were printed in England.[79] The calico craze was in full bloom, prompting riots and violent protests by those employed in the domestic silk and wool industries. In London, for example, a crowd spotted one unfortunate woman who was wearing calico:

> Some People sitting at their Doors, took up her Riding Hood, and seeing her Gown, cry'd out Callicoe, Callico. . . . Whereupon a great Number came down and tore her Gown off all but the Sleeves, her Pocket, the head of her Riding Hood, and abus'd her very much.[80]

In 1721 the use and sale of almost all cotton textiles, whether plain or printed, was banned, a prohibition that was not lifted until 1774, when it became apparent that cotton printed in England was actually a national

---

78. Daniel Defoe, *Defoe's Review*, Facsimile Book II, November 11, 1707 to March 25, 1708 of Vol. IV (New York: AMS Press, 1965 [1708]), 606.

79. Lemire, *Fashion's Favourite*, 33.

80. Cited in Lemire, *Fashion's Favourite*, 36.

manufacture.[81] It was legal, however, to manufacture and sell mixed textiles, such as fustian, a cotton-linen cloth that became a favorite source of cheap clothing until the return of all-cotton clothing toward the end of the century. Even with the ban on imported textiles, the Company continued to make considerable profits on the sale of cotton cloth. The Company was allowed to sell pure cotton textiles for re-export, mostly as coarse, striped "Guinea cloth" for the slave trade or as softer calicos for the American markets. The Company did not itself trade with Africa or the American colonies—that trade was given to other merchants, such as the Royal African Company—but Indian cloth was an important commodity, amounting to about 27 percent of all British exports to Africa during the eighteenth century.[82] We can see the importance of the Company's textile trade to the eighteenth-century British imperial economy in a letter the Company sent to its factors in Bombay two years after the conclusion of the Seven Years War (1757–1763), ordering specific types of Guinea cloth:

> Since the Peace the Slaving Trade to the Coast of Africa has greatly encreased, in course the Demand for Goods proper for that Market is very large; & . . . We are very desirous of contributing so far as lyes in Our Powers to the Encouragement of a Trade on which the well-being of the British plantations in the West Indies so much depends.[83]

The restrictions placed on imported textiles gave rise to a domestic industry situated, for the most part, in Lancashire, a county in the northwest of England.

Its development during the second half of the eighteenth century and the early nineteenth century is one of the key examples of Britain's rapid industrialization. There is much debate on the causes and effects of the Industrial Revolution, or transition, as it is now more commonly called, but a few general conclusions can be made. The shift from relatively small-scale textile manufacturing to large, geographically concentrated mills employing hundreds of workers was possible because of new technology, new work practices creating new efficiencies, and new markets.

---

81. Lemire, *Fashion's Favourite*, 41 and footnote 128.

82. Calculated from Riello, *Cotton*, 138.

83. Cited in Sven Beckert, *Empire of Cotton: A Global History* (New York: Alfred A. Knopf, 2014), 46.

Eighteenth-century inventions such as the flying shuttle, the spinning jenny, and the water frame allowed English manufacturers to compete with lower-priced Indian textiles. Capitalists exploited these developments by establishing large mills requiring a regulated workforce operating on a regular schedule. The new mills created such efficiencies that between 1780 and 1830 the cost of producing a yard of cotton cloth tumbled by 83 percent.[84] Indeed, by the early nineteenth century these cost efficiencies had created an extraordinary situation: because the cost of producing a yard of cloth was now linked to the quantity produced—the more produced, the lower the cost—Lancashire industrialists sought out markets where they could sell their cloth, even at a loss, so long as they could still compete in profitable European or North American markets. By the end of the Company's life, India had become a major market for English-made cloth, which decimated indigenous manufacturing. The Indian cotton industry was further reduced during the second half of the eighteenth century by restrictive contracts that bound weavers to merchants and the Company in ways that led to their steady impoverishment.

Domestic Rivals and the New Company

The opposition to the Company's cotton trade was not an isolated phenomenon. Throughout the century the Company had to contend with rival English merchants, called interlopers, who tried to find ways to defy the Company's monopoly. Interlopers were a thorn in the Company's side. They did not buy a license from the Company but still sent ships to Asia. The Company lobbied to have their ships impounded and was forced to spend considerable resources to fend off these challenges. Ultimately, the Company was successful, but it was faced with its gravest threat of the century when in 1698 the king granted a rival English company a charter to trade to the East Indies.

One of the first signs of trouble for the Company occurred in 1604, when Sir Edward Michelborne (ca. 1562–1609) persuaded King James I (1566–1625) to grant him permission to trade to Asia. Michelborne was an early supporter of the Company but had become disaffected when it refused to give him the command of a ship. His own adventure turned

---

84. Riello, *Cotton*, 214.

out to be little more than piracy, but it affected the Company because it had to explain to its new trading partners that it had no part in his actions. Shortly afterward, in 1607, just as the Company was beginning to show a profit to its subscribers, the king gave permission to another adventurer, Richard Penkevell (no known dates) to form the Colleagues for the Discovery of a Northern Passage to China, Cathay, and other parts of the East Indies. This venture also proved to be short-lived, but it was evident that, even at a very early stage, there were merchants who wished to compete against the Company. The Company also received an early lesson in the fickle ways of monarchs.[85]

In addition to the unwanted competition, the Company faced opposition to its trading privileges. The first serious salvo came in 1615, when Robert Kayll (no known dates) published *The Trades Increase* under the initials J. R. Although Kayll focused on the value of the fishing industry to the nation (and especially the herring catch), he criticized other trades, including the Company's ventures to the East Indies.[86] For example, he noted that in the fourteen years since the Company began to trade, a large number of ships had been lost, that more than two thousand men had died during the voyages, that its ships returned in very poor condition, that the increased need for wood for shipbuilding meant that English forests were being cut down, that provisioning the ships caused inflation, and that the Company's commodities were unnecessary. In what may have been a slight to the Company, Kayll gave his book a title that was the same as the name of the Company's largest and most magnificent ship. Tragically, the ship *Trades Increase* had run aground and had been abandoned at Bantam. Kayll's criticisms were ones that the Company and its supporters countered, with some even dismissing them offhandedly. Indeed, Dudly (or Dudley) Digges (1582/3–1639), writing on behalf of the Company, introduced his defense with the remark "When I first heard of an Invective publisht by some unknowne busie Person, against the *East Indian Trade*: I must confesse, I held it . . . worthy only of that

---

85. For further details and a full chronology concerning the Company's competition and opposition, see William Robert Scott, *The Constitution and Finance of English, Scottish and Irish Joint-Stock Companies to 1720, Vol. II: Companies for Foreign Trade, Colonization, Fishing and Mining* (Cambridge: Cambridge University Press, 1910), 89–207.

86. For a full discussion of this publication and the Company's response, see Miles Ogborn, *Indian Ink: Script and Print in the Making of the English East India Company* (Chicago: University of Chicago, 2007), 107–20.

Companies contempt." Nevertheless, he then rebutted Kayll's objections point by point. For example, Digges addressed the complaint that when mariners died they left behind poor widows and unpaid creditors by noting a little facetiously that the Company chose single men, that they were paid "extraordinarie wages," and that if they happened to die on their return, the great profit from their voyages "soone dries the eies of friends and creditors, as it might doe widowes."[87] Perhaps his most important defense was that the Company's trade had reduced the price of pepper and spices.

Digges did his best to blunt the criticisms leveled at the Company, but Kayll's most damaging observations were ones that would haunt the Company in one way or another for more than two centuries. The first was that the Company was exporting vast quantities of silver, the source of the nation's wealth and, ultimately, power. Kayll drew a parallel between the Company and the Portuguese, who, in the previous century, had been criticized by Charles V, the Holy Roman Emperor. To Kayll the Company, like the Portuguese, "were the enemies to Christendome, for they caried away the treasure of Europe to enrich the heathen." The second major criticism was that no one was allowed to trade freely to the East Indies: "How much more we, murmuring at this iniquity, may affirme that we are all *Britaines*, all subjects of one royall King, all combined together in one naturall league, and therefore not to be barred from Trading equally to all places?"[88] In order for someone in England to benefit from the East India trade, that person had to buy shares in the Company or buy a costly license from the Company. He or she was not allowed to trade independently except when in Asia, and then only as part of the country trade. As the century progressed these shares often sold at above par, meaning they were expensive. Moreover, the Company resisted efforts to increase the number of shares in order to allow more investors. Both issues remained sources of frustration for those who wanted to profit from the Asia trade.

For the Company there was an uncomfortable truth to the charge that it was exporting a very large, perhaps excessive, quantity of silver. Indeed,

---

87. Dudly Digges, *The Defence of Trade. In a Letter To Sir Thomas Smith Knight, Governour of the East-India Companie, etc. From One of That Society* (London: William Stansby for John Barnes, 1615), 1, 38.

88. Robert Kayll, *The Trades Increase* (London: Nicholas Okes to be sold by Walter Burre, 1615), 32, 54.

in its first twenty-three years, the Company exported £753,336 in coin and bullion and only £351,236 in other commodities.[89] As we have seen, the Company quickly discovered that it could not sell nearly enough English goods in Asia to balance its purchases. Through its trade it also realized that silver was more valuable in Asia than in Europe, so exporting silver made economic sense. As a result the Company was placed in an awkward situation: it appeared to be shipping the nation's wealth out of England in order to buy luxury foreign goods that were then sold at a premium in London to the benefit of a few stockholders. The perennial question the Company faced was whether it was working against the national interest. That interest was defined by an economic theory that has come to be called mercantilism.

Mercantilists believed that a nation was wealthy or poor depending on how much gold and silver it controlled. Because they thought wealth was finite, the government had a duty to regulate trade to ensure a positive balance of trade, and society had a duty to lessen its appetite for exotic and expensive foreign goods. In these ways, the nation might accumulate a larger share of wealth than its enemies and thus be in a stronger position. To strengthen the nation, exporting gold and silver became illegal in 1615, although the Company was given an exception. However, as England's largest exporter of bullion and principal importer of spices and cotton cloth, the Company found it necessary to defend a system of trade that seemed to run counter to prevailing ideas of what was good for the nation.[90]

Thomas Mun (1571–1641) was a wealthy Company subscriber who rose to become deputy governor. His knowledge of the Company's business and prevailing economic theories made him the ideal man to defend the Company's practices. The Company has often been described as a mercantilist venture, but in the seventeenth century it had to contort itself to fit the definition. In *A Discourse of Trade, from England unto the East-Indies: Answering to Diverse Objections Which Are Usually Made against*

---

89. Chaudhuri, *English*, 115.

90. For a full definition and discussion of mercantilism and the Company, see Erikson, *Between Monopoly and Free Trade*; Philip J. Stern *The Company State: Corporate Sovereignty and the Early Modern Foundations of the British Empire in India* (New York: Oxford University Press, 2011). See also Philip J. Stern, "Companies: Monopoly, Sovereignty, and the East Indies," in *Mercantilism Reimagined: Political Economy in Early Modern Britain and Its Empire*, ed. Philip J. Stern and Carl Wennerlind (Oxford: Oxford University Press, 2014), 177–95.

the Same, Mun identified four objections to the East India trade, many of which had been raised by Kayll, and answered them one by one. The first and most important objection was "The gold, silver, and Coyne . . . of this Kingdome, is exhausted, to buy unnecessarie wares." [91] He answered by asserting that the East India trade actually increased England's wealth, even though every year the Company exported £100,000 of bullion and imported £500,000 of goods. England benefited because the country only consumed the equivalent of £120,000 of goods, with the remainder re-exported and those profits returning to England.[92] The re-export business, therefore, was the key to understanding the ultimate value to the nation of the East India trade. Moreover, as Digges had pointed out earlier, the English consumer gained because the cost of East Indian commodities was now cheaper since the Company transported them by ship rather than by the expensive overland route.

Kayll's second principal accusation was that the East India trade was closed to all but the Company. As we have seen, this was not quite accurate. The Company permitted private country trade and, much to the chagrin of the Company, monarchs did occasionally grant licenses to syndicates or associations of merchants to trade to the East Indies. In theory, some of these licenses were issued with the proviso that the syndicates not intrude on the Company's established trade, but in practice that was very hard to achieve.

One of the most important efforts to break into the East India trade was organized by Sir William Courteen (ca. 1568–1636; sometimes spelled Courten) and, after his death, his son, also Sir William (d. 1655). Their venture began in 1635 and lasted about fifteen years. Their association was never successful and showed how difficult it was to create a viable trade without the Company's infrastructure, investment, and

---

91. Thomas Mun, *A Discourse of Trade, from England unto the East-Indies: Answering to Diverse Objections Which Are Usually Made Against the Same* (London: Nicholas Okes, 1621), 5. The second objection concerned the quantity of materials used to build the Company's ships, which were then not available to the state in times of emergency because they were in Asia or returned, but in poor condition. The third objection combined a number of criticisms: that the Company consumed too many goods when stocking its ships; that there was too high a rate of mortality on voyages; that the Company destroyed all other East India trade and had proven unprofitable even to the Company; and that the nation had not benefitted by the cheapness of spices and indigo. The final objection was that the Company's export of silver had led to a scarcity of English coin.

92. Ibid., 27–28.

overseas contacts. However, it also showed how vulnerable the Company's privileges could be when a monarch turned his support elsewhere.

In 1635 King Charles I (r. 1625–49) gave permission to Sir William and his association, formally known as the Adventurers to Goa and Other Parts, to create a trade to places in India that were not already controlled by the Company. Courteen's efforts to gain royal support were helped by the efforts of a royal favorite, but the king was in serious financial difficulties and needed help. He had developed an unsteady relationship with the Company, which had refused to allow him to buy shares and denied him a loan of £10,000. Later, in 1640, the king forced the Company to sell to him its pepper stock, but he only paid for a portion.[93] Knowing the king's urgent financial needs, Courteen gave Charles a £10,000 stake in the association.

The association sent a number of ships to the Indian Ocean in 1636, over the Company's objections, and was given another charter the following year. Despite these efforts, the trade was poorly managed, died down, was revived in 1641, but never flourished. In fact, it relied on violence and even resorted to circulating debased coins that it minted at its settlement on the island of Assada, just off the northwest coast of Madagascar.[94] The association, along with the Company, suffered during the Civil Wars in England and, at their conclusion, Oliver Cromwell (in power 1649–58) urged the two to find an accommodation. In 1649 they decided that the Company would handle the port to port India trade while the association would be responsible for trade from Madagascar.[95] In 1650 a number of association merchants joined the Company in issuing a new united joint-stock, which further reduced the threat to the Company. However, some merchants did not join and continued as interlopers.

Despite the continued presence of interlopers, the decades after the Civil Wars were profitable ones for the Company. This was largely due to the increased use of cotton in clothing and draperies, but it was also because the Company had secured its long-term financial future with a permanent joint-stock in 1657 and had deftly navigated the potentially treacherous political seas, first during the Civil Wars by gaining a charter from Cromwell, despite his initial reluctance to support a monopoly,

---

93. Scott, *Constitution*, 116.

94. Jenson, *Journal and Letter Book*, 10.

95. Pickett, *Bibliography*, 26.

and then at the Restoration in 1660. When the new king, Charles II, came to the throne (r. 1660–85), the Company quickly asked for a new charter and gave him valuable presents. The following year the Company received a charter, the most important new provision being the right "to make Peace or War with any Prince or People, that are not Christians, in any Places of their Trade, as shall be most for the Advantage and Benefit of The said *Governor and Company*, and of their Trade."[96] This clause would have profound implications, especially in the next century.

The Company's largess to the king continued through the rules of Charles II and his successor, James II (1685–88). In 1662 the Company loaned Charles £10,000, increasing it to £50,000 in 1666 and then £70,000 in 1667. From 1681 until the Revolution of 1688 the Company gave the king 10,000 guineas a year, a guinea being a gold coin then equivalent to a pound sterling. All this, plus more, helped the Company renew its charter and ward off demands for a rival company.

The king's support was certainly crucial to the Company's survival, but it did not mean that domestic opposition was quashed. The last quarter of the seventeenth century was a politically challenging time for the Company as it tried to fend off interlopers and other rival merchants who wanted to trade privately, wind up its joint-stock in order to broaden the subscription, or replace it with a new Company.

The Company responded in several ways. One author, writing under the pseudonym Philopatris, stated baldly on his pamphlet's title page "that the *East-India* Trade is the most National of all Foreign Trades" and that any "Clamors, Aspersions and Objections" were "Sinister, Selfish and Groundless." He went on to argue that the security of the nation depended on the success of its East India trade and that the trade could only be conducted successfully by a joint-stock company.[97] Even though only a small number of stockholders profited directly from the trade, the Company argued that it ultimately enriched the nation and provided a base for its strength.

Another line of argument was to defend the Company's monopoly by asserting that it was not actually a monopoly. The Company famously adopted this approach during a court case in 1683–85 involving Thomas Sandys, an interloper. Sandys had tried to send a ship to the East Indies,

---

96. *Charters Granted to the East India Company from 1601 ...* (1772?), 76.

97. Philopatris, Title Page in *A Treatise* (London: Printed for T. F. for Robert Boulton, 1681). For a discussion of authorship, see Stern, *The Company State*, 48.

but it had been stopped and the Company initiated legal proceedings against him. Both sides hired high-profile lawyers and the case quickly focused on the question of whether the king could give a company a monopoly of trade.[98] Sandys accused the Company of monopolizing commodities and controlling the prices "for the great and excessive advantages of the few."[99] The presiding lord chief justice, George Jeffreys, ruled against Sandys and agreed with the Company that it did not constitute an illegal monopoly. A monopoly, according to his definition, was a person or company who had been given an exclusive privilege to buy or sell "whereby any Person or Persons . . . are sought to be restrained of any Freedom or Liberty they had before."[100] In other words, a monopoly was a privilege given to one person and stripped from another. In the Company's case, there had never been a direct trade to India before the Company began its voyages—there had never been a "Freedom and Liberty" to trade. Only the Company had created that trade. Therefore, instead of enjoying an illicit monopoly, which benefited only private interest, the Company, to use Philip Stern's phrase, was given a licit exclusive privilege in order to benefit the nation.[101] As a pro-Company pamphleteer had written a few years before:

> Suppose . . . a *Countrey* that for the *difficulty of passage* to it . . . no *English* had traded to formerly; and that some *English* men at their own *Hazard* and *Charges* should . . . *Establish a Trade.* . . . May not the *King* by his *Prerogative* . . . grant the *Privilege* of the Trade to the *Discoverers* and *Adventurers*, and their *Successors*, thereby to encourage others to the like Noble undertakings, for the Generall good of his Kingdome? How could such a *Grant* be within the Compass of a *Monopoly*, Since no *English* man was denied or debarred of any Liberty that he before exercised or enjoy'd? . . . Shall not he that planteth a Vineyard eat the fruit thereof?[102]

---

98. For a full analysis see Stern, *The Company State*, 46–57.

99. Scott, *Constitution*, 148.

100. (George Jeffreys), *The Argument of the Lord Chief Justice of the Court of King's Bench Concerning the Great Case of Monopolies between the East-India Company, Plaintiff, and Thomas Sandys, Defendant* (London: Randal Taylor, 1689), 21.

101. Stern, *The Company State*, 48.

102. *An Answer to Two Letters, Concerning the East-India Company* (1676), 9.

The Company had enjoyed decades of eating its fruit following the formation of the permanent joint-stock in 1657, but its fortunes declined rapidly during the closing years of the century. Imports had risen steadily until 1684, when the total value of all Asian imports amounted to £802,527. The subsequent decline was steep. In 1688 imports came to £158,713 and in 1692 they were a paltry £26,386. Imports would rise again at the end of the century but would not approach their previous peak until the 1720s.[103] The Company's Mughal War, or Child's War, which decimated trade from Bombay, Surat, and Bengal, and the nation's Nine Years' War, which disrupted the re-export trade to the Continent and strained the country's finances, were partially to blame for the slump in trade, but interlopers continued to pose a problem.

The Company's economic woes were compounded in 1688–89, when the Catholic James II was forced from the throne in a "Glorious Revolution" that saw William of Orange (1650–1702) and his wife, Mary (1662–94), James' eldest daughter, installed as joint Protestant monarchs. The Company, under the leadership of Josiah Child, had cultivated the Stuart monarchy and now found itself in a weakened position. Their parliamentary enemies, many of them Whigs, redoubled their efforts to push aside the Company in favor of a new trade to the East Indies. They received backing from the Levant Company, which continued to resent the Company's successes and its inability, by the terms of the Company's charter, to send ships around the Cape of Good Hope to the Red Sea.[104] In addition there were calls for the Company to come to an accommodation with interlopers by winding up the joint-stock in order to re-issue it to a broader community. We should also remember that this was the period when the wool- and silk-weaving industries began to agitate against the Company's calico trade. All in all powerful forces were massing against the Company.[105]

Events moved quickly after the revolution. In 1693 the Company's charter was up for renewal and the Company's first tactic was to bribe

103. Chaudhuri, *Trading*, 508–9.

104. Anonymous, *The Allegations of the Turky Company and Others against the East-India-Company* (1681).

105. For full discussion of these events leading up to the creation of the new company and the eventual union of the new and old companies, see Stern, *The Company State*, 148–63; also Furber, *Rival Empires*, 98–99. Unless otherwise noted, information in the next paragraphs comes from these sources.

its way to royal favor. Vast sums were dispensed to influential members of Parliament and courtiers. Largess was nothing new. The Company had given Charles II an impressive £324,000 over the course of his reign. However, the difficulties in securing a charter in 1693 meant that the Company spent a staggering £170,000 in that year alone. It even offered to lend money to members of Parliament to buy Company stock and promised to buy it back if the profits were unsatisfactory.[106] The extent of the corruption was later revealed by a parliamentary investigation.

The Company's second tactic was to pay a tax on its stock a day late, thus automatically annulling its charter. There is some debate on whether this slight, but potentially disastrous, delay was a mistake or done on purpose, but it seems most likely to have been deliberate. The reasons were that it took the matter out of the hands of a hostile Parliament and put great pressure on the king, who needed income from the Company, to issue a new charter. William did so in November 1693.

With the new charter in hand the Company hoped to build on its momentum by mounting legal cases against interlopers. When these merchants appealed to the House of Commons to allow a new company to exist, it determined that "all subjects of England have equal right to trade to the East Indies, unless prohibited by act of Parliament."[107] This resolution challenged the authority of the king to award a monopoly of trade to a single company and raised the question of Parliament's role in managing the country's trade beyond its borders. As we will see in the next two chapters, the future would see Parliament, not the sovereign, control the terms of the Company's charter and the extent of its trading privileges.

Two decades of crises—the legal challenge of the Sandys case, its disastrous war in India, the flight of its royal patron, the drama surrounding the granting of its new charter, the exposure of its political corruption, and the opposition of the wool and silk manufacturing industries—had damaged the Company's reputation. By 1698 it was in a weakened state politically, and although imports had risen tenfold from its low six years earlier, it was still not in robust economic health. The nation's war with France had squeezed the treasury and made the king and Parliament look for additional sources of income. It was in this climate that the Company proposed to loan the government £700,000 at 4 percent interest.

---

106. Stern, *The Company State*, 154–55.

107. Scott, *Constitution*, 159–60.

The Company's opponents, finally sensing an opening, countered with an enticing £2 million at 8 percent. The government accepted the larger amount, despite the higher interest rate, and a General Society was established in order to raise the funds. Subscribers to that society were allowed to form a new joint-stock company with a new charter (a few merchants opted to trade independently) and, as a result, the English Company trading to the East Indies was formed in September.

This development might have led to the Old Company's death, but under the terms of the agreement the Company was given three years to wind up its affairs and, most importantly, was allowed, as a corporation, to subscribe to the New Company. As a result, it quickly invested £315,000 in shares of the New Company. This was a canny move because it meant that so long as the Old Company owned part of the New Company it could not be abolished. For four years the two companies operated in competition with one another. The rivalry was quite bitter, especially in parts of India, such as Surat, where a contemporary observer wrote:

> The Animosities betwixt the two Companys were carry'd to the greatest Height in this City; and their Servants were so zealous on both sides, that all other Considerations gave place to their Resentments, which has so alienated the Minds of the Old Standers from one another, that to this time they can scarce speak favourably of their Opposers, tho' their interests are the same.[108]

Over the years it became apparent that the Old Company had the advantages of a century of trade, such as commercial and political contacts in Asia and functioning factories, while the New Company had domestic political support. They both recognized that their rivalry diminished profits and that monopoly privileges increased them. They therefore looked for ways to combine forces. In July 1702 an agreement called an "indenture tripartite" between Queen Anne and the two companies began a process that eventually led to their union on April 22, 1709 as the United Company of Merchants of England trading to the East Indies.

The United Company, which we will continue to call the Company, adopted the nomenclature of the New Company. The governor and his

---

108. Lockyer, *Account of the Trade*, 260.

deputy became the chairman and the deputy chairman, while the Court of Committees became the Court of Directors; they remained responsible for running the Company's shipping and trade and were elected by the General Court of Proprietors. The Company changed its flag to reflect the recent union of England and Scotland. The old flag displayed the English Cross of St. George in the canton, or upper left quadrant, together with red and white stripes. The new flag kept the stripes but replaced the cross with the British Union Jack.[109] It also changed its coat of arms and motto. The old motto, "Deus Indicat. Deo Ducente Nil Nocent," or "God Shows the Way. With God Leading They Do No Harm," was changed to acknowledge the emerging importance of Parliament in the affairs of the Company: "Auspicio Regis Et Senatus Angliae," or "Under the Sign (or Auspices) of the King and Parliament of England."[110]

109. Stern, *The Company State*, 163.

110. My thanks to Jane Chaplin for help with the Latin translations.

CHAPTER TWO
The Eighteenth Century

From Merchants to Rulers

The Company experienced enormous change during the eighteenth century. It went from being principally a global trader to becoming a state. At the same time, it also saw its oversight of political and revenue policies gradually shift into the hands of the British state as the interests of the Company and the government began to coalesce. The form of colonial rule that the Company developed over the course of the century was therefore both complex and protean. Some historians see the early emergence of colonial rule and chart its transformation over the decades, while others place more emphasis on characterizing the second half of the century as a period of transition to the form of colonialism that is most easily recognizable to students today, such as the creation and use of racial hierarchies, the deliberate extraction of wealth and resources, and the articulation of a rationale for foreign rule based on paternalistic and evangelical notions of duty to and responsibility for supposedly inferior civilizations. All of these characteristics of colonialism were present in the eighteenth century, but they slowly became more marked and accepted by the British so that by the 1820s, when the so-called era of reform began, the Company's administration can be said to be a fully functioning colonial state.[1] Of course, that state continued to change throughout the nineteenth century, but the main questions for the eighteenth century are how the Company became a ruler and why its rule became colonial.

At the beginning of the century the Company was one of the main sources of wealth for Britain and, although its imports fluctuated over the next decades, its trade remained enormously important to the economic health of both Britain and the textile-exporting regions of India. In

---

1. For discussions of these issues see, P. J. Marshall, "Introduction," in *The Eighteenth Century in Indian History: Evolution or Revolution*, ed. P. J. Marshall (Delhi: Oxford University Press, 2003), 1–49; Durba Ghosh, *Sex and the Family in Colonial India: The Making of Empire* (Cambridge: Cambridge University Press, 2006), especially her introduction.

1700 the Company shipped to London £501,501 worth of goods, which accounted for 13 percent of England's imports.[2] The value of imported goods declined in the next decade but then recovered by 1720. The Company's trade was helped in 1717 by the decision of the Mughal emperor, Farrukhsiyar (1685–1719), to issue an imperial order, or *farman*, that allowed the Company to operate within the empire without paying customs duties. In the decades after 1720 imports remained relatively stable until 1760, which marked the beginning of a new and more aggressive phase of trade, especially to China. During the first half of the century the most important change in the Company's pattern of trade is that between 1726 and 1753 Bengal supplied more than 50 percent of the value of goods exported from Asia.[3] After 1726 the value of goods from both Bombay and Madras declined, while those from China increased, especially after 1746. The shift in trade made Calcutta the most important presidency town and helps explain why, when the town was lost to a local ruler in 1756, its recovery became a priority.

In the 1740s the Company began to assert itself in a more aggressive manner. As we have seen in the previous chapter, the Company had often attacked its Portuguese and Dutch rivals and had even fought the Mughals, but its actions tended to be small in scale. Its forces were designed primarily to protect fortifications, factories, and trade routes and rarely exceeded a few hundred men in any one location. Over the previous decades the Company had also established the structures of a state, such as the power to put on trial anyone who lived within its settlements as well as the right to mint coins, even in its name, but its authority was limited geographically. Two broad trends, one in India and one in Europe, prompted the Company to embark on a series of high-risk military ventures that rapidly expanded its power in ways no one could have foreseen in 1740.

At first, the Company regarded its military engagements as necessary expedients to defend its trade, but once the French and a number of Indian forces had been defeated, the Company's British employees in India, or "servants" as they were known, saw personal and corporate benefits to building an ever-expanding military state. As these changes were occurring during the second half of the century, many directors in London became concerned that the Company's new war footing was too

---

2. Chaudhuri, *Trading*, 508; Erikson, *Between Monopoly and Free Trade*, x.

3. Chaudhuri, *Trading*, 509–10.

costly and dangerous and they often voiced their disapproval. However, a cycle had been established by the 1760s that could not be broken, even by cautious directors: real and imagined threats to trade required a stronger army, and a growing army needed to be paid with ever-increasing quantities of silver. Although the Company continued for a short while to import silver to India, it was insufficient to pay for both its trade investment and its military. As a result, the Company's servants looked to India's land revenue as a seemingly inexhaustible source for its commercial and military investments and embarked on wars to secure those funds.

The second trend that affected the Company's position in India was the outbreak of war in Europe. The War of Austrian Succession (1740–48) and the Seven Years' War (1756–63) saw Britain and France join opposing alliances, with conflict spilling over into the southeastern coast of India. The three Carnatic Wars (1744–48, 1751–54, 1756–63) began with French success, most impressively demonstrated with the capture of Madras in 1746 (the city was returned to the British in 1748), but ended with the Company destroying French military ambitions in India. Over the course of these decades the Company militarized itself and intervened in regional politics, two developments that would only intensify in the following decades.

Anglo-French Rivalry

The French East India Company, La Compagnie des Indes Orientales, had been founded in 1664 ("Orientales" was dropped from the name in 1719), and after a period of low activity it successfully asserted itself in the trade and political networks of southern and central India. Both the British and French companies recognized that their financial health rested on control over the Indian export trade, and so establishing good relations with neighboring Indian rulers was a priority.[4]

By the late 1740s the companies saw the advantages of intervening in regional Indian political struggles. The death of a ruler was an especially

---

4. For a full discussion of the Anglo-French rivalry, see G. J. Bryant, *The Emergence of British Power in India, 1600–1784: A Grand Strategic Interpretation* (Woodbridge: Boydell Press, 2013), 35–106. See also Lawrence James, *Raj: The Making and Unmaking of British India* (New York: St. Martin's Griffin, 2000), 13–29.

dangerous and opportune time: rival sons needed armies to fight for the throne, and both companies were in a position to provide troops. The death of the nizam of Hyderabad, who had ruled a large state in south central India, together with the earlier death of the nawab of the Carnatic, prompted succession struggles in both courts. The French, under the leadership of Joseph-François Dupleix (1697–1763), had close ties to the Hyderabad court and managed to install their preferred candidate on the throne. They were also able to persuade the new nizam to transfer to them, as recompense for their help, a considerable amount of revenue from a large tract of land on the east coast of India known as the Northern Circars (Sarkars).

The French were less successful in the Carnatic, which bordered Madras. The French supported one contender for the throne while the Company backed Muhammad Ali (1717–95; Mohamed Ali Khan). A young Company soldier, Robert Clive (1725–74), captured Arcot, the capital of the Carnatic, on behalf of Muhammad Ali, which eventually led to his installation as ruler. French reverses continued during the Third Carnatic War, with a loss at the Battle of Wandiwash (1760) and the capture of their main factory, Pondicherry (1761). Although Pondicherry was returned to the French at the conclusion of the war, the French would never again pose a credible threat to the Company's trade and would play no substantive role in impeding the Company's rise to power in India.

It is not a coincidence that the decline of French influence in India occurred as the Company began its transition to ruler. The French had been capable of inflicting serious injuries on the Company, but poor decisions, such as the early recall to France of Dupleix, one of the most resourceful of the French company's servants; lack of French state support; and some bad luck tilted the balance in the Company's favor. Importantly, the twenty-three-year-long struggle with the French gave the Company's servants both the ability and the encouragement to turn to military force when problems arose with Indian rulers. The first test came in Bengal in 1756.

The Struggle for Bengal

After decades of enjoying growing profits from the Bengal textile, saltpeter and indigo trades, the Company's position suddenly worsened in April 1756, when the province's ruler, Alivardi Khan (1671–1756), died and his impolitic grandson, Siraj-ud-daula (1731/6?–57), became the nawab. In what seems to have been an effort to assert his authority over his subjects, the young nawab introduced changes in his court and military that, when combined with exorbitant demands for cash from influential bankers, created a climate of disaffection. Siraj-ud-daula also targeted European companies, hoping to reduce their trading privileges. He forced the Dutch and French to pay large sums and, believing the Company's fortifications at Calcutta to be an affront to his authority, he launched an attack on the city on June 18, 1756.[5]

Calcutta and its fort fell quickly and the nawab's forces captured a number of Company employees, some of whom were British. According to John Zephaniah Holwell (1711–98), at that time a junior member of the presidency's governing council, 146 prisoners were forced to spend the night in the fort's prison, colloquially called the "Black Hole." The heat and humidity were so intense that by morning only twenty-three had survived. Holwell's lurid account of his experience is so melodramatic that it is hard to take it seriously:

> Whilst I was at this second window, I was observed by one of my miserable companions on the right of me, in the expedient of allaying my thirst by sucking my shirt-sleeve. He took the hint, and robbed me from time to time of a considerable part of my store . . . and our mouths and noses often met in the contest.[6]

Indeed, research has shown that "at the most only sixty-four persons were confined in the Black Hole, of whom twenty-one survived."[7] Nevertheless, the nineteenth-century British colonial community took Holwell

---

5. For a fuller account of the Company's rise to power in Bengal, see P. J. Marshall, *Bengal: The British Bridgehead, Eastern India, 1740–1828* (Hyderabad: Orient Longman, 1990), 75–92.

6. John Zephaniah Holwell, *A Genuine Narrative of the Deplorable Deaths of the English Gentlemen, and Others, Who Were Suffocated in the Black Hole . . .* in *India Tracts* (London: T. Becket, 1774), 399.

7. Brijen K. Gupta, *Sirajuddaulah and the East India Company, 1756–1757: Background to the Foundation of British Power in India* (Leiden: E. J. Brill, 1962), 78.

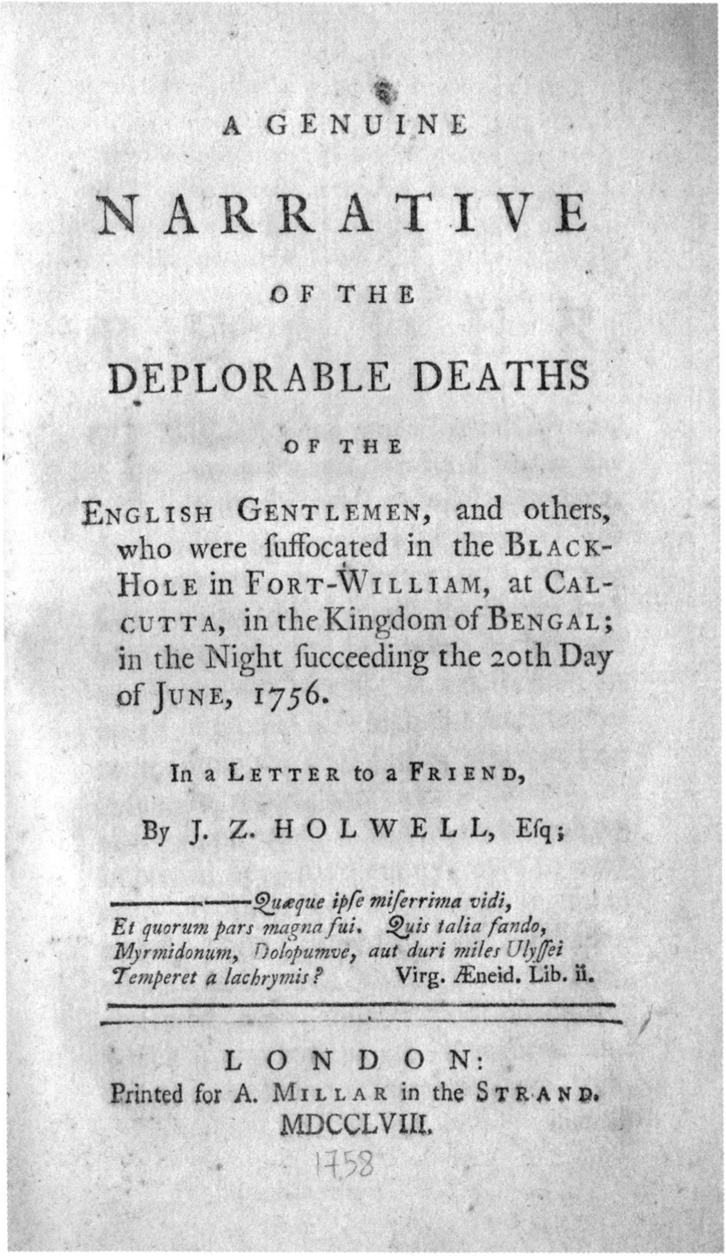

A GENUINE

NARRATIVE

OF THE

DEPLORABLE DEATHS

OF THE

ENGLISH GENTLEMEN, and others,
who were suffocated in the BLACK-
HOLE in FORT-WILLIAM, at CAL-
CUTTA, in the Kingdom of BENGAL;
in the Night succeeding the 20th Day
of JUNE, 1756.

In a LETTER to a FRIEND,

By J. Z. HOLWELL, Esq;

—————————*Quæque ipse miserrima vidi,*
Et quorum pars magna fui. Quis talia fando,
Myrmidonum, Dolopumve, aut duri miles Ulyssei
Temperet a lachrymis?   Virg. Æneid. Lib. ii.

LONDON:
Printed for A. MILLAR in the STRAND.
MDCCLVIII.

1758

Fig. 2. Title Page, J. Z. Holwell's *A Genuine Narrative*
(1758). Middlebury College Special Collections
and Archives, Middlebury, Vermont.

at his word, and the suffering of the Black Hole prisoners became a justi-
fication for the conquest of Bengal.

At the time, the Company's servants in India, especially in Madras,
which was the only settlement capable of providing an army, wanted
to restore the Company's lucrative Bengal trade. A force under the
command of Clive was sent to Bengal, recaptured the town in early
1757, and secured from the nawab the Company's old trading privileges. By June, however, Clive had set his sights on toppling the nawab.
Siraj-ud-daula had made enemies within his court and among his bankers, and some of these men pledged to help Clive. On June 23, 1757,
Clive's army met the nawab's at Plassey, a village between Calcutta and
the province's capital, Murshidabad. As had been secretly agreed, much
of the nawab's army, under the command of Mir Jafar (1691–1765),
held back, resulting in Siraj-ud-daula's defeat. Siraj-ud-daula fled the
battleground but was captured and killed, allowing Mir Jafar to become
the new nawab. The British called these acts of treachery and duplicity
a revolution.

Over the next seven years the affairs of Bengal remained in turmoil.
Mir Jafar found himself increasingly dependent on the Company for
protection against external forces. At the same time, he was compelled
to distribute to both the Company and its leading servants large sums
of money as compensation. When he refused to assign to the Company
the revenue from large and productive districts, the British forced him
to abdicate in September 1760 in favor of his son-in-law Mir Kasim
(?–1777).

Mir Kasim hoped to establish his independence from the British in
the north of Bengal and in Bihar, leaving the southern districts to the
Company.[8] However, his efforts were destroyed when the Company's servants pressed the nawab to give trade concessions to private individuals
(and not just to the Company). This was a step too far, and war broke out
in July 1763. Mir Kasim fled to Awadh, to the west, and the British rein-
stalled Mir Jafar, who died shortly thereafter and was succeeded by his
teenaged son Najm-ud-daula (1750–66). The decisive battle occurred
at Buxar in Bihar in October 1764 and pitted Mir Kasim, Shuja-ud-
daula (1731–75), the nawab wazir of Awadh and the Mughal emperor,
Shah Alam (1728–1806), against the Company's forces. The Company

---

8. Marshall, *Bengal*, 85–87.

defeated its enemies and, at the subsequent Treaty of Allahabad on August 12, 1765, Shah Alam granted the Company the *diwani* for the provinces of Bengal, Bihar, and Orissa "from generation to generation, for ever and ever." In return, the emperor received an annual payment of 2,600,000 rupees from the nawab of Bengal, a sum that was guaranteed by the Company.[9]

The grant of the *diwani* was a defining moment in the Company's history. It was the legal instrument by which the Company gained responsibility over the province's finances. In particular, it meant that the Company could now collect and use the vast land revenues of territories that were more populous than Britain. In the past the nawab of Bengal had been subordinate to the Delhi-based Mughal emperor who had given the nawab the responsibility for the *diwani* and the province's defense and criminal justice. By the third decade of the eighteenth century, it was clear that the nawab of Bengal had become independent in all but name. However, the nawab's legitimacy rested on vestigial ties to and titles from the emperor, and so it was important for anyone who had pretensions to rule Bengal to receive appropriate grants from the emperor. The defeat of Mir Kasim and his allies and the elevation once again of Mir Jafar proved that it was the Company, and not the nawab, who effectively ruled Bengal and Bihar. Once the British gained control over the *diwani*, Robert Clive instituted a policy of dual governance that lasted until 1772. During this period the Company oversaw the collection of revenue while the nawab continued to administer criminal justice and, in theory, the defense of the province.[10] The nawab was subsequently stripped of any remaining authority and lived on a stipend given by the Company.[11]

---

9. East India Company, et al. *Treaties and Grants from the Country Powers to the East India Company: Respecting Their Presidency of Fort St. George, on the Coast of Choromandel, Fort-William, in Bengal, and Bombay, on the Coast of Malabar: From the Year 1756 to 1772* (London, 1774), 133.

10. For an examination of the ideologies underpinning British rule in Bengal, see Robert Travers, *Ideology and Empire in Eighteenth-Century India: The British in Bengal* (Cambridge: Cambridge University Press, 2007).

11. For more on the transition to Company rule, and especially the role of Saiyid Muhammad Reza Khan, an influential and prominent official in the Bengal administration, see Abul Majed Khan, *The Transition in Bengal, 1756–1775: A Study of Saiyid Muhammad Reza Khan* (Cambridge: Cambridge University Press, 1969).

The Company's Internal Organization

The tumultuous situation in Bengal was reflected in increased jockeying and politicking in the Company's London operation.[12] Twenty-four directors ran the Company, operating through twelve committees (the number fluctuated at times), dealing with political, business, and shipping interests. The directors were themselves led by a chairman and a deputy chairman. The committees received the letters from their servants abroad and wrote instructions that covered both high policy questions and day-to-day administrative matters. Their role was, therefore, crucial to the functioning of the Company. However they were paid relatively poorly—£300 annually by the end of the century—but patronage and nepotism brought the greatest financial benefit beyond the dividends they received as stockholders. Every director was given the right to nominate a certain number of young men of their choosing to be writers (in the civil administration) or cadets (in the military establishment), and the two chairmen could nominate twice as many as the directors. Until 1853 there were no entrance exams and so directors could give positions to their own sons and close relatives or sell them. For much of the beginning and middle parts of the eighteenth century, Madras was the most coveted post, but by the end of the century, with the opium and tea trades in full bloom, writerships at Canton were considered the best, followed by those at Calcutta, Madras, Bombay, and, finally, Bencoolen and St. Helena. A director could expect to receive £3,500 for nominating a writer and between £150 and £500 for a cadet. Every year the Company sent out about forty writers and 240 cadets. For a young man whose family could afford to pay, a writership could prove to be very lucrative. The chief supercargo, or agent, at Canton could expect to make £20,000 annually.

When the Company suddenly gained territories in the 1750s and 1760s, with its promises of vast wealth for those in control of the Company, and when newly enriched servants, such as Clive, returned from India with a passion for politics and self-aggrandizement, the stakes at the Company's elections rose considerably. The proprietors met as a general court four times as year, in March, June, September, and December, but they also met in April to elect the directors. In order to

---

12. Unless otherwise noted, information on the Company's organization comes from C. H. Philips, *The East India Company 1784–1834* (Manchester: Manchester University Press, 1961 [1940]), 2–15.

control these elections, wealthy proprietors, such as Clive and his great opponent Laurence Sulivan (ca. 1713–86), resorted to splitting their stock, or transferring ownership of £500 of stock, entitling a person to vote, to a family member or trusted associate in order to increase the votes they commanded. The resulting elections were rancorous and raucous affairs.[13] Reforms in 1767 and 1773 made it a little more difficult to split stock by requiring proprietors to hold stock for at least six months before he or, in theory, she could vote. The reforms also brought in a new voting qualification, whereby only proprietors who owned £1,000, £3,000, £6,000, and £10,000 of stock could vote, with each block of stock entitling the proprietor to one, two, three, or four votes. The effects were to consolidate power in the hands of large stockholders and eliminate stock splitting.[14] By this time it became common for the directors to publish a "house list" of preferred candidates to fill the six open positions every year. Mounting an independent campaign was an expensive proposition, and so the list was usually voted in. Directors served for four years, spent a fifth out of the "direction," but were commonly voted back in. In practice, therefore, about thirty men ran the Company.

Who owned the stock? Table 1 shows the social composition of investors in a typical year. It indicates that proprietors included aristocrats, professionals, and military men. However, the largest categories referred to the middling sort. In other words, the men and, to a lesser extent, women who bought stock were socially respectable and had sufficient income to invest. Politicians also owned stock: in the late 1760s and early 1770s about 23 percent of all members of Parliament owned Company stock.[15] Not shown on this table are the large number of Dutch proprietors, both men and women. In 1774 they owned 33.6 percent of the total stock and constituted 20.3 percent of the accounts.[16]

---

13. For a full discussion of the political milieu and the Company's internal disputes during the second half of the eighteenth century, see Lucy Sutherland, *The East India Company in Eighteenth-Century Politics* (Oxford: Oxford University Press, 1952).

14. For details, see Bowen, *Business*, 70; Ainslee Thomas Embree, *Charles Grant and British Rule in India* (London: George Allen & Unwin LTD, 1962), 124.

15. H. V. Bowen, *Revenue and Reform: The Indian Problem in British Politics 1757–1773* (Cambridge: Cambridge University Press, 1991), 31.

16. Bowen, *Business*, 107–8, 112.

Table 1. Social composition of Company stockholders, 1774,
showing the percentages of the total number of accounts.
For reasons of space not all categories are included.[17]

Male
Titled	5.3%
Esq.	29.8%
Gent.	9.5%
Merchant	8.8%
Profession	7.0%
Army, Navy	3.2%
Trade	3.2%

Female
Titled	1.7%
Wife	0.7%
Widow	5.9%
Spinster	3.2%

The proprietors were often divided and created "interests." The most visible were the shipping and Indian interests. The shipping interest was particularly powerful during the second half of the century and was led by shipping magnates who built the East Indiamen and then leased them to the Company at exorbitant rates. They refused to allow domestic competition and restricted the size of ships so that the cost of freight was very high, especially when compared to American and other European ships.[18] The Indian interest referred to Company servants who had returned home with enough money to buy stock with an eye to making money and influencing policy. A fair number also became politicians, but it is generally agreed by historians that they did not form an active voting bloc in Parliament.

---

17. Excerpted from Bowen, *Business*, 103.

18. James R. Fichter, *So Great a Profit: How the East Indies Trade Transformed Anglo-American Capitalism* (Cambridge: Harvard University Press, 2010), 175.

Financial and Political Crises

Beginning in the 1760s and continuing into the 1790s the Company experienced rapid change. Many historians consider these to be the crucial decades, when the Company transitioned from a trading entity into a pseudosovereign state. It certainly continued to trade goods and found an especially lucrative trade in opium and tea, but the most consequential changes were its assertion of its *diwani* rights in Bengal and its belligerent political and military posture toward its neighboring Indian states. By the end of the century the Company had built a formidable army and had used it to defeat or intimidate many of these states. As a result it controlled, either directly or indirectly, much of the north, east, and south of India and was well positioned to continue its aggression. Moreover, the Company expected to enrich itself by collecting the land revenue of Bengal and other annexed territories. With so much power and wealth behind it, many observers at the time were therefore bewildered when they saw the Company embroiled in serious financial and political crises.

These crises were so serious that they forced the British government to intervene in the Company's affairs. Parliament forced changes to the Company's Indian administrative and legal structures and created a special committee in London to monitor the directors' political decisions. One of the significant consequences of these developments was that, even as the Company gained the kind of power in India that was associated with sovereign authority, its independence in London was, over time, increasingly constrained.

When the news of the 1765 Treaty of Allahabad filtered back to London and once the proprietors understood that the land revenues of Bengal were now available to them, it was widely assumed that the Company would make a lot of money. It was claimed that the influx of revenue would allow the Company to permanently discontinue shipments of silver to India and that there would be more than enough to pay for its investment in Indian export goods, such as textiles; the purchase of Chinese tea; and the maintenance of its army. There was such confidence in the future financial condition of the Company that the proprietors even voted to raise the dividend. However, the early euphoria began to change to deep concern as it became clear by the beginning of the 1770s that the revenues were much less than anticipated and that the costs of the army and administration were ballooning.

During this era of crisis the Company's critics often attacked it on the basis of its monopoly privileges and the fact that it now had responsibilities as both a trader and a ruler. In 1773 Thomas Pownall famously captured the Company's changing roles when he declared, "The merchant is become the sovereign."[19] Adam Smith (1723–90) published *An Inquiry into the Nature and Causes of the Wealth of Nations* in 1776 and attacked the Company as a monopoly. One of his lines of argument was that the Company could not be both a monopoly and a ruler since those interests were directly opposed to one another. For example, he noted that sometimes a Company servant might order peasants to plow up a field of poppies and instead sow rice simply to raise the price of opium. At other times, the same servant might force a reverse course of action in order to increase the production of opium. In both cases, the actions are taken to manipulate the supply of opium to the market for the sole benefit of the Company and its servants. However, the ruler, or sovereign's, interest lies in opening up competition so that more commodities and more valuable commodities could enter the markets, which would lead to an increase in tax revenue for the state. As Smith noted, the Company's

> mercantile habits draw them . . . to prefer upon all ordinary occasions the little and transitory profit of the monopolist to the great and permanent revenue of the sovereign. . . . It is the interest of the East India company considered as sovereigns, that the European goods which are carried to their Indian dominions, should be sold there as cheap as possible; and that the Indian goods . . . should be sold there as dear as possible. But the reverse of this is their interest as merchants.[20]

The result, according to Smith, was that the Company's administration in India remained "subservient to the interest of monopoly," which stunted the "surplus produce of the country to what is barely sufficient for answering the demand of the company."[21]

---

19. Governor Pownall, *The Right, Interest, and Duty, of Government, As Concerned in the Affairs of the East Indies* (London: J. Almon, 1773), 3.

20. Adam Smith, *An Inquiry into the Nature and Causes of the Wealth of Nations* (Chicago: University of Chicago Press, 1976), II.153–55.

21. Ibid.

The Company's dire economic condition and the condition of Bengal gave Smith an opening to attack the Company. In the year before the Company gained the *diwani* it collected £606,132 in land revenue, mostly from lands immediately surrounding Calcutta and from districts on the east coast of India. Based on the optimistic assessments provided by Clive and others, the Company believed that it could count on receiving £4 million every year from just the Bengal revenues. In fact, the most it collected was £1,817,649 in 1765–66, and that figure declined over the next five years.[22] Then, in late 1769 Bengal experienced a terrible famine that lasted for more than a year and had long-term financial consequences for the Company. It is hard to calculate exactly how many died, with figures varying widely, but most historians estimate losses at between a third and a fifth of the population. The lack of data also makes it difficult to establish the number of people who lived in Bengal at the time of the famine, but records suggest that there were about 22 million people in 1789.[23] Given the length of time needed for the population to recover to prefamine levels, this figure may be a fair approximation for the number living in Bengal just before the famine. Charles Grant (1746–1823), a high Company servant, lived in the presidency at this time and later recorded his observations. "It was impossible," he wrote,

> to stir abroad without breathing an offensive air, without hearing frantic cries, and seeing numbers of different ages and sexes in every stage of suffering and death. . . . At length a gloomy calm descended. Death had ended the miseries of a great portion of the people, and when a new crop came forward in August, it had in some parts no owners.[24]

During this period of declining revenues and then famine, the Company was also losing money because the Bengal Council initiated a number of ill-conceived currency reforms. The root of the problem, as understood at the time, was a "silver famine," or a scarcity of silver currency. Once Bengal had been conquered the Company stopped importing silver and instead

22. Bowen, *Revenue*, 104.

23. Sugata Bose, *Peasant Labour and Colonial Capital: Rural Bengal Since 1770*, Indian ed. (Cambridge: Cambridge University Press, 1993), 14, 20.

24. Charles Grant, *Observations on the State of Society among the Asiatic Subjects of Great-Britain* (Cambridge: Cambridge University Press, 2013 [1797]), 19.

relied on land revenues for the money it needed to purchase goods and pay its army and administration. However, in addition to its inability to collect sufficient revenue, the Company's servants complained that there was too little silver in circulation. In order to get to the root of the matter, the Company turned to an experienced economist, James Steuart. In his analysis, published in 1772, he explained that recent experiments with bimetallism, or the introduction of gold mohur coins alongside silver rupees, exacerbated the drain of silver.[25] In 1766, for example, Clive had spearheaded the adoption of bimetallism, with the public intention of bringing hoarded gold into the currency markets. However, instead of setting the exchange rate between the silver and gold coin at the market rate, he and his council overvalued gold. The result was that whatever silver rupees were in circulation were immediately withdrawn by traders since they were unwilling to accept devalued rupees. Without a ready supply of silver coin it became difficult for peasants to pay land rents, which had cascading effects throughout market towns and in the administration. The decision was eventually reversed but not before anyone, such as Clive, who was rich and had prior knowledge of the regulation, was able to buy gold and then sell it for an immediate profit once gold coins became legal tender.

In Madras the Company's administration was insular, riven by faction and also known for its corruption. In the early 1770s one of the most egregious examples occurred when prominent Company servants lent large sums of money to the nawab of Arcot and the Carnatic, Muhammad Ali Khan.[26] The nawab secured these loans with the revenues from tracts of land that were under the control of the raja of Tanjore, the ruler of a nearby state, who, although independent, was nevertheless obliged to pay tribute to the nawab. In 1773 Muhammad Ali, in need of funds and at the same time promising more money to the Company, persuaded the Madras administration to use its troops to annex Tanjore to the nawab's territories. Soon after, the incoming governor of Madras, Lord George Pigot (1719–77), opposed this highly controversial act; he suspended two members of the council and reinstated the raja. However, the majority of the council, encouraged by the nawab, turned on Lord Pigot and

---

25. James Steuart, *The Principles of Money Applied to the Present State of the Coin of Bengal* (1772).

26. For a detailed account of the corruption in Madras, see Nicholas B. Dirks, *The Scandal of Empire: India and the Creation of Imperial Britain* (Cambridge: Belknap Press of Harvard University Press, 2006).

imprisoned him in August 1776. This coup was even supported by the Calcutta-based governor general, Warren Hastings (1732–1818), although once the news reached London the directors rebuked and fined the councilors. Unfortunately, rebukes and fines could not help Lord Pigot. He died in 1777 while still in custody in Madras. The issue of the nawab's enormous debts to Company servants lived on, however, and became a subject of considerable debate for many years, as it became increasingly clear that the Company would have to intervene. The unscrupulous way Company servants lent money to the nawab and the political instability it caused added to the British public's growing odium regarding the Indian affairs and actions of the Company and its servants.

But the Company's crises were not limited to India. The 1770s was a particularly difficult decade for the directors. As a result of an agreement made in 1768, when everyone believed that Bengal's riches would flood Britain, the Company was obliged to pay to the British government £400,000 every year. In addition, though, it faced a chronic trade imbalance, an acute financial shortfall, increased political scrutiny, and resentment among many in the public.

The Nabobs

What caught the public's attention was the return to Britain of Company servants who were suddenly very rich. Their opulent tastes and social extravagance were immediately noticed, as was their ability to buy landed estates and even parliamentary seats. They were popularly termed "nabobs," a corruption of the Arabic and Urdu title "nawab."[27] Life expectancy for the British in Bengal was poor, with at least 57 percent of all civil servants dying before they could return home. The situation was worse among the European recruits to the army: during the 1760s and 1770s about 25 percent of the Company's European soldiers died every year.[28] With an early death more likely than long-term survival, Company servants sought to make as much money as possible as quickly as possible. Many made their

---

27. Tilman W. Nechtman, *Nabobs: Empire and Identity in Eighteenth-Century Britain* (Cambridge: Cambridge University Press, 2010); Percival Spear, *The Nabobs* (Calcutta: Rupa and Co, 1991).

28. P. J. Marshall, *East Indian Fortunes: The British in Bengal in the Eighteenth Century* (Oxford: Oxford University Press, 1976), 218–19.

money from private trade, but others were given fortunes by Indian rulers who were desperate to ingratiate themselves with powerful Company officials on whom they were dependent. Soon after Mir Jafar was installed as the new nawab of Bengal, he gave Company servants the staggering sum of £1,750,000. Even after this initial outlay, the money continued to flow and the man who benefited the most was Clive. He estimated that by 1767, following his two stints as governor of Bengal (1757–60, 1765–67), he was worth £401,102. In addition, he claimed an annual rent from land in Bengal, known as his jagir, amounting to £27,000.[29] The jagir became a highly controversial perquisite—his enemies claimed the rent was really the Company's—but he managed to retain it and, together with the fortune he brought back from India in the form of diamonds, silver, and bills of exchange, he became one of the wealthiest men in Britain.

Like many nabobs, Clive was both greatly admired and intensely disliked. During the time he was governor for the second time, a large number of Bengal army officers turned against him because he had reduced their field pay, or batta, in an effort to rein in spending. It has been suggested that the first biography of Clive was written by a number of disaffected army officers under a pen name, probably in the mid to late 1770s. The biography is scurrilous and largely incoherent, but it gives a taste of how his enemies wished to portray him. Lord Clive, the pseudonymous biographer writes,

> displayed where ever he went the ostentatious pageantry of an Asiatic sovereign. . . . Amongst his weighty and momentary regulations, he indulged himself now and then with the relaxation of transient amours. He thought his rank, his fortune and his power, were sure to conquer the women, with the same facility that he ruled over the company's servants; effectively he found several ladies of easy virtue, who, like other commodities, came readily into the scheme of his monopolies, and composed (his) little seraglio.[30]

Many nabobs were seen as having adopted the supposed licentious ways of "Oriental" rulers, which, on their return, made them both fascinating and dangerous.

---

29. Ibid., 236.

30. Charles Caraccioli, *The Life of Robert Lord Clive* . . . (London: T. Bell, 1786), 1.447.

In Britain, Clive became the most visible symbol of the corruption of the Company. In 1772, at the height of the Company's financial crisis, to which we will return shortly, Clive delivered an extraordinary address to the House of Commons. The principal reason for his appearance was to defend himself against charges of corruption, but he also used the occasion to explain how and why Company servants made fortunes in Bengal and what the consequences were. He began by noting that the indigenous form of government in India is an "absolute despotic" one and that the general population are "servile, mean, submissive and humble," while the elites are "luxurious, effeminate, tyrannical, treacherous, venal, cruel." As a result of silver flowing into Bengal and only goods coming out, a culture of extravagance had developed. "Presents," as he put it, were routinely given,

> and I will take upon me to assert, that there has not been an Officer commanding his Majesty's Fleet, nor an Officer commanding his Majesty's Army; not a Governor, not a Member of Council, not any other Person, civil or military, in such a station as to have connection with the Country Government, who has not received Presents.

Receiving these presents did not mean that the Company's servants were oppressive; any case of extortion, he claimed, was the work of banyans, or Indian intermediaries who acted as agents to unwitting Europeans. Clive likened these agents to a beautiful wife who seduces her husband's best friend. Just as a seductress can find a man's weakness, so these banyans could take advantage of impressionable and naïve men coming to Bengal at the age of sixteen. Before the assembled members of Parliament, Clive explained that as soon as one of these young men landed in Calcutta,

> a Banyan, worth perhaps one hundred thousand pounds, desires he may have the honor of serving this young Gentleman, at four shillings and six-pence *per* month. The Company has provided chambers for him, but they are not good enough; the Banyan finds better. The young man takes a walk about the town, he observes that other writers, arrived only a year before him, live in splendid apartments . . . ride upon fine prancing Arabian Horses, and in Palanqueens and Chaises; that they keep Seraglios, make Entertainments, and treat

with Champaigne and Claret. . . . The Banyan . . . furnishes
him with money; he is then at his mercy. The advantages
of the Banyan, advance with the rank of his master, who in
acquiring one fortune generally spends three . . . he is in a
state of dependence under the Banyan, who commits such
acts of violence and oppression, as his interest prompts him
to, under the pretended sanction and authority of the Company's servant. Hence, Sir, arises the clamor against the English Gentlemen in India.

Clive concluded this flourish by asking his listeners to look at retired
Company servants who were now living in Britain to see if there was evidence of "any thing tyrannical in their disposition towards their inferiors."
Instead, these supposed nabobs were good, humane, charitable, benevo-
lent, generous, hospitable, and honorable men. If any one of them was
sufficiently villainous as to be depicted on the London stage by the well-
known playwright Samuel Foote, it was only because he had been placed
in a situation in Bengal in which he was "subject to little or no controul."[31]

It turned out that Samuel Foote did indeed write a play about a particularly dissolute and immoral nabob. *The Nabob* was first performed
in 1772 and pulls no punches: Sir John Oldham, a respectable man, has
fallen on hard times and finds himself indebted to a returning nabob,
Sir Matthew Mite. The problem is that Sir Matthew does not have any
social standing, having come from the poorer classes, and so is looking
to marry into the gentry. Moreover, we come to learn that Sir Matthew
is a gambler, "profusely scattering the spoils of ruined provinces"; a phi-
landerer; and an extortionist.[32] He threatens to send Sir John to debt-
or's prison unless he is allowed to marry Sir John's beautiful daughter,
Sophy. It looks as though the nabob will get his way when, at the last
minute, Sir John's brother, a wealthy and honorable merchant, produces
the money to pay the debt. This unexpected, but happy, conclusion allows
Sophy to become engaged to her cousin. Audiences at the time would
have delighted in the caricature of the nabob and felt reassured that his
Oriental schemes had been foiled and that the old and natural order had
been reestablished.

---

31. Robert Clive, *Lord Clive's Speech in the House of Commons, on the Motion Made for an
Inquiry into the Nature, State, and Condition, of the East India Company* . . . (1772).

32. Samuel Foote, *The Nabob; A Comedy, in Three Acts* (London: T. Cadell, 1778), 4.

The outrage against nabobs and the corruption of the Company, both in its elections and management in London and in its administration in India, was intensified by the Company's surprisingly grave financial position. By the beginning of the 1770s the Company found that it was having difficulty auctioning all its stock. For example, in 1772 it had £3,260,072 worth of goods, much of it tea, lying in its warehouses. In this chapter's final section we will focus on the Company's tea and opium trades, but suffice it to say here that high import duties on tea, problems selling tea to the American colonies, and the prevalence of smuggling all meant that the Company was saddled with much more than it could sell.[33] The Company also found that over the previous decade it had been spending an exorbitant amount of money on its army, calculated at 44 percent of its Bengal budget, and that the costs were not diminishing.[34] Moreover, in 1771 the dividend was unwisely raised from 6 percent to 12.5 percent in the mistaken belief that the Company would meet its revenue targets in Bengal. All of this meant that in 1773 the Company's deficit was an eye-popping £1,948,549.

The crisis came to a head when bills of exchange began to arrive in London in unprecedented amounts.[35] Beginning in 1769 the Bengal Council issued large numbers of bills, far exceeding its authority. Instead of borrowing money from Indian bankers, the council chose to raise money from Europeans who wanted to remit part or all of their fortune. The result was that by 1771/72 the London office found itself responsible for £1,577,959, five times more than the year before. Honoring these bills placed intolerable pressure on the Company's already depleted treasury and precipitated the crisis that led to the first efforts by the British government to reform the Company.

---

33. Unless indicated otherwise, information in this and the next paragraph comes from Bowen, *Revenue*, 117–21.

34. Marshall, *Bengal*, 135.

35. For information on the role of agency houses in extending credit, remitting funds, and developing agricultural and other business ventures, see, Anthony Webster, *The Richest East India Merchant: The Life and Business of John Palmer of Calcutta, 1767–1836* (New Delhi: Viva Books, 2009); Anthony Webster, *Twilight of the East India Company: The Evolution of Anglo-Asian Commerce and Politics, 1790–1860* (Woodbridge: Boydell Press, 2009). For a discussion of the development of a banking system, see Amiya Kumar Bagchi, *The Evolution of the State Bank of India: The Roots, 1806–1876. Part I: The Early Years, 1806–1860* (Bombay: Oxford University Press, 1987).

The Regulating and India Acts

The Company had previously attempted to implement reform when it formed a commission for inquiry into Bengal affairs and sent Henry Vansittart (1732–70?), Luke Scrafton (1732–70?), and Francis Forde (ca. 1718–70?) to Calcutta as supervisors in 1769. Vansittart and Scrafton represented opposing parties within the Company, one led by a past and future chairman, Laurence Sulivan, and the other by Clive, while Forde was added to break any tie. Their charge was to reorganize the Company's financial and administrative affairs in India, and they were given vast powers. Unfortunately they all died when their ship was lost at sea in the Indian Ocean.

By 1772 everyone knew that the supervisors had drowned and that the Company's affairs were getting worse. In that year the Company defaulted on its £400,000 payment to the state and was forced to ask for financial help from the government. In return for that assistance Parliament passed the Regulating Act the following year. The most important provisions were that it established a governor general, who was to live in Calcutta and to whom the governors of Madras and Bombay would report, and that it created a supreme court of four judges, also based in Calcutta. Warren Hastings, then the governor of Bengal, was promoted to be the first governor general in 1774. The act also reformed the Company's election system to make it harder for factions to control votes.

The significance of the act was that it marked the first time that the British Parliament intervened in the running of the Company's Indian territories. The role, rights, and responsibilities of the British king and Parliament in the administration of the Company's settlements had never been fully established. The 1698 charter gave the Company the right to establish courts and raise forces to defend its settlements, but it also reserved the "sovereign Right, Power and Dominion" over the Company's "Forts, Places, and Plantations."[36] In practice, the Company ran its presidencies without royal or parliamentary oversight or interference. However, the Company's problems during the 1770s became a national preoccupation. The Regulating Act marked the beginning of a slow erosion of the Company's powers and independence, and an increasing government interest in the affairs of India. There has been much debate

---

36. *Charters Granted to the East-India Company from 1601* . . . (probably after 1772), 239.

about when the "colonial" appears in India, with some arguing that the Company established a colonial state or exhibited colonial attributes with the conquest of Bengal, or even earlier, and others making the case for a gradual transition to colonialism. This book supports those who see the Company's colonial state developing over the course of the second half of the eighteenth century, but if we want to point to a particularly important moment in that transition, it might be fair to see the Regulating Act of 1773 as marking the beginning of a trend that saw the blending of the interests of the Company and the British state.[37]

The Regulating Act did not result in clearer lines of authority in India. As we will see, the Bengal Council was, for many years, notoriously divided. In 1783 a parliamentary bill proposed to establish greater control over the turbulent affairs of the Company by transferring for a period of four years the directors' powers to seven commissioners, who were to be named by Parliament. However, the bill died in the House of Lords due to concerns that too much patronage, and therefore money, would pass into the hands of politicians. A new prime minister, William Pitt (1759–1806), came to power in 1784 and managed to pass different legislation, known as the India Act, increasing the authority of the governor general over his council in Calcutta and, importantly, establishing in London the Board of Control with the power "to superintend, direct, and controul, all acts, operations, and concerns, which in any wise relate to the civil or military government or revenues of the British territorial possessions in the East Indies."[38] Under the act, patronage remained the directors' prerogative. The directors also had full control over matters of trade and, in theory, the appointment of its administration. In fact, the Board of Control exercised enormous sway over the appointments of governors and although it did not often write the letters that were sent to the presidencies, it did monitor and influence the instructions. The act created what was, in effect, a system of dual oversight over the Company's

---

37. We can also see the transition in the Company's decisions to spend money in ways and on projects that are usually only done by states. A well-known example is the Company's support for ambitious and relatively expensive surveys, such as James Rennell's mapping of Bengal in the 1760s and 1770s and, a generation later, William Lambton and George Everest's trigonometrical survey of India. Ian J. Barrow, *Making History, Drawing Territory: British Mapping in India, c. 1756–1905* (Delhi: Oxford University Press, 2003); Matthew H. Edney, *Mapping an Empire: The Geographical Construction of British India, 1765–1843* (Chicago: University of Chicago Press, 1997).

38. Cited in Bowen, *Business*, 73.

political and revenue affairs. The board consisted of one of the secretaries of state, the chancellor of the exchequer, and four other members of the Privy Council.[39] In practice, one man, Henry Dundas (1742–1811), came to dominate the board, first as a member and then, from 1793 until 1801, as president. The establishment of the board and the domineering personality of Dundas clearly shifted some, but not all, political power over the Company's presidencies away from the court and toward the British government. This shift became a trend when the Company's charter came up for renewal in 1793, 1813, and 1833. By then, the interests of the Company and those of the British state were inextricably intertwined.

The Rise and Fall of Warren Hastings

One of the unanticipated effects of the Regulating Act was that it encouraged the emergence of two opposing factions within the reconstituted Bengal Council. The inability of the governor general to overrule the majority on the council led directly to the reforms contained in the India Act but also magnified the governor general's actions that made him a political target both in Bengal and Britain.

The three men who went to India as part of the Bengal Council were General John Clavering (?–1777), Colonel George Monson (1730–76), and, most importantly, Philip Francis (1740–1818). They arrived in Bengal in October 1774 determined to root out corruption and correct any maladministration they could find and immediately locked horns with the two other members of the council who were already in Calcutta: Richard Barwell (1741–1804) and Warren Hastings, the new governor general. Although Hastings now had authority over the other two presidencies, he found himself in the minority in the Bengal Council. It was not until the death of Monson in September 1776 that he was able to assert himself. However, his feud with Francis continued and quickly degenerated into personal attack. When Francis was caught climbing out of his married paramour's window, Hastings, himself no stranger to infidelity, jumped at the chance to publically embarrass his enemy. Hastings turned to one of his allies, the chief justice, Elijah Impey (1732–1809), who forced Francis to make amends by paying a large sum

---

39. Philips, *East India Company*, 33.

to the young woman's husband.[40] Eventually, the rivalry became so bitter that in August 1780 the two men even fought a duel, ostensibly about the Company's policies toward the Marathas. According to contemporary accounts, the two men and their seconds found an appropriate spot on the outskirts of Calcutta. There they stood fourteen paces apart and fired simultaneously:

> Mr. Francis's ball missed, but that of Mr. Hastings pierced the right side of Mr. Francis, but was prevented by a rib, which turned the ball, from entering the thorax. It went obliquely upwards, passed the backbone without injuring it, and was extracted about an inch on the left side of it.[41]

Francis himself wrote that when the bullet hit him his immediate thoughts were that his back had been broken and that he was about to die. In fact, he survived and, soon after, left for London, where he continued to attack Hastings whenever the opportunity arose.

There were several reasons Francis and his two allies in the council opposed Hastings. They came to India believing that the Company's servants were corrupt and that Hastings headed a venal administration. Once in India they saw Hastings adopting policies that they thought were reckless. Francis was also ambitious and wanted to replace Hastings as the governor general, a goal that he never achieved.

One of the first decisions that the majority on the council opposed was a war Hastings had championed in early 1774 against the Rohillas in northern India. Following the decline of Mughal authority, the Afghan Rohillas had established a state on the western border of Awadh. The two states had once been allies, but the wazir of Awadh, needing additional revenue, decided to attack his neighbor. When he asked for the Company's military help, Hastings supplied an army in exchange for a considerable sum. The Company destroyed the Rohilla army, allowing Awadh to annex the territory. Hastings' opponents noted that the Rohillas had posed no threat to the Company and argued that the war had been unjustified.

---

40. Dirks, *Scandal of Empire*, 96–97.

41. H. E. Busteed, *Echoes of Old Calcutta: Being Chiefly Reminiscences of the Days of Warren Hastings, Francis and Impey* (Calcutta: Thacker, Spink and Co., 1888), 113.

By 1774 Hastings was under considerable pressure to increase revenues. Two years earlier he had tried to reform the land revenue system
by "farming" out, or auctioning, the rights to the collection of revenues
to zamindars and others for five years. To his dismay, the zamindars had
overbid and the collections were disappointing. Despite further changes
to the Company's relationship with zamindars the land revenue totals
were insufficient to pay for the Company's growing army and its investment in goods for sale in Britain and elsewhere. The assertion of monopoly rights over opium and other commodities helped, but the Bengal
presidency was in deep debt and Hastings looked to allies to replenish
the Company's treasury.

By the end of the 1770s Hastings fixed his attention on the revenues
of the raja of Benares, Chait Singh (?–1810).[42] (The raja's domains were
located to the southeast of Awadh and bordered the Company's lands.)
When Singh inherited his state in 1770 he was the nominal subordinate
to the wazir of Awadh. However, when the wazir died in 1775, the majority of the Bengal Council, over Hastings' objections, took the opportunity
to renegotiate the Company's treaty with Awadh and demanded that the
revenues that Benares had previously paid to the wazir now be paid to the
Company. This arrangement worked until rising financial and military
pressures prompted Hastings in 1778 to demand and receive a considerable additional payment of £50,000. Chait Singh was again pressured
to pay the same amount in 1779 and 1780. The raja reluctantly agreed to
provide the additional amount, but he deliberately delayed the payments.
At a meeting between Hastings and Singh in August 1781, Hastings complained about the tardiness of the payments and threatened to impose a
fine of £500,000. An attempt by Hastings to arrest Singh prompted violent resistance and forced Hastings to escape to a nearby fort for safety.
Once reinforcements arrived the British deposed Singh, installed a more
compliant ruler, and nearly doubled the annual revenue demands, which
reportedly led to the impoverishment of the region.

The need for resources was great enough for Hastings to look beyond
Benares. In the same year that he deposed Chait Singh, Hastings forced

---

42. Information on Hastings' dealings with Chait Singh, the Begums of Awadh, and
the trial at large comes from P. J. Marshall, *The Impeachment of Warren Hastings* (Lon-
don: Oxford University Press, 1965), 88–129. Additional context and discussion of the
Company's public relations crisis and Hastings' trial can be found in Kate Teltscher, *India
Inscribed: European and British Writing on India, 1600–1800* (Delhi: Oxford University
Press, 1995).

Fig. 3. James Gillray, *The Bow to the Throne* (1788), showing
the governor general, Warren Hastings, dressed in "Oriental"
clothing and sitting on a toilet, distributing bags of gold coins
to the prime minister, the lord chancellor, and the queen.
Meanwhile the king is scooping coins from the toilet.

a crisis with the family of the nawab wazir of Awadh, Asaf-ud-daula
(1748–97). The problem facing Hastings was that the wazir owed the
Company a large sum of money. In 1773 Asaf-ud-daula's father had
agreed to station Company troops within his territories at his expense.
The troops were ostensibly sent to protect Awadh, but they functioned as
a check on the wazir's power and as a source of income for the Company
and its officers. In the years after the treaty was signed, Asaf-ud-daula,
who had been installed as wazir in 1775, failed to pay the full amount. By
1781 the amount owed was considerable, about £440,000, and Hastings
knew that two begums, wives of the two preceding wazirs, held jagirs, or
rights to land revenue, and treasure that could be used to pay Asaf-ud-
daula's debts to the Company. On the pretext that the begums had supported Chait Singh's rebellion, Hastings pressured the wazir to resume
their jagirs while a Company officer forcibly entered the begums' palaces

and, after torturing eunuchs who knew where the treasure was hidden, managed to extract £550,000.

Hastings' tenure as governor general ended when he returned to England in February 1785. He used his fortune to buy back his family estate and expected that he would be welcomed home by the political establishment. Instead he found that his old enemy, Philip Francis, had become friends with members of Parliament, especially Edmund Burke (1729/30–1797), who had turned against the Company and were hostile to Hastings. Francis provided them with the details of what Hastings had done during his thirteen years at the head of the Company's Indian administration, and, as a result, a decision was made to bring charges of high crimes and misdemeanors against Hastings.

In February 1786 Burke and other managers, as the prosecutors were termed, presented twenty-two articles of charge to the House of Commons. Hastings was accused of initiating an unprovoked war against the Rohillas and extorting payments from the raja of Benares and the begums of Awadh. He was also accused of inappropriately giving government contracts to his friends and supporters and of accepting bribes. The most sordid example dated to his early days as governor of Bengal, when it was said that he had received more than £35,000 from the nawab of Bengal. This payment came to light in 1775, when an influential Indian administrator, Nandakumar, complained to the majority on the Bengal Council. Nandakumar was then quickly charged with forgery, convicted, and, by the orders of Hastings' good friend Elijah Impey, hanged. It was a shocking case of judicial retribution and murder—forgery, although in theory a capital crime in Britain, should not have resulted in Nandakumar's execution.

In what was something of a surprise, given the power of the Company in London political life and the assumption that the Pitt ministry would not support the charges, the House of Commons voted to impeach Hastings in May 1787. The Rohilla charge was defeated but other charges, including those focusing on Benares, the begums, contracts, and "presents," or bribes, were upheld. In all, twenty articles of impeachment were brought before the House of Lords.

The trial began on February 13, 1788 and the opening was a social sensation. Tickets were hard to get and only the most politically and socially connected were able to enter Westminster Hall to view the spectacle. Fanny Burney (1752–1840) was one of the fortunate and, like many who crowded the boxes and galleries overlooking the floor, she had strong views about Burke and Hastings.

> I shuddered, and drew involuntarily back, when, as the doors were flung open, I saw Mr. Burke . . . make his solemn entry. He held a scroll in his hand, and walked alone, his brow knit with corroding care and deep labouring thought,—a brow how different to that which had proved so alluring to my warmest admiration when first I met him! . . . How did I grieve to behold him now the cruel Prosecutor (such to me he appeared) of an injured and innocent man![43]

The charges Burke and the managers brought were clearly attempts to bring Hastings to account for his alleged corruption and policies of state extortion and violence. But they were also an indictment of a style of governance that was termed despotic. Commentators often represented Indian or "Oriental" governments as despotic because the ruler, whether a nawab, a raja, or a Mughal emperor, governed according to his whim and fancy without any kind of restraint to the exercise of his power. In Britain, by contrast, the claim was that Parliament, through the laws that it passed in regularly scheduled meetings, provided a check to the king's ability to impose his economic, religious, or political will on his subjects.[44] As early as 1772 William Bolts (1739–1808), a disaffected former Company servant, wrote a blistering exposé of the Company, arguing that it should not continue to operate as both a merchant and a state. Part of his argument rested on the idea that the impoverishment of Bengal was due to the exercise of monopolistic and arbitrary power: "Under such despotism, supported by military violence, the whole interior country, where neither the laws of England reach, or the laws or customs of those countries are permitted to have their course, is no better than in a state of nature."[45]

---

43. (Fanny Burney), *Diary and Letters of Madame D'Arblay (1778–1840), as Edited by Her Niece, Charlotte Barrett* (London: Macmillan and Co, 1905), III.411.

44. For further discussion of despotism, as understood by the British in the 1770s and 1780s, see Jon E. Wilson, *Modern Governance in Eastern India, 1780–1835* (Basingstoke: Palgrave Macmillan, 2010), 63–65.

45. William Bolts, *Considerations on India Affairs; Particularly Respecting the Present State of Bengal and its Dependencies* (London: J. Almon, 1772), viii.

On the fourth day of the trial in the House of Lords, Burke accused Hastings of basing his defense on the idea that actions in India do not have the same moral meaning as they do in Britain and that he was therefore constructing a "geographical morality," whereby once a man crossed the equator his virtues died, "as they say some insects die as they cross the line." Burke denied that morality was relative and said that Hastings could not hide behind the argument that he had governed in the despotic fashion because Indians were only accustomed to arbitrary rule. "My Lords," Burke said,

> the East-India Company have not arbitrary power to give him; the king has no arbitrary power to give him; your lordships have not; nor the Commons. . . . We have no arbitrary power to give, because arbitrary power is a thing which neither man can hold nor any man can give.[46]

In his defense Hastings asked their lordships to recollect that over the course of his tenure as governor general Britain lost its North American empire and doubled its debt. Meanwhile, Hastings not only had managed to keep the Company's Indian empire but had increased its population and trade. He went on to state:

> Although your Lordships have been told by the House of Commons, that my measures have disgraced and degraded the British character in India, I appeal to the general sense of mankind, to confirm what I am now going to say, that the British name and character never stood higher, or were more respected in India, than when I left it.[47]

He then lamented, "I gave you all, and you have rewarded me with confiscation, disgrace, and a life of impeachment."

Hastings was finally acquitted on April 23, 1795. The length of the trial was largely due to the fact that Hastings had successfully argued that a vote should only be held once all the charges had been heard and defended. Moreover, since the lords had other business to conduct the trial was only held irregularly. In the end the managers were able to

---

46. *The Works of the Right Honourable Edmund Burke, Vol. VII. Speeches on the Impeachment of Warren Hastings* (London: Henry G. Bohn, 1857), 93–94, 99.

47. Cited in Dirks, *Scandal of Empire,* 122–23.

present complete evidence for just four of the charges and by then the verdict was a foregone conclusion. The French Revolution, a rise in patriotic fervor, and a renewed appreciation of the value of the Company's empire meant that Hasting's acquittal was not in doubt. However, the long trial proved to be immensely expensive. Hastings had had to raise £40,000 for his bail (half of which was provided by two Company supporters), and his final legal fees came to £67,528. To help him cover his costs the Court of Directors in 1796 gave him £42,000 to pay for expenses accrued since 1785, a £4,000 annuity, and an interest-free loan of £50,000. The managers' final costs came to £39,887.[48]

Hastings is sometimes depicted as representing an era when the Company's British servants were sympathetic to and had an appreciation for the customs and cultures of Indians. He reformed the civil and criminal courts so that cases were tried with an ear to Hindu and Muslim legal traditions. Many British men married or lived with Indian women. Some adopted Indian dress and living arrangements and, in the arts, a syncretic style of painting arose that would come to be known as Company style painting.[49] Hastings himself arranged for the translation into English of a number of classical Indian works and even wrote an approving preface to Charles Wilkins' translation of the important philosophical poem the *Bhagavad Gita*. While Hastings and his era can be contrasted with the violent racism that characterizes the last half-century of Company rule, it should be remembered that Hastings was a ruthless empire builder and that his effort to understand Indian culture was, at least in part, a way of extending his control. As he notes in his otherwise celebrated preface to Wilkins' translation:

Orientalism

> Every accumulation of knowledge, and especially such as is obtained by social communication with people over whom we exercise a dominion founded on the right of conquest, is useful to the state . . . it lessens the weight of the chain by which the natives are held in subjection.[50]

---

48. Marshall, *Impeachment*, 58, 77.

49. Mildred Archer, assisted by Graham Parlett, *Company Paintings: Indian Paintings of the British Period* (Singapore: Victoria and Albert Museum, 1992).

50. Charles Wilkins, *The Bhagvat-Geeta, or Dialogues of Kreeshna and Arjoon; in Eighteen Lectures; with Notes* (London: C. Nourse, 1785), 13.

The Permanent Settlement

Most Indians were peasants, and so for them subjection came in the form of land revenue. Peasants would sell their produce at markets and, at regular periods throughout the year, pay a high proportion of their income to middlemen, called zamindars, who, after having taken a cut, would then pay the Company through its representatives. Year after year, the amount collected by the Company fell far short of what it demanded or needed, given its rising military costs and its investments in Indian and Chinese products. To secure its revenue the Company often had to resort to violence or the threat of violence, but doing so could be counterproductive, as peasants could abandon their fields while zamindars might themselves respond violently to Company pressure. Moreover, a series of revenue collection reforms that began in the late 1760s and continued through the 1770s failed to squeeze out the expected revenue.

The situation changed dramatically after 1786, when a Whig aristocrat, Charles Cornwallis (1738–1805), arrived in India as governor general. Lord Cornwallis was appointed to bring stability to and reduce corruption in the Company's administration. He quickly realized that private or "country" trade encouraged administrators to divert their time and energies away from official duties and so he stifled those opportunities. He also embarked on legal reforms, separating the previously joined roles of judge and revenue collector, and fought a war in southern India with the ruler of Mysore. He is best known, however, for his 1793 Bengal revenue reform known as the Permanent Settlement.

The Permanent Settlement became law in March 1793, after many years of discussion and review. At the time it was controversial, but it has since become one of the most discussed, debated, and researched pieces of British legislation in India. Philip Francis first raised the idea for settling or fixing forever the revenue demand during his debates with Hastings. He was influenced by French physiocrats, who believed that prosperity could be ensured through the development, or, as it was termed "improvement," of land. His proposals were defeated in the council, but they eventually found a new advocate in Cornwallis, although the governor general disliked Francis and never acknowledged his role.

The core assumptions of the Permanent Settlement were that revenue could never be guaranteed, let alone increased, until zamindars were given security over land, which could be best achieved by making zamindars landholders or owners of land and by fixing forever the revenue they paid. The entire settlement came to 28.6 million rupees.[51] The change this brought about was enormous. Previously, zamindars had been given the right to collect the revenue from specified villages or plots of land. They had been told how much they were to collect, and it was their responsibility to deliver that amount by a certain date. If they extracted more from the peasantry than the Company demanded, they were free to keep the additional amount. However, it was understood that zamindars did not own the land, since land was owned by the Company or, in theory, the Mughal emperor who had awarded the *diwani* to the Company. The new regulation turned these collectors of revenue into landholders and made the peasantry their tenants. Cornwallis expected that zamindars, now secure in their property and knowing that they and their successors would never pay a single rupee more in revenue than was demanded in 1793, would invest in the improvement of their lands. Cornwallis believed that an "improving" landholder would drain swamps and cut forests in order to expand agricultural production. More food would, in turn, stimulate population growth and return Bengal to its former economic glory.

The principal disagreement among British administrators was whether to make the settlement permanent, as Cornwallis wanted, or only for ten years. In 1789, at the height of the debate, Cornwallis wrote,

> As I have a clear conviction in my own mind of the utility of the system, I shall think it a duty I owe to them (that is, the Court of Directors), to my country, and to humanity, to recommend it most earnestly to the Court of Directors to lose no time in declaring the permanency of the settlement . . . and not to postpone for ten years the commencement of the prosperity and solid improvement of the country.[52]

In practice, the Permanent Settlement caused agricultural and social turmoil, with the reverberations lasting well into the twentieth century. Many zamindars were unable to pay the revenue demand, which had been

---

51. C. A. Bayly, *Indian Society and the Making of the British Empire* (Hyderabad: Orient Longman, 1990), 66.

52. Cited in Ranajit Guha, *A Rule of Property for Bengal: An Essay on the Idea of Permanent Settlement* (New Delhi: Orient Longman LTD, 1982), 169.

set at a very high level, and so the Company put their lands up for auction. It has been calculated that in the decade after its passage "45 percent of the annual value of the land revenues of Bengal" passed from one owner to another.[53] The ten largest zamindars fared the worst, losing 61 percent of their lands, while the smaller landholders lost 26 percent of their property. New landholders initially found that they, too, had difficulty collecting rents, especially when they did not have strong patronage ties to local communities. The large-scale sale of lands began to stop by the turn of the century, when regulations in 1799, 1812, and 1816 reinforced the zamindars' powers of eviction and gave them greater control over the terms that they set with tenants. This stability encouraged many zamindars to become absentee landholders, often living in Calcutta. Instead of investing in their property, they commonly sold the rights to collect rents to others, who then sometimes sold those rights to a third party. Particularly common in the western parts of the presidency, the result of this "subinfeudation" was that tenants were forced to pay higher and higher rents. Many peasants, already poor, were pushed into cycles of debt that sometimes lasted a lifetime. It was only after the Company ceased to exist that the new British administration tried to put a halt to the progressive immiseration of rural Bengal by passing laws to protect tenants from rack-renting, but those efforts had limited success. At the other end of the spectrum, absentee landlords and their families lived comfortably in Calcutta. They were disproportionately Hindu, whereas their tenants, especially in eastern Bengal, were largely Muslim, and they formed part of the increasingly influential and visible elite *bhadralok* community.

The Company quickly realized that the Permanent Settlement was not resulting in the improvement of Bengal, and so other forms of revenue settlement were adopted in its other territories. In the south, for instance, the Company, through the governor of Madras, Thomas Munro, chose to fix contracts directly with the cultivator, a system that was termed the ryotwari (raiyatwari) settlement.[54] As the Company conquered new territory, one of its priorities was to extract as much revenue as possible without sparking rural unrest. Land revenue constituted the vast majority of its Indian income, especially after it lost its India and China trading monopolies

53. Sirajul Islam, *The Permanent Settlement in Bengal: A Study of Its Operation, 1790–1819* (Dacca: Bangla Academy, 1979), 157.

54. Burton Stein, *Thomas Munro: The Origins of the Colonial State and His Vision of Empire* (Delhi: Oxford University Press, 1989).

in the early nineteenth century. Therefore, it adopted a conservative approach to agrarian relations, on the one hand using the threat of force by its vast military to ensure payments and on the other hand reluctant to sanction change that might lessen the burden on the peasantry.

Tea and Opium

In the late 1660s an advertisement appeared in London announcing the sale of tea. "All Persons of Eminency and Quality, Gentlemen and others" were invited to go to Thomas Garway's coffeehouse in Exchange Alley, where they could buy tea for between sixteen and fifty shillings a pound. In his advertisement Garway spelled out the many advantages of drinking tea. For example, "It vanquisheth heavy Dreams, easeth the Brain, and strengtheneth the Memory." Garway also noted that it gave people an appetite, "particularly for Men of a corpulent Body, and such as are great eaters of Flesh." Students reading the advertisement must have also taken heart since tea "overcometh superfluous Sleep . . . so that without trouble whole nights may be spent in study without hurt to the body."[55]

Garway is often credited for being the first to sell tea to the public in England. At this time tea was an expensive and rare commodity since it was only grown in China and brought to Europe in very small quantities. In 1664 the Company imported just two pounds, two ounces of tea, most of which was given away as political presents. Over the course of the next 170 years, consumption of tea in Britain rose astonishingly. In 1706 the Company auctioned 100,000 pounds of tea. By 1760 the figure had risen to five million pounds and in the 1830s, just before it lost its China monopoly and no longer remained a trading organization, it sold thirty million pounds of tea.[56] Company tea did not just stay in Britain. For example, every year between 1770 and 1773 it sold 300,000 pounds for the colonial American market.[57]

---

55. Thomas Garway, *An Exact Description of the Growth, Quality and Vertues of the Leaf Tea.*

56. Figures from Michael Greenberg, *British Trade and the Opening of China, 1800–1842* (New York: Monthly Review Press, n.d., reprint of Cambridge University Press, 1951), 3; Carl A. Trocki, *Opium, Empire and the Global Political Economy* (London: Routledge, 1999), 39.

57. T. H. Breen, *The Marketplace of Revolution: How Consumer Politics Shaped American Independence* (New York: Oxford University Press, 2004), 300.

The story of tea is also the story of opium. Beginning in the mid-1760s, when the Company gained easy access to India's inland opium fields, the sale of opium and the purchase of tea became inextricably and tragically linked. In December 1799 the receiver general of the Chinese Board of Revenue, who was known to the Company as the Hoppo (Hubu), issued an edict at Canton (Guangzhou) prohibiting the sale of opium. He announced that an investigation had revealed large-scale smuggling and that opium was now widely used throughout society and was no longer limited to "vagrants and disreputable persons." Its high cost bankrupted addicts, with the result that many became thieves. It also had a terrible effect on the body:

> When at length the gradual and progressive effects of this poison have pervaded the lungs and the whole bodily frame, the sufferers with the pale and sickly hue of Doves or small fluttering birds, are no longer within reach of Medical assistance: desirous but in vain of quitting so dreadful a practice, they would willingly end it with their lives by tearing out their entrails in despair.[58]

The best opium came from the districts around Patna and Benares in northern India, and once the Company had conquered these regions it became much easier to transport the drug to China. Because the Chinese government banned opium, it had to be smuggled. During the last quarter of the eighteenth century, about four thousand chests were loaded onto ships bound for China every year. A chest contained forty specially prepared and packed balls of opium, each weighing about 3.5 pounds. The number of chests smuggled into China increased significantly over the next decades. In 1822–23 the figure was 7,773, largely because of the addition of opium from Malwa, in western India.[59] In 1833–34, 20,486 chests were imported. Thereafter the numbers increased even more rapidly, so that by 1838–39 more than 40,000 chests entered China.[60] Imports again nearly doubled by 1855. The opium trade was, according

---

58. Hosea Ballou Morse, *The Chronicles of the East India Company Trading to China, 1635–1834* (Cambridge: Cambridge University Press, 1926), vol. II, appendix M, 344–45.

59. For an analysis of the Malwa-China opium trade, see Anne Bulley, *The Bombay Country Ships: 1790–1833* (Richmond: Curzon Press, 2000), 151–74.

60. Trocki, *Opium*, 70–73, 95.

to at least one historian, "the world's most valuable single commodity trade of the nineteenth century."[61]

The production and sale of tea and opium were closely linked and were themselves part of worldwide triangular trades that both enabled and complemented the development of capitalism and industrialization. In order to understand the rise of tea consumption in Britain and the importance of opium to the Company's financial health, we must first appreciate the significance of sugar within the principal triangular trade of the Atlantic Ocean.

In the previous chapter we saw that in the seventeenth and early eighteenth centuries the Company bought silver from the New World to fund its purchase of Indian cotton textiles that were then either bartered for pepper in Southeast Asia or shipped directly back to England. Some of those bolts of fabric, called Guinea cloth, were re-exported to parts of West Africa, where they were traded for slaves, many of whom were transported to sugar plantations on British-controlled islands in the West Indies.

The growth in the consumption of sugar in Britain during the eighteenth century matches the growth of tea. Per capita use of sugar in 1700 was four pounds; by 1800 it had risen to eighteen pounds. It rose a further 233 percent during the next thirty years and would continue to rise into the twentieth century.[62] To first create and then meet the growing demand for sugar, plantation owners established industrial processes in Barbados, Jamaica, and other sugar islands that anticipated industrialization in Britain. For example, there was close control over labor and time (slave or, in Britain, cheap labor was organized in shifts), capital investment in the machinery, and, importantly, a drive toward large-scale production in order to reduce the cost to the consumer and thereby attract more buyers. The result was that by the end of the eighteenth century sugar was inexpensive. Indeed, it was cheaper for a laborer in England to drink a cup of tea with sugar imported from the West Indies and tea shipped from China than to drink a mug of local beer.[63]

---

61. Frederic Wakeman, "The Canton Trade and the Opium War," in *The Cambridge History of China*, ed. John King Fairbank (Cambridge: Cambridge University Press, 1978), 10.4.163–212, 172.

62. Sidney Mintz, *Sweetness and Power: The Place of Sugar in Modern History* (New York: Penguin Books, 1986), 67, 73.

63. Ibid., 115.

The cheapness of sugar is one reason tea became so popular. The other reason is that tea itself became cheap. How did the Company make tea affordable? It found an answer in opium. One of the long-standing problems for the Company was that few Asians, whether south Indian textile manufacturers or Sumatran pepper growers, had much need for British exports. The Chinese were no different and would only accept silver for tea. When the Company conquered Bengal it hoped that it could use the excess land revenue it now collected as its investment in tea. However, famine, poor land management and corruption by its servants, and an expensive and growing Bengal army meant that Bengal could not reliably provide sufficient silver for the purchase of tea.

Although deeply disappointed by its financial difficulties in Bengal, the Company was aware that the Chinese would buy two Indian commodities over which it now had control: cotton and opium. The cotton trade to China was the Company's main source of revenue until 1823. Opium, however, was typically a more stable and, ultimately, profitable commodity since it was addictive and was only grown in India (some opium from the Ottoman Empire did make it to China, but it was considered of inferior quality). The Company, therefore, made it a priority to control the production and sale of opium. In 1773 it asserted a monopoly over all sales of opium and in 1797 it established control over all aspects of its growth and production.

The production of opium was similar in scale and complexity to the production of sugar. It was very capital and labor intensive and time sensitive and required the establishment of a factory in order to create a sellable product. The crop was planted in October or November and harvested around March. Farmers cut incisions into the poppy and collected the sap, with the first batch considered the best quality. The raw, moist opium was then transported to the collecting points in Patna and Benares, where it was weighed, cleaned, and formed into balls. About 1,000 ball makers worked in shifts during the hot months of April and May and together they produced as many as 20,000 balls a day. The balls were placed in vast warehouses that could hold as many as 300,000 balls. Each ball was turned a quarter turn every six days, a process that required sixty-five boys for every 10,000 balls. The drying process took about six months, and once the balls were ready for shipment they were carefully packed in chests and sent by boat to Calcutta, where they were auctioned. Until 1820 the Company typically held two auctions a year, but after that date it began to hold monthly auctions in response to the rapid rise in demand.[64]

The Company knew that the sale of opium to the Chinese was illegal, and so it pretended that it had no hand in its distribution. It auctioned the opium to private traders, many of whom were British, who transported the chests on ships that had to be licensed by the Company. About a third of the opium went to Southeast Asia, but almost all of the remainder went directly to China. Once the ships reached the southern coast of China, the traders smuggled the opium ashore and received silver as payment.

Some smugglers chose to transport their silver back to India, a practice that was itself illegal under Chinese law, but many decided the safer route was to deposit the silver in the Company's factory in Canton. In return they were given bills that were payable in either Calcutta or London. The Company charged a commission on those bills and so made a profit (and the private traders could themselves barter or sell their bills), but the great benefit to the Company was that it now had significant quantities of silver with which its supercargoes, or servants in Canton, could buy tea.

Beginning in 1760, the Chinese government imposed strict conditions on foreign purchases of tea and all other goods. For example, tea could only be loaded onto ships at the Whampoa (Huangpu) anchorage, ten miles from Canton, and the trade was limited to certain months of the year, after which the supercargoes had to leave. The most important limitation of this "Canton System" was that the Company and all other foreigners could only buy from a special guild called the Cohong (Gonghang). There were no more than thirteen Cohong and, in theory, they set the price for the tea, although the price was usually set after a process of negotiation with the Company.

The Company's opium for tea triangular trade was immensely and increasingly profitable. In 1788 a chest of Patna opium typically sold at auction for 466 rupees.[65] By 1821 the price had risen to 4,259 rupees, giving the Company a profit of ten times its investment. Between the 1770s and the 1830s opium became indispensable to the Company's financial health. During the first seventeen years of its opium monopoly

---

64. Information in this paragraph from Trocki, *Opium*, 70–73.

65. Unless noted otherwise, figures in this paragraph are from Trocki, *Opium*, 65, 73–74.

the Company made £1,277,000 in profit.[66] By the 1820s it was the Company's largest Indian export item and accounted for 15 percent of the Company's Indian revenue.

For much of the eighteenth century the Company also made a profit on tea, although by the 1770s high duties on the import of tea limited sales and promoted smuggling. Tea was smuggled from continental Europe and sold throughout Britain at prices that were far below the auction rate. The loss of revenue was particularly painful for the Company since it was simultaneously experiencing a land revenue crisis in Bengal. The British government enacted some measures to help the Company, notably reducing the duties on tea bound for the American colonies (a move which prompted the Boston Tea Party, since Americans still had to pay a tax on tea) and passing the Commutation Act in 1784, which reduced duties in Britain from an average of 106 percent to 12.5 percent. The Commutation Act was unpopular because the government created a tax on windows to recoup the revenue shortfall. As one observer wrote, "A tax upon a luxury which none need have, was exchanged for a tax upon a necessary, which all must have. Was this a fair commutation?"[67] Although duties on tea would rise again during the wars with revolutionary and Napoleonic France, their temporary reduction did eliminate much of the smuggling and encouraged legitimate sales. By the 1830s the Company derived all of its profits from tea, and tea duties gave the British government 10 percent of its annual revenue.[68]

Over the course of the eighteenth century, tea went from being an expensive luxury consumed only by the wealthy to becoming the common, national drink for all classes. Its cheapness and availability in Britain masked its origins on slave plantations and in opium fields and factories. Its sweetness obscured the transformations in British society that made tea so well suited to sustaining the emerging working classes: it was easily brewed at work, reducing the need to return home and thus improving productivity; it was a stimulant without being intoxicating; and, above all, it was inexpensive. The Company's opium and tea trade was therefore at the heart of changing tastes and changing economic structures. It was

---

66. Marshall, *Impeachment*, 166.

67. Anonymous, *The Conduct of the Present Parliament Considered, Previous to Its Dissolution* (London: J. Ridgway, 1789), 21.

68. Greenberg, *British Trade*, 3–4.

also, with Indian land revenue, the financial backbone of the Company's Indian empire.

The end of the Company's monopoly of trade to China in 1833 was also the end of its trading days. It sold its stocks and factories and concentrated on the administration of its vast territories. The Company's free trade critics, who had first emerged as a major opposition group during the financial crises of the 1770s, finally persuaded Parliament that the wealth of the British nation and the health of its empire would be better served by allowing any British trader direct access to China. So-called free trade may have benefited British traders, but the costs to China mounted to such an extent that the opium crisis became intolerable. The influx of new traders resented the Cohong and their influence, and the smugglers' relentless imports of opium drained China of its silver and prompted inflation. Energetic efforts by Chinese officials in 1839 to prevent the trade, most notably by Lin Zexu (1785–1850), who seized and destroyed the entire stock of opium at Canton, initiated a war with Britain. The British ostensibly fought to defend the principles of free trade, and the Treaty of Nanjing in 1842 forced the Chinese to accept the importation of opium, abolish the Cohong, pay an indemnity for the destroyed opium and the cost of the war, and cede the island of Hong Kong. With no restrictions in place, opium imports surged in the following years, rising to well above seventy thousand chests a year by the mid-1850s.

CHAPTER THREE
The Nineteenth Century

The Company's Army

The Company's transition to a territorial state and the creation of Britain's eastern empire was due, in large part, to the growth and success of the Company's army or, more accurately, armies, since each presidency had its own army. By the mid-seventeenth century the Company's charter gave it the right to raise troops to defend its warehouses and forts, and the first European regiment was formed in Bombay in 1668. The presidencies were so distant from each other that their armies recruited separately and developed different traditions. The Company's army was also distinct from the British army, although the Company paid to garrison large numbers of British regiments in India. By the late eighteenth century British army regiments were sent to India on twenty-year tours of duty and so became a permanent fixture in India, fighting alongside the Company's army.

At first the Company allowed Europeans, not just British men, and even Indians to become officers, but reforms in 1785 and concern about loyalty meant that by the end of the eighteenth century almost all officers were British and none was Indian. Many British men also served as enlisted soldiers. Although officers were British the army recruited Indians, known as sepoys, a corruption of the Persian *sipahi*. Recruitment was so successful that for most of the eighteenth and all of the nineteenth centuries sepoys far outnumbered Europeans. It is one of the great ironies of the Company's history that its Indian empire was effectively won by its Indian troops.

During the late seventeenth century the army was small and unimpressive by Indian standards, and it was only after the assumption of the *diwani* in 1765 that the army grew rapidly (see Table 1).

Table 1. Army strength, 1763–1823[1]

	Bengal	Madras	Bombay
1763	6,680	9,000	2,550
1782	52,400	48,000	15,000
1805	64,000	64,000	26,500
1823	129,473	71,423	36,475

Once it began to grow it quickly became one of the largest armies in the world, even larger than Britain's. In 1815, at the conclusion of the Napoleonic Wars, the British army numbered 233,952 men, but this declined to 102,529 in 1828, then 91,388 in 1838 before rising again to 116,434 in 1846.[2] About a fifth of these troops were stationed in India. The strength of the Company's armies also declined toward the end of the 1820s as a result of a poor Indian economy, but the change was only slight and temporary. By 1857 its strength had rebounded, so that the Bengal army alone numbered 150,000 men, comprising 127,000 Indians and 23,000 British.[3] The total of its three armies amounted to 280,000, making it one of the world's largest armies.[4]

Just as sepoys far outnumbered British soldiers, so those soldiers outnumbered all other Europeans in India. In 1830, for example, the Company garrisoned 36,409 British soldiers but employed only 3,500 civil servants and permitted just 2,149 businessmen and other Europeans to live in India. The resources needed to sustain both its army and part of

1. Raymond Callahan, *The East India Company and Army Reform, 1783–1798* (Cambridge: Harvard University Press, 1972), 6; Douglas M. Peers, *Between Mars and Mammon: Colonial Armies and the Garrison State in India 1819–1835* (London: I. B. Tauris Publishers, 1995), 129.

2. Peter Burroughs, "An Unreformed Army? 1815–1868," in *The Oxford History of the British Army*, ed. David G. Chandler and Ian Beckett (Oxford: Oxford University Press, 1994), 164.

3. Thomas R. Metcalf, *The Aftermath of Revolt: India, 1857–1870* (Princeton: Princeton University Press, 1964), 24, 46.

4. Heather Streets, *Martial Races: The Military, Race and Masculinity in British Imperial Culture, 1857–1943* (Manchester: Manchester University Press, 2004), 24.

the British army were extraordinary, prompting one scholar to note that the Company's state could accurately be called a "garrison state."[5]

The Bengal army was the most prestigious of the three presidency armies, offering the best opportunity to gain a fortune and return to Britain. The pay was low, although extra pay, known as batta, was given to soldiers when they were stationed outside of their presidency. Soldiers were also entitled, according to their rank, to a share of any "prize money" gained as a result of a military victory. The only sure way to make a lot of money, though, was through a myriad of privileges that allowed officers to profit from supplying and clothing the army. These privileges were a form of state-sanctioned corruption, and it was not until the 1790s that even modest reforms were attempted. A young man could hope to become rich as an officer, but prospects were better in the civil administration and even better as a merchant.

The bulk of the recruits to the three armies were Indian peasants. In both Bombay and Madras the Company recruited widely, in terms of caste and religion, but in Bengal the infantry was largely high-caste Hindus and Muslims from Bihar and other regions adjacent to the Bengal presidency, notably Benares and the state of Awadh. Hindus were attracted to the army because it afforded them higher status than their peasant origins gave them in society.[6]

The military success of the Company's army is a vexing question. Its Indian enemies were often highly militarized and wealthy states, accustomed to offensive and defensive warfare and well equipped with effective artillery and small arms. Some states, such as the Marathas and the Sikhs, adapted to changing military circumstances and adopted tactics and weapons that resulted in battles that might have been won by either side. The Sikhs, in particular, went to great lengths to train their troops along European lines and even paid their infantry more than the Company. The Company did not have significantly better troops, training, or weapons, especially when factoring in the distance between Britain and India.[7] Indeed, the Company had many disadvantages.

One important disadvantage was that, until the early nineteenth century, the Company had almost no cavalry.[8] This made its infantry, gunners,

---

5. Figures on the European population from Peers, *Between*, 54.

6. Seema Alavi, *The Sepoys and the Company: Tradition and Transition in Northern India 1770–1830* (Delhi: Oxford University Press, 1995), 5.

7. Ibid., 3.

8. See Callahan, *East India Company*, for a full account of the Company's army in the late eighteenth century and its uneasy partnership with the British army.

and lines of communication both vulnerable to attack by highly skilled enemy cavalry and dependent on the cavalry of allied Indian states. A second disadvantage was that officers were promoted solely on the basis of seniority, not ability. Third, the army was divided in significant ways: it was divided into presidency armies that fueled jealousy and, sometimes, confusion since they were trained and governed by different traditions (the three armies were not joined as one Indian army until 1895); it was divided between its Indian recruits and European officer class; and it was divided between itself and British army troops who were also stationed in India. There was considerable hostility between the Company's officers and the king's officers since the Company, for financial reasons, did not sanction as many high ranks and did not promote as quickly as the British army. As a result, young British army officers often outranked older Company officers, causing widespread disaffection. An effort at the end of the century to fold the Company's army into the British army failed, although some reforms did improve the relative position of the Company's officers. A final disadvantage was that the Company's territory was not contiguous, which made it challenging to defend its long boundaries against potential enemies.

Disease was a particularly disabling issue for the Company. It is difficult to compare the Company's army to its Indian adversaries since little research has been conducted on morbidity and mortality rates in Indian armies, but studies on the Company's army suggest that disease was a chronic problem. Soldiers were certainly killed in action. The Madras army, for instance, experienced 111 deaths per thousand during the Mysore War of 1799 but only 57 deaths per thousand per year between 1812 and 1816, when it was not at war. However, waterborne diseases such as dysentery and cholera reduced the fighting effectiveness of the army to an astonishing extent. Just living in India, even during peacetime, significantly increased a British man's chance of an early death. In 1830, for example, there were 9.5 deaths per thousand soldiers in Britain, but in Bengal, the unhealthiest presidency for Europeans, the figure was a staggering 61.9 deaths per thousand.[9] Venereal diseases were also a constant problem for the army. Soldiers would go to brothels in cantonment bazaars, and it has been estimated that more than 30 percent of British soldiers in India during the 1820s and 1830s were hospitalized at some point because they had contracted syphilis or some other sexually

---

9. Philip D. Curtin, *Death by Migration: Europe's Encounters with the Tropical World in the Nineteenth Century* (Cambridge: Cambridge University Press, 1995), 23, 181, 194.

transmitted disease.[10] The army tried to regulate the brothels but eventually determined that the most effective way to contain the spread of venereal diseases was to establish "lock hospitals" where registered, army-approved prostitutes would be examined periodically and, if found to have a disease, forced to remain in the hospital for treatment. The idea behind this was that disease could be contained through the control of women.

What, then, accounts for the string of Company victories in the late eighteenth and early nineteenth centuries? What tipped the balance was a combination of a diplomatic strategy that divided Indians, financial resources with which Indians could not compete, and control of the sea. By using treaties and threats, the Company was able to isolate neighboring states so that it rarely had to fight a combined force. As we will see, its triple alliance with the Marathas and the nizam of Hyderabad made it possible for the Company to prosecute a war against Tipu Sultan. Had a similar alliance been formed against the Company, the Madras presidency may have been imperiled. Each conquest gave the Company additional land revenue that, in conjunction with the sale of cotton and opium to China, provided the Company with the money to pay for an enormous standing army. The Company had a navy, the Bombay Marine, but it was small and mostly directed against piracy. It was really the British navy that gained control over the Indian Ocean and in so doing gave the Company the ability to transport troops and money from Britain and from presidency to presidency while denying its Indian enemies the ability to resupply by sea.

Military Conquests in South, Central, and North India

Beginning in the 1740s the Company fought at least one major war every decade. After its initial conquests in the mid-eighteenth century, the Company fought three important wars that expanded its territory significantly and established it as the dominant power in India. These wars were against Tipu Sultan, the Marathas, and the Sikhs. There were certainly other victorious campaigns and even some that it lost, such as

---

10. Philippa Levine, *Prostitution, Race and Politics: Policing Venereal Disease in the British Empire* (Routledge: New York, 2003), 38.

when its army was famously decimated while leaving Afghanistan in 1842, but the three campaigns are crucial to understanding how and why the Company expanded in India after the 1780s. An examination of these three campaigns will give us an understanding of the political and military culture of rival states and the specific reasons for their eventual defeat. The next section will cover the Company's expansion in the Malay Peninsula and Burma.

Tipu Sultan

By the 1760s the southern Indian state of Mysore had emerged as a formidable military threat to the Madras Presidency. A new Muslim ruler, Haider Ali (1722–82), had reformed the state's revenue and tax structures and used his wealth to fight two impressive wars with the Company in 1767–69 and 1780–84. He captured a large number of British soldiers, and although many were later released, some converted to Islam, were given wives, and were incorporated into his army.[11]

Haider Ali's son, Tipu Sultan (1750–99), sought to increase the prosperity of his father's kingdom by introducing a range of currency, agricultural, and military initiatives.[12] Tipu found it increasingly difficult, however, to withstand the burgeoning power of the Company. War broke out again in 1790 when the governor general, Lord Cornwallis, determined that a growing and bitter dispute between Tipu and the raja of Travancore endangered the Company's position in South India. Cornwallis recognized the need for allies in the Company's struggle against Tipu and so signed treaties with Tipu's greatest enemies, the Marathas and the nizam of Hyderabad, creating the triple alliance. Although Tipu experienced some initial success, the third Anglo-Mysore war was a disaster for Mysore. The Treaty of Seringapatam (Srirangapatna) in 1792 forced Tipu to pay a huge indemnity, lose half his territory, and surrender two of his sons to be kept as Company hostages.

---

11. At least two "captivity narratives" were written by British men: James Bristow, *Narrative of the Sufferings of James Bristow, Belonging to the Bengal Arilley* [sic], *during Ten Years Captivity with Hyder Ally and Tippoo Saheb* (London: J. Murray, 1793); James Scurry, *The Captivity, Sufferings and Escape of James Scurry, Who Was Detained a Prisoner during Ten Years, in the Dominions of Hyder Ali and Tippoo Saib* (London: H. Fisher, 1824).

12. Kate Brittlebank, *Tipu Sultan's Search for Legitimacy: Islam and Kingship in a Hindu Domain* (Delhi: Oxford University Press, 1997).

Fig. 4. James Gillray, *The Coming-on of the Monsoons* (1791).
The caricature shows Tipu Sultan urinating on the governor
general, Lord Cornwallis. Although Gillray shows the British
in retreat, the war ended in the Company's favor.

An enfeebled Mysore was still considered a threat by the Company
hawks in India, especially in the context of the ongoing war with France.
Even before he became the governor general in 1798, Richard Wellesley
(1760–1842) determined that he would pursue a "forward policy"
toward Indian states to force them into "subsidiary alliances." These alliances would typically give the Company control over the external affairs
of the Indian states; impose a resident, or a Company ambassador, who
would keep a close eye on developments in the court; and garrison Company troops in the state and at the state's expense. The states of Arcot,
Awadh, and Hyderabad were high on Wellesley's list, but Mysore posed a
particularly pressing problem since Wellesley and his similarly truculent
military officers believed Tipu was seeking an alliance with Napoleon.
Fearful, perhaps paranoid, that the French were intent and even able to
dislodge the British from India, despite their failure to capture Egypt in

1798, Wellesley decided to launch a war against Tipu. The Company's Fourth Mysore War ended on May 4, 1799, when Tipu was killed by a musket ball that entered his right temple as he fought at one of the gates to his palace at Seringapatam. Wellesley annexed large portions of Mysore and installed as ruler of the rump state a descendant of the Hindu ruler that Haider Ali had pushed aside in 1761.

The British had developed a fascination with Tipu and considered him to be a tyrannical ruler. William Kirkpatrick (1754–1812), a colonel in the Company's army and a friend of Wellesley, encapsulated the British sentiment when, based on some of Tipu's letters that he had translated, he described the ruler "as the cruel and relentless enemy; the intolerant bigot or furious fanatic; the oppressive and unjust ruler; the harsh and rigid master; the sanguinary tyrant; the perfidious negociator [*sic*]; the frivolous and capricious innovator; the mean and minute economist; the peddling trader; and even the retail shop-keeper."[13] British writers at the time regularly used similarly pejorative and demeaning adjectives to characterize Indians, not just Tipu Sultan. The tendency to see Indians as morally, intellectually, and even physically inferior to the British became commonplace later in the nineteenth century. *orientalism*

Marathas

The second series of campaigns that extended Company control into central India was fought in 1803–4 and 1817–18 against the Marathas, an alliance of powerful Hindu military families.[14] During the second half of the seventeenth century, under the leadership of Shivaji (1627 or 1630–80) and his successors, the Marathas had challenged the supremacy of the Mughal emperor, Aurangzeb, in western India. When Mughal authority declined in the decades following Aurangzeb's death in 1707, the Marathas were able to expand their territory into central and northern India. At first, the locus of power lay with the Maratha king, or raja,

13. William Kirkpatrick, *Select Letters of Tippoo Sultan* . . . (London: Black, Parry, and Kingsbury, 1811), x.

14. Stewart Gordon, *The Marathas, 1600–1818* (Cambridge: Cambridge University Press, 1993); Randolf G. S. Cooper, *The Anglo-Maratha Campaigns and the Contest for India: The Struggle for Control of the South Asian Military Economy* (Cambridge: Cambridge University Press, 2003).

but by the 1740s real control had shifted to his prime minister, known as the peshwa, who was based at Pune. Moreover, as the Marathas extended their control of territory beyond Delhi in the north and as far as Orissa in the east, regions of the new Maratha state came to be dominated by commanders and their families. These commanders, known by their title or family names, such as the Gaikwad, Sindia (or Scindia/Sindhia), Holkar, and Bhonsle came to control vast territories centered on the cities of Baroda, Gwalior, Indore, and Nagpur. In theory, these commanders were under the direction of the Peshwa, who was himself nominally subordinate to the raja, but by the end of the eighteenth century all were acting independently and in competition with one another.

Once Tipu Sultan had been defeated and his kingdom divided, the Company saw the Marathas as the last major Indian military force that could pose a direct and credible threat to Company territory. Moreover, many Company officials in India, including the governor general, Lord Wellesley, continued to believe, erroneously, that France posed a danger to the Company. Wellesley therefore pursued a belligerent policy toward the Marathas, hoping to constrain them through the subsidiary alliance system.

Wellesley found his opportunity to dominate Maratha politics when, on the last day of 1802, the peshwa, Baji Rao II (1775–1851), signed the Treaty of Bassein. By the terms of the treaty the Company promised the peshwa military aid, but in return the peshwa accepted a resident at his court and agreed to pay for the maintenance of those Company troops assigned to protect him. The treaty was a classic example of a subsidiary alliance in that it effectively made the peshwa a Company puppet, at his expense. The peshwa was compelled to sign the treaty because he was militarily weak and needed Company troops to defeat his Maratha rivals.

Once the treaty had been signed, the Company confronted the forces of Daulat Rao Sindia (1779–1827) and Raghuji Bhonsle II (?–1816). The third important Maratha ruler, Jaswant Rao Holkar (1776–1811), remained neutral, believing that by doing so he might benefit from a drawn-out fight that diminished both the Company and his rivals' forces.[15] The war was fought on two fronts: a northern front, which saw the Company's commander-in-chief, General Gerard Lake (1744–1808), defeat Sindia's forces and capture Delhi, and a central Indian front, which pitted the governor general's younger brother, Arthur Wellesley (1769–1852; later known as the duke of Wellington as a result of his

---

15. Cooper, *Anglo-Maratha Campaigns*, 10.

victory over Napoleon), against Bhonsle and Sindia's forces. Lake and Wellesley's successes resulted in subsidiary alliances with the Marathas, all the Rajput states that had previously been subordinate to the Marathas, and the annexation of Orissa. The Company also acquired vast territories around Agra and Delhi as well as lands annexed from Awadh, which were collectively to form the Company's new Ceded and Conquered Provinces.[16]

The wars against Tipu Sultan and the Marathas were enormously expensive and exposed differences among the directors in London and between the directors and the Board of Control. Two powerful men, Henry Dundas, the president of the board, and David Scott (1746–1805), a director, chairman, and member of the Secret Committee, supported Wellesley in his efforts to subdue the remaining independent Indian states. In January 1800 Wellesley promised them that, if they were patient, "the death of the Nizam will probably enable me to gratify your *voracious appetite for lands and fortresses.* Seringapatam ought, I think, to stay your stomach awhile. . . . Perhaps I may be able to give you a supper of Oudh and the Carnatic, if you should still be hungry."[17] Despite their support, many other directors opposed Wellesley for two principal reasons. The first was that, in their estimation, he was leading the Company to financial ruin. To avert catastrophe, they ordered the Company to borrow money in order to buy additional goods in India for sale in Britain. Wellesley received the money and, despite warnings not to do so, promptly spent it on his wars. The second reason a group of directors opposed Wellesley was that they formed the "shipping interest" within the court and disliked his association with Scott and others who wished to open up the lucrative shipping contracts. Many of the directors also disliked Wellesley's efforts to establish a college in Calcutta, although they did think it was a good idea to establish civil and military colleges in England. In 1806 they opened the East India College at Haileybury, just to the north of London, and in 1809 they established a military seminary at Addiscombe in Surrey.

Once Dundas left the Board of Control in 1801, Wellesley's position was less secure. The directors recalled him in 1805 and sent

---

16. Gordon, *Marathas*, 176.

17. Cited in C. H. Philips, *The Correspondence of David Scott, Director and Chairman of the East India Company, Relating to Indian Affairs, 1787–1805* (London: Offices of the Royal Historical Society, 1951), xx. Information on Wellesley in this paragraph is also drawn from Philips' introduction, especially pages xx–xxii.

Lord Cornwallis for his second tour as governor general. Cornwallis wished to establish peace with the Marathas but he died shortly after arriving in India and was buried in Ghazipur. After Cornwallis' death a period of quiet hostility ensued until war broke out again in 1817. Tension had been mounting between the Marathas and the Company, specifically over Company efforts to expand its political influence and the Company's irritation with roving bands of former regular and irregular Maratha troops looting Company lands. When war was declared the Company quickly overwhelmed a weakened Maratha alliance. Their collapse signaled the end of any meaningful independence for almost all remaining states in India. Only the Sikh kingdom had sufficient military and financial resources to withstand a war against the Company. The rest of India was now divided between Company-controlled presidencies and provinces, which were increasingly referred to as British India, and a large number of Indian states, as many as six hundred, often known as Princely India. Every state was bound to the Company by a treaty, the terms of which helped the Company categorize states as tributary, subsidiary, or protected. British India now amounted to more than half a million square miles and contained 93.7 million people paying an estimated £22,718,794 a year in taxes.[18]

Sikhs

The Company's final territorial conquests were in Punjab, a region in north India that for many years had been ruled by a politically astute and militarily adept Sikh leader. Ranjit Singh (1780–1839) was at first only one of several Sikh military commanders, each controlling patches of land, but in 1799 he rose to prominence by capturing the large and important city of Lahore.[19] He rapidly expanded his control over most of Punjab by using a combination of military pressure and diplomatic overtures, including marriage alliances, which resulted in the creation of a unified and centralized Sikh state.[20] He transformed the army, known as the Khalsa, into a force that could rival the Company's by introducing

---

18. These figures are for 1833. Bowen, *Business*, 5.

19. J. S. Grewal, *The Sikhs of the Punjab* (Cambridge: Cambridge University Press, 1990).

20. Purnima Dhavan, *When Sparrows Became Hawks: The Making of the Sikh Warrior Tradition, 1699–1799* (New York: Oxford University Press, 2011), 175–76.

heavy artillery while maintaining the Khalsa's traditional strength in its cavalry. Beginning in the 1820s he also hired European officers, most notably Jean-Francois Allard and Jean-Baptiste Ventura, to teach French and British drilling techniques in order to improve the infantry's cohesion and effectiveness. His army was better paid than the Company's, but it was constantly in arrears, which became a source of discontent once the state had ceased to expand and the promise of prize money disappeared.

In 1838 Emily Eden accompanied her brother, the governor general, on a tour to visit Ranjit Singh, whom she famously described as "exactly like an old mouse, with grey whiskers and one eye," having lost it in childhood as a result of smallpox. Her account of their meeting conveys the British ambivalence toward Ranjit Singh and his powerful state. On the one hand he was "a very drunken old profligate," but on the other hand he "has conquered a great many powerful enemies; he is remarkably just in his government . . . he hardly ever takes away life, which is wonderful in a despot; and he is excessively beloved by his people."[21] She also noted that the British officers who were invited to witness an impressive Sikh military parade were left second-guessing their contempt for the Sikh army: "Nobody knows what to say about it, so they say nothing, except that they are sure the Sikhs would run away in a real fight. It is a sad blow to our vanities!"[22]

After Ranjit Singh's death in 1839 the Sikh state entered a period of crisis. There was considerable tension between the court and the army and even between commanders, which was intensified by the rapid deaths of three of Ranjit's successors. In 1843 Ranjit's youngest son, Dalip Singh (1838–93), who was then only five years old, was installed as ruler with his mother acting as regent. The Company was well aware of the disunity of the Sikhs and saw an opportunity to strengthen its position on its northwest borders. At this time the Company had made significant and, to the Sikhs, alarming military advances on all sides of the Sikh state. To the west, the Sikhs witnessed a protracted Afghan-Company war (1838–42) that at first led to the installation of the Company's preferred candidate on the Afghan throne. To the south, General Charles Napier (1782–1853), in an unprovoked move, annexed Sind to Company territory in 1843. To the southeast, across the river Sutlej, the Company

---

21. Emily Eden, *"Up the Country": Letters Written to Her Sister from the Upper Provinces of India* (London: Richard Bentley, 1867), 198.

22. Ibid., 209.

had rapidly increased its garrison strength to more than forty thousand troops.[23] By 1845 it appeared to many Sikhs that the Company's aggressive posture was threatening its own security. Indeed, in the words of a British military historian writing in 1911, the Company believed it had a "geographical and political necessity for . . . expansion."[24]

The First Sikh War broke out in December 1845 when Sikh troops crossed the Sutlej. It lasted just under three months, during which time five major battles were fought. The war was not convincingly won: despite being on a war footing the Company was poorly led and its army was, at times, saved from potential defeat by treacherous decisions made by the Sikh army's commanders. Some of those commanders, who were alienated from the troops, had allied themselves with Dalip Singh's regent, who wanted to reduce the army's power over the court. The Company's victory was due, in part, to Sikh divisions.

The price of defeat was a diminished state. The Company recognized Dalip Singh as ruler, but his state was broken apart. Kashmir was established as a Company-controlled state, while extensive tracts in Punjab were annexed to Company territory. The governor general, Lord Hardinge (1785–1856), revealed the extent of British power in a letter he wrote to the Company's agent at Lahore:

> By the treaty of Lahore (March 1846) the Punjab was never intended to be an independent state. By the clause I added, the Chief of state can neither make war nor peace, nor exchange nor sell an acre of territory, nor admit a European officer, nor refuse us a thoroughfare through its territories, nor in fact, perform any act (except in its own internal administration) without our permission. In fact the native prince is in fetters and under our protection, and must do our bidding.[25]

The Company had difficulty pacifying Punjab and it was not long before opposition emerged, especially in areas that were distant from the capital. The Second Sikh War (1848–49) was fought in the south

---

23. Further context provided in Sita Ram Kohli, *Sunset of the Sikh Empire* (Bombay: Orient Longmans, 1967), 102.

24. Reginald George Burton, *The First and Second Sikh Wars: An Official British Army History* (Yardley: Westholm Publishing, 2008 [1911]), 8.

25. Cited in Kohli, *Sunset of the Sikh Empire*, 118–19.

and west of the Sikh state, beginning at Multan and then moving to the lands bordering the rivers Chenab and Jhelum. The Company's army was eventually victorious, but the siege of Multan and the three major battles in the west were hard-fought and bloody. The result was the complete annexation of Punjab and the installation of a body of administrators, most notably the brothers John and Henry Lawrence (1811–79; 1806–57), who would be lauded as the quintessential colonial civil servants. Their devotion to duty and God, their paternalistic approach to Punjabis, and their efforts to transform the agrarian society through irrigation works and revenue reform made them "titans" to later colonial historians who were eager to see great British men make a positive difference to Indian lives. Philip Mason, for example, writing under the pseudonym Philip Woodruff, praised their manly vigor when he noted that the 1840s and early 1850s was a time "when two or three dozen men [toiled] with fierce nervous energy at tasks more than mortal."[26]

Expansion in Southeast Asia

The Company did not expand just in India. It acquired several important settlements in Southeast Asia, with the hope of strengthening its country and China trades as well as protecting itself from any growth of Dutch influence. The first settlement was established on Penang Island, in what is today Malaysia, in 1786, when Captain Francis Light took advantage of military difficulties facing the sultan of Kedah. The Company changed the island's name to Prince of Wales Island, built a fort in the new town of George Town, and, within a few years, pressured the sultan to cede more territory on the mainland, which was then called Province Wellesley. To the south, the British acted to preempt their European enemy, the French, from controlling Dutch possessions and so seized Malacca (Melaka) from the Dutch in 1795. The Company controlled the settlement until 1818, when it was returned to the Dutch. However, a treaty with the Dutch in 1824 saw the Company exchange Bencoolen (Bengkulu), their old pepper port on the island of Sumatra, for Malacca. Both Penang and Malacca were considered strategically important since they were at the north and center of the Strait of Malacca, a crucial shipping lane

---

26. Philip Woodruff, *The Men Who Ruled India: The Founders of Modern India* (New York: St. Martin's Press, 1954), 324.

for trade between Bengal and China. In 1819 a Company officer, Thomas Stamford Raffles (1781–1826), founded Singapore, at the very southern end of the Strait, and all three territories, Penang, Malacca, and Singapore, were joined administratively in 1826. They were collectively called the Straits Settlements and became the Company's fourth presidency.[27]

Although Singapore would prove to be by far the most successful of the three Settlements, none was particularly valuable to the Company. There was relatively little revenue to support their defenses and administration. All three were trading ports, but, once the Company lost its China monopoly, their value as entrepôts diminished considerably. Nevertheless, the Settlements became a principal destination for Indian convict and indentured labor. It has been calculated that at least fifteen thousand to twenty thousand convicts were sent to the Settlements between 1790 and 1860, mostly to Singapore.[28] Laborers came from the Madras presidency and usually went to the sugar plantations in Penang and Province Wellesley. Their indentures specified the terms of employment and could be renewed: in return for working for a certain length of time, typically three years, laborers would receive a wage but not their passage. In reality, indentured labor was a brutal system and has been called a new form of slavery. Laborers often had to borrow money to pay their passage to the Settlements, a sum they were never able to repay. They were then trapped for years in abysmal working conditions far from home only to be given subsistence-level wages. The indentured labor system would come to underpin many British colonial economies, from the West Indies to South Africa to Ceylon (Sri Lanka). Between 1844 and 1910 approximately 250,000 Indians went just to Malaya (which included the Straits Settlements) as indentured laborers.[29]

---

27. Penang had been named a presidency in 1805, but it was never considered equal to Bombay or Madras. In 1830, the Settlements were incorporated into the Bengal Presidency and remained under Calcutta's control until 1867, when they became a Crown Colony. For more information on the Straits Settlements, see C. M. Turnbull, *The Straits Settlements, 1826–67: Indian Presidency to Crown Colony* (London: University of London, Athlone Press, 1972) and Marcus Langdon, *Penang: The Fourth Presidency of India, 1805–1830. Volume 1: Ships, Men and Mansions* (Penang: Areca Books, 2013).

28. Richard B. Allen, *European Slave Trading in the Indian Ocean, 1500–1850* (Athens: Ohio University Press, 2014), 204.

29. Ravindra K. Jain, "South Indian Labour in Malaya, 1840–1920: Asylum, Stability and Involution," in *Indentured Labour in the British Empire, 1834–1920*, ed. Kay Saunders (London: Croom Helm, 1984), 158–82.

Other Indian communities were either already living in Malacca or came to the Straits Settlements voluntarily. Three prominent communities included the Chitty Malacca (or Melaka), who were descendants of south Indian Hindu merchants who first came to Malacca in the fifteenth century and subsequently intermarried with Malays. They were also called the Indian Peranakan, Peranakan being a Malay word for "born of" and suggesting mixed parentage. Indian Muslim traders had also settled in Malacca and were known as the Jawi Peranakans. Finally, the Chettiars, Hindu Tamils, arrived much later and generally did not marry outside of their caste. They quickly developed into an important merchant and banking community.

Many Chinese also came to the Straits Settlements. At first they came as traders, attracted by the commercial advantages given to these "free ports." Large numbers married Malays and became the most famous of the Peranakan communities. They were also called the Straits Chinese and were influential in the affairs of the Settlements. In the 1840s tin was discovered inland, prompting many more southern Chinese to travel on indentures to the Settlements en route to the mines. As a result of these migrations from China and India, the Settlements had especially diverse populations.

To the north of the Straits Settlements, the Company fought two wars against Burma and gained substantial territory. The first war was to have lasted two months, but the planning was so disastrous and the assessment of Burmese strength so ill informed that the war lasted three years. As it dragged on it became one of the most expensive British wars of the nineteenth century. Rangoon was captured in the very early stages of the war, but instead of receiving the invaders as liberators, as had been expected in Calcutta, the local Burmese destroyed crops and fled. Malnutrition and disease sapped the army's strength in Rangoon, while conditions on other military fronts were similarly discouraging. Eventually, the Company was able, in the words of the governor general, to "conquer a peace with the Burmese."[30] The 1826 Treaty of Yandabo was harsher than that envisioned at the beginning of the war, because the British had developed a need to overcome any doubts about their military superiority. The treaty forced the Burmese to pay an indemnity, cede Arakan and Tennasserim, and forgo any claim to Assam, which was subsequently annexed to India. After the second war in 1852 the Burmese lost the province of Pegu,

---

30. Peers, *Between*, 161.

which the British renamed Lower Burma. Later, in 1885, Upper Burma
was also forcibly annexed to the British Indian Empire. In the Atlantic Ocean the Company continued to govern St. Helena, even housing
Napoleon Bonaparte (1769–1821) during his final exile from 1815 to
1821. However, when the Company lost its monopoly in 1833 it also lost
its authority over the island.

Religion and the Company

In 1792, the year before he set sail for Bengal as a Baptist missionary,
William Carey (1761–1834) published *An Enquiry into the Obligations
of Christians, to Use Means for the Conversion of the Heathens*. Toward
the end of his book Carey explicitly compares the work of the East India
Company to that of a missionary:

> When a trading company have obtained their charter they
> usually go to its utmost limits. . . . They cross the widest
> and most tempestuous seas, and . . . they introduce them-
> selves into the most barbarous nations. . . . Christians are
> a body whose truest interest lies in the exaltation of the
> Messiah's kingdom. Their charter is very extensive, their
> encouragements exceeding great, and the returns prom-
> ised infinitely superior to all the gains of the most lucrative
> fellowship.[31]

The parallel Carey makes between the Company and Christians raises
a number of important questions: To what degree was the Company a
Christian corporation? Did the Company encourage missionary activity?
And what were the connections between the Company, missionaries, and
the rise of the colonial state?

The Company's approach to religion changed dramatically over the
course of its existence and mirrors social, religious, and political developments in both Britain and India. Before tracing those changes it is
important to understand that there were few other issues that divided the

---

31. William Carey, *An Enquiry into the Obligations of Christians, to Use Means for the
Conversion of the Heathens* (Leicester: Ann Ireland, 1792), 81–82.

British more than religion.[32] The Church of England, or more broadly the Anglican and Episcopal churches, was the "established" or official church. It was practiced by many, but not by all, in England, Scotland, and Wales and by a minority in Ireland. Large numbers of English and Scots were followers of other protestant churches, such as the Baptist, Presbyterian, and, after the death of John Wesley in 1791, Methodist churches and were known collectively as Dissenters, or, toward the end of the Company's era, Nonconformists. Catholics formed a majority in Ireland but were a minority in Scotland and England. Throughout the seventeenth and eighteenth centuries Parliament passed laws that severely curtailed the rights, freedoms, and employment of both Dissenters and, to an even greater degree, Catholics. For example, until the late 1820s Dissenters and Catholics were forbidden from holding public offices. The two main political parties that passed those laws, the Whigs and the Tories, defined themselves, in part, by their attitude toward non-Anglicans. At the risk of being overly simplistic, we can understand the Whigs as an anti-Catholic party and more tolerant of Dissenters, while the Tories were opposed to Dissenters, believing they posed a greater danger to the state and its religion than Catholics. More generally, Whigs were seen as defenders of the people's rights and, by the nineteenth century, support-ers of political reform, while Tories were supporters of the power of the king and opposed to reform. Tories found allies with High Churchmen, who comprised a section of the Church of England, while Whigs, who were often of the "middling sort," such as traders, were friends with Low Churchmen. By the end of the eighteenth century Dissenters were par-ticularly suspect since some voiced support for republican and democratic ideas that had become the basis for revolution in the American colonies and in France. This period also saw the spread of evangelical movements in Britain, and evangelicals could be found among both Dissenters and Anglicans, although not among High Churchmen, who frowned on what was termed "enthusiasm." Evangelicals, as Penelope Carson notes, had an "awareness of sinfulness, a feeling of spiritual insufficiency and a desire for a personal assurance of salvation through the atoning death of Christ." Many of them also had experienced a moment of spiritual

---

32. Information in this paragraph is drawn from Paul Kléber Monod, *Imperial Island: A History of Britain and Its Empire, 1660–1837* (Chichester: Wiley-Blackwell, 2009), 51–54.

crisis and rebirth that made them devote their lives to God.[33] Evangelicals would come to play an important role in shaping the Company in the first half of the nineteenth century.

From its early years the politics of religion informed the Company's policies, but religion became a particularly important issue after the 1790s, when British Baptist missionaries, including Carey, entered Bengal. Over the next four decades the central debate focused on whether the Company had a responsibility to introduce Christianity into its territories and what the risks of mutiny and rebellion might be if missionaries were given free access to Indians. The issue was argued fiercely within the Company, Parliament, and the press in Britain and was only settled by the Charter of 1833, which removed all restrictions on missionaries. Their success was an expression of a growing British contempt for Hinduism and Islam, a conviction that the Company, as a government, had a duty to improve the lives of its subjects, the new prominence of evangelicals, and the ongoing competition between Dissenters and Anglicans.

During the seventeenth and for much of the eighteenth centuries, the Company tried to keep chaplains and missionaries at arm's length. Its 1698 charter stipulated that it had to employ chaplains appointed by the archbishop of Canterbury or the bishop of London. The chaplains were expected to learn Portuguese within a year of arriving in India and to start learning an Indian language in order to teach the Company's slaves and Indian servants the principles of Protestantism. The Company was also required to build churches at its major settlements. In reality, very few chaplains were sent and even fewer churches were built. It also habitually skirted a law that required a chaplain for every vessel leaving England with more than one hundred men by hiring only ninety-nine sailors.[34] These were financial decisions: it was expensive to keep chaplains and build churches. There were also political considerations. The Company usually recognized that it was weak militarily and highly dependent on Indians for trade, and so it tried to avoid what it saw as the mistakes of the Portuguese, who were thought to have lost their Asian empire as a result of overzealous proselytization. It also recognized that

---

33. Penelope Carson, *The East India Company and Religion, 1698–1858* (Woodbridge: Boydell Press, 2012), 25. Carson's book provides the most comprehensive treatment of the Company's religious policies.

34. Anthony Farrington, *Trading Places: The East India Company and Asia 1600–1834* (London: British Library, 2002), 29.

some of its subjects, especially in Bombay, were Catholics and so, much to the anger of some Anglicans, it allowed priests to conduct Mass. The Company's grudging tolerance of chaplains in its settlements only went so far, however: chaplains were permitted to serve their congregations but were generally not allowed to engage in missionary activity. In theory the Company had complete control over who traveled to its settlements, although in practice missionaries who were determined to go could slip in by sailing on Danish or Dutch ships. Such a move was risky since governors had the authority to deport undesirable men.

These policies appalled some who wanted to see the Company take a more active religious role. As early as 1694 the Reverend Humphrey Prideaux (1648–1724), dean of Norwich, complained that the Company had "fallen almost to nothing" in comparison to the Dutch and attributed that collapse of power and wealth to a lack of interest in conversion.[35] He also noted with disgust that in all of the Company's Indian settlements Muslims, Jews, and Hindus had their places of worship. Even the Portuguese had their churches,

> where they corrupt Christianity to a degree worse than Heathenism. But there is not so much as a Chapel in any of them for the true Religion of *Jesus Christ*. . . . Nor is there any the least care taken to propagate the Gospel among the natives. . . . But, on the contrary, they are so careless and impiously unconcerned in this matter, that they permit the Popish Priests to come into the families of the *English* settled there, and pervert their servants and slaves to their idolatrous superstition, which is there practiced in the grossest manner in the world.[36]

Prideaux's arguments made little headway with the Company and for the next century only a trickle of chaplains and a handful of German Lutheran missionaries traveled to its settlements. However, as its

---

35. Humphrey Prideaux, "An Account of the English Settlements in the East-Indies, Together with Some Proposals for the Propagation of Christianity in Those Parts of the World," in *The Life of the Reverend Humphrey Prideaux . . . With Several Tracts and Letters of His, upon Various Subjects. Never before Published.* (London: J. and P. Knapton, 1748), 167.

36. Ibid., 163–64.

territories and armies expanded, the Company did begin to take a more active role as a patron of Hindu and Muslim traditions and places of worship. Its new subjects and soldiers expected it to assume the roles that were common to its Indian predecessors and rivals. Many Indian states routinely gave grants of land to religious institutions, and the Company began to assume that role by disbursing grants, underwriting religious festivals, funding religious schools, and even collecting a Hindu pilgrimage tax at the famous Jagannath temple.

The contradiction of failing to promote Christianity while patronizing Hindu and Muslim traditions was not lost on the Company's critics in Britain. The first important call for change came from within the Company. Charles Grant was an evangelical Anglican who had spent more than twenty years in Bengal working on revenue and trade matters.[37] Once he had made his fortune, he returned to England in 1790 and began a long career as a Company director, rising to become chairman on three occasions. He was also a member of Parliament and was known for his opposition to Lord Wellesley's bellicose policies in India and, later, his support for the Company's unsuccessful efforts to retain its monopoly on trade to India. However, his most consequential contribution came in 1792, when he distributed and later published his *Observations on the State of Society among the Asiatic Subjects of Great Britain.*

Grant's chief observations were that Hindus were "depraved" and that they lived in a "wretched" state. He had little better to say about Muslims—"successive treacheries, assassinations, and usurpations, mark their history"—but his focus was on Hinduism. He supported his claims by noting that Hindu men were dishonest, avaricious, and quarrelsome and that while they confined their "suffering" wives at home they elsewhere enjoyed "licentious connections" with dancing women. He even suggested that Hindus engaged in the "unnatural practices of the ancient Heathens, though in these the Mahomedans are still more abandoned."[38]

His argument was that Hindus were living in such a low state because they were ignorant. They did not know that they could be redeemed through Jesus Christ, and so it was the responsibility of the Company

---

37. For a full biography see Ainslee Thomas Embree, *Charles Grant and British Rule in India* (London: George Allen & Unwin LTD, 1962).

38. Quotations from Charles Grant, *Observations on the State of Society among the Asiatic Subjects of Great Britain, Particularly with Respect to Morals and on the Means of Improving It* (1792), 216, 70, 53.

to allow missionaries to live in India. Closer religious ties, he promised, would strengthen Company rule. He also assumed that the Company was a Christian organization, but he was frustrated that it generally rebuffed missionaries.

Grant found evangelical allies outside of the Company. William Wilberforce (1759–1833), who was instrumental in bringing about the end of the British slave trade in 1807, helped Grant prepare a "Pious Clause" to be inserted in the revised Charter of 1793 requiring the Company to send out and pay for missionaries. Despite Grant's growing influence within the Company and with the Board of Control, the clause was withdrawn due to widespread opposition by stockholders, who were afraid of the consequences and wary of the cost.

The defeat of the Pious Clause was only the beginning of a fierce and important debate. In 1805 Reverend Claudius Buchanan (1766–1815) published a book to pressure Parliament and the Company into sending bishops to India and thus create what would effectively be an Anglican Church of India.[39] Having a bishop live in India was important because only he could ordain clergymen. Without him, all ordinations had to take place in Britain. To prove the need for such a church he described all of the depravities that he saw in Hindus and concluded that they have no morality: robbers, prostitutes, infants, and priest all pray to "an horrible idol of clay painted red, deformed and disgusting as the vices which are practiced before it."[40] Buchanan shared Grant's belief that it was the Company's duty, as an arm of a Christian nation, to "civilize" Indians— indeed, one of his chapters is titled "On the Practicability of Civilizing the Natives." But he went further than Grant in thinking that "Providence" had arranged for the conquest of India for the very purpose of converting Hindus and Muslims and even intimating that conversion could be imposed, especially on the children of the poor.[41]

Buchanan's book set off a "pamphlet war" between supporters of the status quo and the evangelicals and their allies. The significance of the debate is that it revealed the growing acceptance of the evangelical

---

39. Claudius Buchanan, *Memoir of the Expediency of an Ecclesiastical Establishment for British India; Both as the Means of Perpetuating the Christian Religion among Our Own Countrymen; and as a Foundation for the Ultimate Civilization of the Natives* (London: T. Cadell and W. Davies, 1805).

40. Ibid., 33.

41. Ibid., 31.

movement's claim that the Company had a responsibility to improve the morality of its Indian subjects. Many in the Company continued to oppose the work of missionaries, but this period saw a sympathy develop between the goals and practices of missionaries and those of the Company. Missionaries and their supporters saw clear benefits for the Company: providing a moral, Christian education that was supported by the government would endear the Company to Indians and ultimately strengthen the Company's control over India. There was disagreement as to whether that education should be in English (Grant and Buchanan) or in the vernacular (Carey), but its value to the empire was obvious.

Except it was not obvious. In July 1806 a mutiny broke out among troops of the Madras army at Vellore, in Southern India.[42] The mutiny was suppressed within hours but not before more than one hundred British officers and men had been killed. The Madras troops mutinied for a number of reasons, largely to do with offensive new regulations and clothing. However, the debate within the Company and in Britain hinged on whether the troops had been driven to action by the threat of conversion by the few missionaries who lived and traveled in the presidency or whether they were inspired by the family of Tipu Sultan, the Company's former enemy in Mysore, whom they were guarding in the fort. For the antimissionary lobby, the mutiny became the most important example of the dangers of opening the door to proselytization. Indians, they claimed, would not be able to distinguish missionaries from the government and would assume that the Company endorsed and encouraged conversion. Their arguments were given added weight when, in 1807, a grotesque pamphlet was distributed in Bengal. The pamphlet was written in Persian and targeted Muslims: "We are come to convert you from a distant country," it began, and it included a highly derogatory biographical sketch of the "tyrant" Muhammad and his "creed, which is only the source of mental darkness." It ended by urging Muslims to "Quit, O brethren! the lying religion which you have been taught to believe, and embrace the faith of Jesus Christ."[43]

The governor general, scared that Bengali Muslims would assume that the Company had endorsed the pamphlet, ordered the destruction of all the undistributed copies. Shortly afterward, in Britain, the Reverend

---

42. James W. Hoover, *Men without Hats: Dialogue, Discipline and Discontent in the Madras Army, 1806–1807* (New Delhi: Manohar, 2007).

43. *Papers Relating to East India Affairs (Resident Europeans Police—Missionaries—Weavers, and Investments)* (House of Commons, April 14, 1813), 48–49.

Sydney Smith (1771–1845), who had close family ties to the Company, published an acerbic review of missionary work in India and concluded that these "quite insane" men "would deliberately, piously, and conscientiously expose our whole Eastern empire to destruction, for the sake of converting half a dozen Brahmans, who, after stuffing themselves with rum and rice . . . would run away."[44] Others also pointed to the danger of proselytization, but one author went further and defended the character and morality of Hindus.

Charles Stuart (1757/8–1828) was a former Bengal army officer who was known as "Hindoo Stuart" because of his affection for Hinduism, his collection of Hindu statues, and his lifestyle, which included an Indian mistress. He was outraged by Buchanan's book, calling it "the chaff and rubbish of the harvest" and proceeded to rebut it point by point.[45] One of his most striking assertions was that, contrary to what Buchanan claimed, Hindu texts were profound and produced moral and decent people. Stuart cautioned his readers not to denigrate or laugh at what evangelicals considered childish stories about Hindu gods: "Wherever I look around me, in the vast region of Hindoo Mythology, I discover Piety in the garb of allegory; and I see Morality, at every turn, blended with every tale . . . it appears the most complete and ample system of Moral Allegory, that the world has ever produced."[46] Although much of what Stuart wrote was broadminded for the time, his view of Hindus and how the Company should interact with them was based on the common trope that Hindus were, by nature, passive and that the empire was secure so long as they were not unnecessarily provoked. He therefore supported the Company's efforts to deny admission to most missionaries.

Despite their rhetorical force, such defenses of the Company's policy on religion were increasingly seen as passé. The mood in Parliament had shifted by 1813, and Grant, Wilberforce, and their supporters were able to persuade the members to establish an Anglican Indian Church and to insert the Pious Clause into the new charter. The clause stipulated that Britain had a duty "to promote the interests and happiness" of Indians and that the Company had to pay for "facilities," meaning schools and churches, in order to introduce useful knowledge as well as religious and

---

44. Sydney Smith, *The Edinburgh Review*, Article IX (April 1808), 151–81, 173.

45. A Bengal Officer, *Vindication of the Hindoos from the Aspersions of the Reverend Claudius Buchanan* . . . (London: R. and J. Rodwell, 1808), 13.

46. Ibid., 97.

moral improvement.[47] Missionaries still had to obtain a license from the Company to work in India, a restriction that was only lifted twenty years later, and the clause did specify that one of the principles of the government was the free exercise of religion, but a new era had begun.

Reform in the Colonial State

The evangelical victory initiated the start of a series of social and administrative reforms that, in conjunction with the earlier zamindari and ryotwari settlements, solidified the Company's colonial state. The significance of the reforms has been debated, with recent scholarship tending to suggest that they had limited effects, especially when compared to the rapid social and economic transformations ushered in by the railways, telegraphs, and censuses during the middle and second half of the century. The majority of Indians were hardly affected by the ban on widow immolation, known as sati, or the introduction of English as the official language of instruction and administration, but the reforms did signal a new approach to governance. Moreover, the sweeping currency reform of 1835 had profound implications for the development of an all-India economy and, toward the end of the century, the rise of Indian nationalism.

The reforms have usually been dated to the 1828–35 period, when Lord William Bentinck (1774–1839) was governor general.[48] He was joined by men whose views on politics, economy, and society were shaped by the post-Napoleonic order in Europe and who were now enjoying Company dominance in India at the conclusion of the Maratha wars. Many of them believed in the Liberal ideas of "peace, retrenchment and reform" (of the British franchise—there was no Indian franchise at this time), while others were attracted to utilitarian arguments that the government should promote "the greatest happiness of the greatest number" of people through such measures as public education. Yet others, as we have seen, were evangelicals.[49] What they all had in common was a belief

---

47. For the exact language see Carson, *East India Company*, 250.

48. John Rosselli, *Lord William Bentinck: The Making of a Liberal Imperialist 1774–1839* (Berkeley and Los Angeles: University of California Press, 1974).

49. For a full discussion see Eric Stokes, *The English Utilitarians in India* (Oxford: Oxford University Press, 1959).

that a government should do more than simply impose taxes and raise an army to defend the king, country, and established church. The emergence of an educated middle class in Britain and the growth of the Company's empire, followed by a period of relative peace, encouraged the idea that in India the government had a responsibility to improve the material and moral lives of those it governed.

This period also saw free traders win two of their greatest victories: Parliament ended the Company's monopoly on trade, first to India in 1813 and then to China in 1833. One of the consequences of the loss of the India monopoly was that Lancashire mill owners sent vast quantities of cheaply made cotton cloth to India, with devastating effects on the indigenous Indian textile industry and to the Indian economy more generally, since the influx of cheap goods led to a devaluation of the rupee. The loss of the China monopoly meant that the Company was no longer a trading outfit and was only a government in India, the Straits Settlements, and its other territories. These developments concentrated the Company's attention on its role as a government and not on its vanishing commercial obligations.

It should also be emphasized that although the British began to see the Company's government in a different light, it did not mean that they wanted the government to intervene in either economic or social life beyond what was absolutely necessary. Administrators were attracted to the doctrine of laissez-faire, which encouraged a hands-off approach to industry, and they continued to worry that too much social change would prompt mutinies or peasant revolts. This nervousness was heightened by the realization that the economy was in a slump by the 1820s and that famine had returned to parts of India by the late 1830s. At the time, Bentinck was known (and reviled) for his cuts to the state's budget and to the army's batta. Nevertheless, much of the new thinking in the Company was about reform.

Lord Bentinck was not new to India. He had been governor of Madras when the Vellore mutiny occurred, and for a while his career had suffered. When he returned to India in 1828 as governor general, he was well aware of the dangers, both to his own standing and to the Company's situation, of provoking Indians with the threat of conversion. However, ten years of peace in India and the growing influence of evangelicals and missionaries, such as William Carey, convinced him that the time was right to declare sati illegal. Sati was occasionally practiced in the Company's territories, especially in Bengal, and involved a widow being burnt to death with her husband on his pyre.

By the 1820s many British missionaries, government officials, and the public saw sati, or concremation as it was sometimes called at the time, as a symbol of the degraded state of Hindu society and a marker of the low moral standing of the Company's government. Although the vast majority of Hindu widows did not become satis—there were, on average, between five hundred and six hundred a year[50]—evangelicals chose to focus on the practice because it was so emotive and therefore had the best chance of pushing the government to condemn an aspect of Hinduism. For reformers this was the first step in a larger civilizational battle: would the Company now disassociate itself from Hinduism and begin to promote values that reformers characterized as universal but were really Christian? When he issued his regulation abolishing sati in November 1829, Bentinck explained that his motivation was to benefit Hindus: "I know nothing so important to the improvement of their future condition," he wrote, "as the establishment of a purer morality . . . and a more just conception of the will of God." By separating religion from "blood and murder" and now seeing their previous "error," Hindus would be ready to make further reforms. He hoped that "thus emancipated from those chains and shackles upon their minds and actions, they may no longer continue . . . the slaves of every foreign conqueror, but that they may assume their first places among the great families of mankind." He insisted, perhaps with a wry smile, that his decision was not an attempt at conversion.[51]

In making his case to abolish sati, Bentinck relied heavily on the arguments made by a number of elite, high-caste, English-speaking "Bhadralok" Bengalis, such as Rammohan Roy (1772–1833).[52] Roy had worked for the Company in Calcutta and had become interested in the Unitarian idea that a combination of rational faith and social reform through education could lead to human progress.[53] He was also influenced by Sufi traditions, but he was most attracted to the Hindu

---

50. Lata Mani, *Contentious Traditions: The Debate on Sati in Colonial India* (Berkeley: University of California Press, 1998), 21.

51. A. Berriedale Keith, ed., *Speeches and Documents on Indian Policy, 1750–1921* (London: Humphrey Milford, Oxford University Press, 1922), 1.225.

52. S. Cromwell Crawford, *Ram Mohan Roy: Social, Political, and Religious Reform in 19th Century India* (New York: Paragon House Publishers, 1987).

53. David Kopf, *The Brahmo Samaj and the Shaping of the Modern Indian Mind* (Princeton: Princeton University Press, 1979), 3.

Fig. 5. Rammohan Roy by Rembrandt Peale (1833).

Upanishads, also known as the Vedanta.[54] Roy was convinced that the Vedanta was a way to understand the universal nature of God and believed that contemporary Hindus had abandoned that path in favor of debased idol worship. For these reasons he became involved in the establishment of colleges; founded the Brahmo Sabha, a society to promote

54. Gavin Flood, *An Introduction to Hinduism* (Cambridge: Cambridge University Press, 1999), 251–53.

the Vedanta and universal monotheism; and campaigned against sati on the basis that it had no religious sanction.

Indian men such as Roy were indispensable to the smooth running of the administration. The Company had always relied heavily on Indians to fulfill a wide variety of roles such as trading partner, interpreter, and moneylender, but as its administration grew during the first decades of the eighteenth century it needed to employ greater numbers. The need became more acute during Bentinck's governor generalship since, for reasons of economy, some lower-level bureaucratic positions were, for the first time, given to Indians.

The appropriate role for Indians in the administration was a matter of debate. It went to the heart of the rationale for colonial rule that was crystalizing during the 1820s and 1830s and would continue into the next century. Thomas Babington Macaulay (1800–59), then a member of Parliament but soon to be the legal member of council in Calcutta, addressed this issue during the parliamentary debates on the renewal of the charter in 1833.[55] The broad questions before Parliament were whether the Company should continue to exist, whether it should retain its monopoly of trade to China, and what role the Company should play if allowed to continue to exist but without its monopoly. Bound up in the last question was the political future for Indians.

Macaulay argued that the Company, rather than the British Crown, should govern India, even without its monopoly. But how should the Company rule? The issue for Macaulay was that India had had a long history of moral decline and that over time it must be raised. As a result India was unlike Britain, where the people were sufficiently "competent" to participate in government through "representative institutions." The purpose of imperial rule, therefore, was "to give a good government to a people to whom we cannot give a free government." He hoped that good government would "educate our subjects into a capacity for better government" which, one day in the distant future, could see Indians "demand European institutions."[56] In the meantime Indians had to be educated.

When Macaulay arrived in India as a high official, he immediately entered a fierce debate on whether the Company should continue to fund colleges that taught in Arabic and Sanskrit, as well as those that taught in

55. Lady Trevelyan, ed., *Miscellaneous Works of Lord Macaulay* (New York: Harper & Brothers, 1880), 5.131–67.

56. Quotations in this paragraph are from Treveleyan, *Miscellaneous Works*, 141 and 167.

English, or only support colleges that taught in English. Macaulay sided with the "Anglicists" against the "Orientalists" and famously argued that "a single shelf of a good European library was worth the whole native literature of India and Arabia."[57] Only English, he maintained, could convey true science, philosophy, and history, and only English would civilize India. He recognized that the government had limited funds and could not educate all Indians, and so he suggested that the few Indians who could be educated in English would become a class of "interpreters between us and the millions whom we govern; a class of persons, Indian in blood and colour, but English in taste, in opinions, in morals, and in intellect."[58] An additional benefit of such an education was that it would dispel superstition. In a private letter to his father, Macaulay wrote that within thirty years there would no longer be a Hindu among "the respectable classes."[59] Macaulay and the Anglicists succeeded in redirecting funds to English-medium institutions, at least in the short term. By the end of the decade the government changed its position again and began to support education in both English and Indian languages.

As with the abolition of sati, the debate on the role of English in education and government (English replaced Persian in courts and the administration by the end of the 1830s) had a limited impact. Most Indians were not directly affected by the governor general's decisions. Nor were they affected by the government's highly publicized campaign against *thagi*, from which the English word "thug" is derived, but which then meant the murder by strangulation of wealthy travelers by itinerant gangs. Nevertheless, the reforms did indicate a shift in perspective, tenor, and approach to Indians and to governance. They also revealed the by-then commonplace racist attitudes among the Company's British officials. It was widely believed that Indian civilization had been in a long decline and that one of the benefits of British rule was that there was now an opportunity to arrest that decline. James Mill (1773–1836), a powerful figure in the Company's London administration and the father

---

57. Thomas Babington Macaulay, "Minute on Indian Education," in John Clive and Thomas Pinney, eds., *Thomas Babington Macaulay, Selected Writings*, ed. John Clive and Thomas Pinney (Chicago: University of Chicago Press, 1972), 241.

58. Ibid., 249.

59. Letter of October 12, 1836 in Thomas Pinney, ed., *The Letters of Thomas Babington Macaulay, Vol. III: January 1834–August 1841* (Cambridge: Cambridge University Press, 1976), 193.

of John Stuart Mill (1806–73), who also worked for the Company, published a history of British India that argued that Indian civilization had never advanced over thousands of years: "By conversing with the Hindus of the present day, we, in some measure, converse with the Chaldeans and Babylonians of the time of Cyrus; with the Persians and Egyptians of the time of Alexander."[60] Many colonial officials agreed with Mill and believed that Indians had a need to be ruled by foreigners.

Perhaps the most consequential reform, but one that has received relatively little attention until recently, was the creation in 1835 of a uniform coinage for the Company's Indian territories.[61] From the time of its very first voyage the Company had always taken a keen interest in coinage, and this interest remained even after land revenues displaced trade as the principal source of its income. In each of its three presidencies the Company had been given valuable concessions from the Mughal emperor or local ruler to issue its own coins. This meant that the Company did not have to pay a commission to Indian mints when it wanted to coin its bullion. The coins that it did mint in India or in Britain were usually immediately accepted by moneychangers, traders, and soldiers because, compared to some Indian states, they were not debased, meaning that they retained a high silver or gold content. The perennial difficulty, however, was that each presidency had its own currency and coinage. The silver rupees of Bengal were of a different size, weight, and design than those of Bombay or Madras, and while Bengal and Bombay were on a silver standard, Madras had a silver and gold standard. Indeed, there were dozens of different types of coin in legal circulation. For example, someone traveling through Bengal in the early nineteenth century could come across at least four different rupees: the Benares and Farrukhabad rupees in upper Bengal, the Arcot rupee in eastern Bengal, and the heavier Murshidabad or Sicca (Sikka) rupee in the areas surrounding Calcutta that were known as lower Bengal. The Company had for many years tried to rationalize its various currencies by creating an imaginary currency, the current rupee, which was used only for bookkeeping. Nevertheless, this

60. James Mill, *The History of British India*, abridged and introd. William Thomas (Chicago: University of Chicago Press, 1975), 248–49.

61. The details of the Company's currency reforms can be found in Sanjay Garg, *The Sikka and the Raj: A History of Currency Legislations of the East India Company, 1772–1835* (New Delhi: Manohar, 2013); Peter R. Thompson, *The East India Company and Its Coins* (Honiton: Token Publishing, 2010).

state of affairs naturally caused confusion and was one of the reasons, in 1806, the directors ordered their presidencies to create a single coinage with a new design.

Over the next twenty-seven years governors and mint masters slowly abandoned bimetallism, discontinued coins, closed mints, installed mint machines, and gradually introduced rupees in each presidency that had a uniform weight and purity. This was a significant achievement, but there was still no uniform coin. In order to create the Company rupee in 1835, Lord Bentinck and his successor, Sir Charles Metcalfe (1785–1846), had to overcome a longstanding problem: all rupees were in the name of a former Mughal emperor, Shah Alam II (1728–1806). The Sicca rupee, for example, had a Persian couplet on the obverse that read: "Defender of the religion of Muhammad, Shah Alam, Emperor, shadow of the divine favor, put his stamp on the seven climes." The reverse noted that the coin had been "Struck at Murshidabad in the 19th year of his reign of tranquil prosperity." The Company had not changed the design since 1777, the nineteenth year of Shah Alam's reign, even though he was dead and even though the coins were minted at Calcutta. The Company had kept the same language on the coins, including the reference to the nineteenth regnal year, because it wanted to stop Indian moneychangers, who controlled the flow of money to the peasantry, from discounting coins by as much as 3 and 2 percent in the second and third years after their issue, as had been the case in the past. The Company had also been worried that moving away from a coin that was in a familiar idiom, prominently mentioning a Mughal emperor and written only in Persian, would cause a crisis of confidence in the Company's currency.

By 1835, however, the Company felt it was sufficiently secure to issue a new coin in the Greco-Roman tradition. The new Company coin symbolically established the British—not just the Company—as the dominant power in India and created one of the conditions for the emergence of a national economy. It replaced the name of Shah Alam with a portrait and the name of King William IV (1765–1837), and, on the reverse, the value of the coin was written in English and Persian, all set within a wreath of laurel.

The introduction onto the Company rupee of the king's face, name, and title and the prominent use of English mark the moment when the Company finally felt sufficiently secure and confident to sweep away Indian tradition and declare the British king as sovereign of its Indian territories. The making of the colonial state had been a gradual process, beginning more than seventy years before, but it could be said that the unveiling of the Company rupee was also the unveiling of the colonial state. It is true that there was still a Mughal emperor, Muin ud Din Akbar II (1760–1837) until 1837 and then the poet-emperor Bahadur Shah II (1775–1862), but an entrenched colonial rule had been established. Colonialism is notoriously difficult to define, precisely because, as we have seen, the Company's settlements and state changed dramatically over two centuries, but as a result of territorial conquests, the Cornwallis and Bentinck reforms, and a deepening racism among the British, a state emerged that would form the basis of British rule until independence in 1947. At its core was an English-speaking civil service that was backed by an imposing army, funded by land revenues, and convinced that its mission was to keep the peace and gradually improve the moral and material condition of peoples it considered less civilized than Europeans. Another important feature of this form of colonialism was the assertion, through the new coin, that Indians were now subjects of the British king.

The Company rupee did not just signal the end of a process of state formation; it also helped bring about a new phase of colonial rule, one characterized by accelerating economic integration. The rupee was now legal tender throughout British India, and its ubiquity and inherent value meant that it was even accepted in the Princely States that had their own currencies. Commerce across India became easier, and when railways were introduced in 1853, travel became faster as well. The new all-India economy would play an important part in helping to stimulate ideas of nationalism during the second half of the nineteenth century. Economic ties helped to create a sense of national identity, and by the turn of the twentieth century, Indian scholars and nationalists were framing their early arguments against imperial rule in terms of a "drain" of national wealth.

Indian Responses and the Rebellion

What did Indians think of the Company's rule? Rammohan Roy answered this very question in 1831. He identified three classes of Indian, each with a different opinion. Peasants, he wrote, were not particularly knowledgeable about or interested in the form of government, whether British or Indian, but were focused on the government official with whom they interacted most and who had the greatest ability to make their lives better or worse. Those who were of an "aspiring character" or who were part of a family that had suffered economically "consider it derogatory to accept the trifling public situations which natives are allowed to hold under the British Government, and are decidedly disaffected to it." Only those who were doing well economically or who had benefited from the Permanent Settlement "and such as have sufficient intelligence to foresee the probability of future improvement . . . are not only reconciled to it, but view it as a blessing to the country."[62]

It is certainly true that some Indians, like Roy and those who depended on the Company for their livelihoods, were supporters of the colonial government. It is also accurate that some were frustrated that Indians could not hold responsible positions in government or in the army. However, Roy's assessment also reflects a patrician disdain for the peasantry. Peasants were very politically aware and, when faced with excessive or unfair taxes and revenue demands, sometimes rebelled against their landlords and the state. The British regarded these rebellions as law-and-order issues, but their frequency suggests that there was widespread hostility toward the revenue systems as well as the police and courts that enforced the revenue laws.

The most important rebellion occurred in northern India and began in May 1857. The Company was taken by surprise and was unprepared to meet the challenge of such a broad-based, sustained, and effective rebellion. Within weeks of its start the Company had lost much of the North-Western Provinces (or what had previously been called the Ceded and Conquered Provinces) as well as the annexed state of Awadh. In order not to lose its Indian Empire the Company had to scramble to find and deploy loyal troops from other parts of India and was forced to rely on British Crown troops that had to be sent from Britain and elsewhere. The rebellion was eventually suppressed, with most fighting ending by late 1858, but the cost in terms of lives—especially Indian lives—and property was enormous. Accurate figures are difficult to find, but historians have estimated that 2,600 British enlisted soldiers and 157 officers (or 2.7 and 4 percent, respectively, of the total) were killed. Another 8,000 died of heatstroke and disease, while 3,000 were severely injured. Indian deaths from the war and the resulting famines and epidemics may have reached 800,000.[63]

62. Bruce Carlisle Robertson, ed., *The Essential Writings of Raja Rammohan Ray* (Delhi: Oxford University Press, 1999), 195.

63. Lawrence James, *Raj: The Making and Unmaking of British India* (New York: St Martin's Griffin, 2000), 254–55; Douglas M. Peers, *India under Colonial Rule: 1700–1885* (Harlow: Pearson Longman, 2006), 64. Peers suggests that six thousand British died.

What the rebellion was (and what it subsequently meant) is one of the great debates of South Asian and British imperial history. From its inception there has even been uncertainty and disagreement over what to call it. In 1858, for example, Charles Raikes (1812–85) inadvertently revealed the confusion when he struggled to give a label to what was happening. "I attribute the origin of our existing disturbances in India," he wrote,

> to a mutiny in the Bengal army, and to that cause alone; I mean that the exciting and immediate cause of the revolution is to be found in the mutiny. That we have in many parts of the country drifted from mutiny into rebellion, is all too true; but I repeat my assertion, that we have to deal now with a revolt caused by a mutiny, not with a mutiny growing out of a national discontent.[64]

Raikes supplied many of the terms that have been used to characterize the events: mutiny, revolution, revolt, and national discontent. Writers also saw it as an uprising and rebellion. In the twentieth century, others added war of independence and nationalist war. The distinctions sometimes reveal political or ideological positions. For example, in Britain at the time, conservatives believed that they were witnessing a national revolt that was caused by deep opposition to the reforms that had begun under Lord Bentinck. Liberals and supporters of the Company, such as Raikes, who wished to protect it from being wound up by Parliament, argued that the fighting was simply the product of a mutiny and was not caused by the Company's efforts to improve India.[65] If there were men who joined the mutiny, they did so because they were credulous and had been hoodwinked into believing false information about the Company and its intentions. Imperialist historians tended to highlight the role of the mutineers, and so for many decades it was often referred to as the Sepoy Mutiny or the Great Mutiny. This perspective downplayed both

---

64. Charles Raikes, *Notes on the Revolt in the North-Western Provinces of India* (London: Longman, Brown, Green, Longmans & Roberts, 1858), 156. This passage is quoted and given additional context in Gautam Chakravarty, *The Indian Mutiny and the British Imagination* (Cambridge: Cambridge University Press, 2005), 23.

65. Thomas R. Metcalf, *The Aftermath of Revolt: India, 1857–1870* (Princeton: Princeton University Press, 1964), 72–75.

the "national" character of the rebellion—meaning that all sections of Indian society actively participated—and any "nationalist" interpretation. By the early twentieth century, Indian nationalists saw the beginnings of their movement in the rebellion, while Marxist historians focused on the prominent role of the peasantry. Many historians today use the term "rebellion" because it signals that although large sections of the Bengal army did mutiny they were joined and even led by a broad spectrum of north Indian society, from aristocrats to landlords, merchants to peasants. The term also encompasses the strong anticolonial nature of the war but does not necessarily go so far as to suggest it was a nationalist struggle.

Much of the difficulty in characterizing and understanding the rebellion is that there were many causes and goals and many theaters of war. The initial outbreak occurred in Meerut, less then forty miles from the northeast of Delhi. Indian soldiers belonging to regiments of the Bengal army attacked and killed their British officers on May 10, 1857. They did so because the day before they had been forced to witness eighty-five sepoys sentenced to ten years' imprisonment for refusing to use cartridges for the new Enfield rifle, which were thought to have been greased using pig and cow fat. The soldiers then marched to Delhi, captured the city, and declared the aging (and utterly surprised and unprepared) Mughal emperor, Bahadur Shah, their leader. News of their success spread rapidly and within weeks the British had lost control over much of northern India, with the exception of Bengal and the newly conquered Punjab. The soldiers were joined by landlords, peasants, and merchants, Muslims as well as Hindus, which historians have interpreted as a sign that there was widespread hostility to the colonial government and that opposition had been growing for many years.

Discontent was particularly strong within the Bengal army. The sepoys' main complaints focused on how they were treated by their officers and on their pay. Some were concerned that their officers and the government were eager to see troops convert to Christianity. Rumors had circulated that the new cartridges were a ruse to force conversion, which was why there was such consternation and disobedience among troops in May 1857. Although the cartridges were not greased with pig or cow fat, it was true that some prominent officers did proselytize. Soldiers were also anxious about new regulations that meant that they were now obliged to serve anywhere ordered (previously, regiments had successfully resisted serving overseas, since for some Hindus traveling over the ocean was

considered a threat to caste status). Finally, there was general unhap-
piness over pay, which had not been raised in about fifty years. Cost of
living increases, especially for food, meant that a sepoy's pay was worth
half of what it had been worth in 1800.[66] Batta, a traditional way to
supplement the pay of those who served outside the presidency, had
also been cut.

About a third of the sepoys in the Bengal army were recruited from
the state of Awadh. This connection was crucial for the spread of the
rebellion, since the Company's actions in Awadh had ripple effects in the
Bengal army. Awadh, usually spelled Oudh or Oude by the British, had
been one of the largest and wealthiest states to emerge from the dissolution of the Mughal Empire at the beginning of the eighteenth century. It
was governed by a Shia dynasty and was based in Lucknow. Despite its
size and wealth it had gradually been weakened by the Company, which
had seized territory and forced its rulers to garrison and pay for a contingent of Company troops, who were to be given batta for their service
in the state.

Awadh's final indignity occurred in 1856, when the governor general,
Lord Dalhousie (1812–60), decided to depose the king and annex the
state. He did so based on an argument that the Company was legally
permitted to annex a state if it determined that the state had been mis-
governed. At the same time, Dalhousie also articulated a "doctrine of
lapse," whereby the Company assumed complete control over an Indian
state if, on the death of the ruler, there was no direct heir. The two doc-
trines were, to some degree, pretexts since Dalhousie's motivation behind
the annexations was a belief that India could never be improved if it
were burdened by a hodgepodge of states ruled by Indians. Dalhousie
annexed six other states during his period as governor general from
1848–56, the most consequential for the subsequent rebellion being the
Maratha states of Satara and Jhansi. The ruling families were under-
standably angered by these measures, but it would become clear that
many of their subjects also felt humiliated and had sympathies for their
former rulers.

Another consequence of the annexation of Awadh was that the British introduced a new landholding and revenue scheme. Many of the losers were previously dominant (and still powerful) landholders, known as
taluqdars. Many had been dispossessed of their rights to collect revenue

---

66. Saul David, *The Indian Mutiny, 1857* (London: Viking, 2002), 28.

while the remainder faced higher revenue demands. Society in Awadh was largely agricultural, and so these changes disrupted social relations and created anxiety and hostility that reverberated throughout the region and cut across caste and religious lines. High revenue demands also affected agricultural communities in the adjacent North-Western Provinces.

Taluqdar and peasant discontent was an important reason the mutiny was transformed so quickly into a popular rebellion, but there were other reasons. In 1858 the rebels issued a proclamation to persuade five sections of Indian society to join the rebellion. Although issued toward the end of the war, the proclamation nevertheless suggests why different communities supported the rebellion. The document first addressed landholders and reiterated that they had suffered under high revenue assessments and promised relief if they fought against the colonial government. The document then reminds merchants that the British had "appropriated to themselves the monopoly of all lucrative trades such as indigo, opium, cloth" and that the new indigenous government would open up these trades to Indians. Government workers, or "men of service," were promised higher ranking and higher paying posts, while artisans could expect to regain work that they had lost to British manufacturers. Finally, Hindu and Muslim religious figures could look forward to state support from the rebel government.[67]

Once the war began both sides had advantages and disadvantages. The rebels had surprised the British and had effectively expelled them from much of northern India. They had a vast numerical superiority, seasoned and well-trained troops from the old Bengal army, and sufficient materiel to prosecute a war. A number of impressive leaders emerged, including Nana Sahib (1824–?), the adopted son of the last Maratha peshwa, whose state of Satara had been annexed; Tantia Tope (Topi; ?–1859), son of a Maratha courtier; and Rani Lakshmi Bai (1835–58), the queen of the annexed state of Jhansi.[68] The Mughal emperor was also a recognized figurehead, although he did not actively participate in the campaigns.

---

67. S. Mahdi Husain, *Bahadur Shah Zafar: And the War of 1857 in Delhi* (Delhi: Aakar Books, 2006), xlvi–li.

68. Harleen Singh, *The Rani of Jhansi: Gender, History, and Fable in India* (Cambridge: Cambridge University Press, 2014); Joyce Lebra-Chapman, *The Rani of Jhansi: A Study in Female Heroism in India* (Honolulu: University of Hawaii Press, 1986).

The rebels' principal disadvantages were that a singular goal never materialized (some wanted to see a powerful Mughal Empire reappear, others fought for the independence of annexed states, while others had more personal reasons to oppose the British), and they were not able to capitalize on their early momentum. Large numbers of troops were often left unused for months and the war quickly became defensive.

The Company initially found itself on its back foot. It had lost control over much of its largest army, which had found allies and recruits among the local population. Its loyal Indian and British troops were widely scattered, and it had to wait for fresh troops to arrive from overseas. However, the Company, together with the British public and government, never contemplated anything other than the reconquest of lost territories and devoted considerable money and troops to that effort. The British were also helped by the nature of the fighting. There was often poor coordination among all of the rebel armies, and so the British were able to prosecute the war in a manner that best suited them. Finally, the Company could also rely on large numbers of loyal troops and new recruits, most notably from Punjab.

Once the war began, one of the Company's first priorities was the recapture of Delhi. Over the summer the British massed European and Sikh troops on the Ridge, to the city's northwest, and finally attacked the city in September. The city fell after six days of desperate fighting. Bahadur Shah was imprisoned, put on trial for "the crimes of Mutiny and Rebellion against the State," and exiled to Burma.[69] His sons had been summarily executed at the time of their capture. The British tended to blame Muslims for the mutiny, believing that religious agitators had hoodwinked Hindus into joining the fighting on behalf of a renewed Mughal Empire. In revenge, British troops often targeted Muslims. The great Urdu poet Ghalib was in Delhi at the time of its capture and wrote a vivid and harrowing account of life in the city before, during, and after the fighting. Ghalib had been both a court poet for the Mughal emperor (or, as the British preferred to call him, the king of Delhi) and a pensioner under the Company. Like many, therefore, his loyalties might have been divided at the start of the war, but once Delhi had been captured he sent his account to the British as a proof of his suffering and loyalty and to request the resumption of his pension. Ghalib's account has the

69. Pramod K. Nayar, ed., *The Trial of Bahadur Shah Zafar* (Hyderabad: Orient Longman, 2007), 3.

PUNCH, OR THE LONDON CHARIVARI.—September 12, 1857.

JUSTICE.

Fig. 6. "Justice." *Punch*, September 12, 1857.

weariness of defeat, and although he praises the British and curses the rebels for causing the war, he nevertheless reveals the violence the British inflicted on Delhi and, especially, on Muslims. He notes, for example, that most of the city's population had fled, but large numbers were held in two prisons, one outside and one inside Delhi. "The angel of death," he writes, "alone knows how many people have been hanged by the neck in these two prisons."[70]

For many British soldiers and for much of the British public, the rebellion quickly became a war of retribution and racial dominance. Attention focused on cases in which British officers and their wives and children had been killed in cold blood. The most notorious example was a massacre at Kanpur (Cawnpore) in June 1857. There the British found themselves besieged by troops led by Nana Sahib and Tantia Tope. After three weeks, the garrison surrendered in exchange for safe passage by boat. However, for reasons that are not clear but have been much debated, the British were attacked soon after boarding the boats. A few men managed to escape, but most died. As many as two hundred women and children were held prisoner for a few days but, just before a relief force of British troops arrived, they, too, were killed, and their bodies were thrown down a well.

The Kanpur massacre prompted calls for vengeance in Britain and provided the pretext for the razing of villages, humiliation, and indiscriminate slaughter. Indians who were captured were usually subject to spurious legal proceedings, and large numbers were either hanged or blown from cannon. Mutiny was already punishable by death, but under the terms of Act XIV (June 1857) anyone found guilty of "seducing" a sepoy to mutiny could be executed. However, within a month of signing the act, the governor general, Lord Canning (1812–62), realized that unchecked violence could be counterproductive and issued a resolution on July 31, 1857 to give specific guidelines on how captives should be treated, "lest measures of extreme severity should be too hastily resorted to, or carried too far."[71] The resolution was met with widespread contempt among the British, and the governor general was famously mocked as Clemency Canning. As the rebellion was slowly suppressed, the resolution may have restrained some magistrates and officers, but vindictive violence remained common.

If, to the British, the Kanpur massacre proved Indian treachery and the need for retribution, the siege of the Residency at Lucknow displayed British heroism and gallantry. The Residency was an easily fortified complex, and once the rebellion reached Lucknow on July 1, 1857,

---

70. Mirza Asadullah Khan Ghalib, *Dastanbuy: A Diary of the Indian Revolt of 1857*, trans. from Persian by Khwaja Ahmad Faruqi (New York: Asia Publishing House, 1970), 60.

71. Michael Maclagan, *"Clemency" Canning: Charles John, 1st Earl Canning, Governor-General and Viceroy of India, 1856–1862* (London: Macmillan & Co LTD, 1962), 324.

it became the refuge for the British contingent in the city. It was surrounded and then attacked and bombarded frequently, causing many casualties. British troops arrived in late September and tried to relieve the siege but were only able to fight their way to the Residency. Indian forces remained strong enough to prevent them leaving until November 17, when the siege was finally lifted. The courage and resourcefulness shown by the besieged were so moving to the British that, once control had been established over the province, the Residency's Union Jack flag was never lowered at sunset until the independence of India in 1947.

The rebellion was not just confined to the Delhi-Kanpur-Lucknow region. It also spread south to Gwalior and Jhansi. There the rebels were led by Lakshmi Bai, the Rani of Jhansi, whose state had been one of those annexed by Lord Dalhousie. The British defeated her troops at Jhansi in early 1858, but she made a dramatic escape and, joined by Tantia Tope, overran Gwalior. However, their resistance did not last much longer. She was killed in battle in June 1858, and he was eventually betrayed and executed in April 1859. Nana Sahib was never captured or killed but instead escaped into Nepal.

Even before the end of the war it was clear to many in Britain that the Company could not be allowed to continue as a government. It had managed to renew its charter in 1853, but not for the customary twenty-year period and only because it replaced its patronage system for entry into its civil service with competitive examinations. At that time there was a concern that if the Company were pushed aside political parties might be too tempted, and perhaps corrupted, by the chance to appoint civil servants to India.[72] The rebellion quickly changed the mood in Britain and, despite some last-minute attempts by the Company to delay the inevitable,[73] the Company's remaining powers were transferred to Parliament under the Government of India Act of August 2, 1858.

The act did not officially abolish the Company. The proprietors, or shareholders, continued to receive a dividend that had been guaranteed in 1834, when the Company lost its commercial privileges for a period of forty years. At the same time a "sinking fund" had been established in order

---

72. Francis Hutchins, *The Illusion of Permanence: British Imperialism in India* (Princeton: Princeton University Press, 1967), 88.

73. John Stuart Mill, *Memorandum of the Improvements in the Administration of India during the Last Thirty Years and the Petition of the East-India Company to Parliament* (London: Wm. H. Allen & Co., 1858).

to eventually redeem the dividend. After the Company was stripped of its power in 1858, the government of India continued to pay the expensive dividend, which amounted to 10.5 percent of the Company's capital. In 1873 the British Parliament, eager to redeem the dividend and thereby save the colonial government £450,000 a year, passed a law to reimburse the proprietors by the end of April 1874 and close the Company's books shortly afterward. Having begun operations on the last day of 1600, the East India Company ceased to exist on June 1, 1874.

CONCLUSION

When the Company was effectively closed in late 1858, all of its remaining responsibilities were transferred to the British government. In some respects the change was momentous. A company that had, over the course of 258 years, altered fashion and consumption patterns in Europe and Asia, built an Indian and Southeast Asian empire through conquest, and then established colonial rule was suddenly no more. The transfer of power to the Crown made it easier for the British public to see a unified British Empire, eventually incorporating Asian, African, Caribbean, and Middle Eastern lands, even if those territories were governed very differently. India was so important, in terms of size, population, wealth, and prestige, that in the popular British imagination it became the "Crown Jewel" of the empire. The transfer of power also made it easier to create a more integrated imperial economy, where raw goods could be transported to Britain to be manufactured into clothes or machines and then sold back to its colonies.

In India the creation of the Raj, as the new administration was often termed, led to important changes in policy. The most visible had to do with the army. To ensure that another mutiny would not catch the colonial administration flatfooted, the British decided to station much larger numbers of British troops in India and reduce the size of the Indian army. In 1857 the Company had about 40,000 British troops stationed in the country, but by 1867 that number had increased to over 61,000. Over the same period the number of Indian troops declined from roughly 260,000 to 120,000. This meant that the ratio of sepoys to British troops also declined, from about seven and a half to one at the start of the Rebellion to just two to one twenty years later.[1] At the same time, the army stopped recruiting high-caste northern Indians and instead turned its attention to so-called martial races, which included Sikhs, Muslims from the northwest frontier, and Gurkhas from Nepal. This reformed army became the empire's most valuable asset, controlling the population in India while fighting imperial and world wars abroad.

---

1. Statistics from "Lord Lawrence to Lord Canborne, 4 January 1867," in C. H. Philips, *The Evolution of India and Pakistan, 1858–1947: Select Documents* (London: Oxford University Press, 1962), 509.

A second, important change in policy was a decision to abandon attempts to annex Indian states. Many in Britain believed that the Company's Indian administration had been too eager to interfere in Indian social customs and religious affairs and had pursued misguided policies toward the Indian states. These interventions were thought to have been a major cause of the Rebellion, and so it was decided that the new government would be much more conservative in its dealings with both Indian society and so-called princely states. In November 1858 Queen Victoria issued a proclamation in which she promised that Indians would not be "molested or disquieted, by reason of their religious faith" and that treaties between the Company and "native princes" would be honored by her government. She added, "We desire no extension of our present territorial possessions; and, while we will permit no aggression upon our dominions or our rights to be attempted with impunity, we shall sanction no encroachment on those of others."[2] The hope was that this new attitude would encourage the princes to become loyal bulwarks against popular insurrection. Indeed, the princes, secure in their thrones and protected by British India, were usually reliable collaborators with the British, often suppressing dissent and stifling economic competition within their states. Historians have pointed to the famous imperial assemblage held in Delhi in 1877 as the classic late nineteenth-century example of the strange symbiosis that existed between the British and the princes. The assemblage was intended as a dramatic display of British domination over India and as evidence of complete British assumption of the symbolic and real power once held by the Mughal emperors. The sixty-three princes who attended the event, held at a specially constructed site just to the northwest of the old Mughal capital, were told that Queen Victoria had now assumed the title of empress of India. They were given special silk banners by the viceroy and participated in ceremonies that symbolically tied them to their British rulers and ranked them in order of importance. Victoria had long been fascinated by India and was eager to see her titles match the level of prestige she believed Britain had gained with the creation of an empire. The British enjoyed the self-aggrandizing pageantry of these kinds of events and held two more assemblages, which they termed *darbars*, in 1903 and 1911.

---

2. "Proclamation by the Queen to the Princes, Chiefs, and the People of India, 1 November 1858," in *Speeches and Documents on Indian Policy, 1750–1921*, ed. A. Berriedale Keith (London: Humphrey Milford, Oxford University Press, 1922), 1.383.

If the post-Company period was partly defined by the new, race-based Indian army and the government's conservative and theatrical approach to the princely states, it was also defined by continuities. The structure of the new government was similar to the old Company structure, and many of the men who served the Company, both in London and India, retained their posts or assumed new ones that were not much different from what they had held before.[3] In India, Lord Canning, the Company's governor general, kept his post and added viceroy to his official titles. In London the Court of Directors and the Board of Control were abolished and replaced with the Council of India. The Council advised the new secretary of state for India, who became a member of the British Cabinet. The first two secretaries happened to be the former presidents of the Board of Control. Moreover, seven of the fifteen members of the new Council were former members of the Court of Directors. The government clearly valued continuity over rapid or thoroughgoing change.

There was also continuity in the ideology behind British rule over Indians. Even if the new government was now determined not to interfere with religious or social customs, colonial officials and British scholars alike, echoing arguments that had first been made earlier in the century, insisted that the role of empire was to ensure peace in India and promote civilization. Sir John Strachey (1823–1907), a prominent colonial official and historian, wrote "that there is not, and never was an India, or even any country of India, possessing, according to European ideas, any sort of unity, physical, political, social, or religious; no Indian nation, and especially no 'people of India,' of which we hear so much."[4] Strachey's insistence that there was no Indian nation—despite the appearance of a nationalist movement at that very moment—was coupled with the claim that only colonial rule could keep the peace. Victorian historians firmly believed that India "descended" into chaos and violence after the decline of the Mughal Empire in the first decades of the eighteenth century. According to their interpretation, India had so many castes, communities, religions, and races that they were in a permanent state of conflict. They therefore argued that the wars of the eighteenth century reflected India's natural state and that peace could only be established through foreign and imperial rule. Historians today reject this characterization, preferring to

---

3. For details, see Francis Hutchins, *The Illusion of Permanence: British Imperialism in India* (Princeton: Princeton University Press, 1967), 87.

4. Sir John Strachey, *India* (London: Kegan Paul, Trench, Trübner & Co., Ltd., 1894), 5.

see viable, stable, and wealthy states emerge after the dissolution of the Mughal Empire. For earlier generations of historians, however, the struggles of the eighteenth century were a convenient explanation for both the decline in Indian civilization and the need for British rule.

According to late Victorian scholars, peace was not the only benefit that colonialism could provide. Sir James Fitzjames Stephen (1829–94), a legal member of the Supreme Council in Calcutta, wrote in 1883 that the role of the colonial state was to promote the welfare of Indians by introducing "the essential parts of European civilisation into a country densely peopled, grossly ignorant, steeped in idolatrous superstition, un-energetic, fatalistic." According to his reasoning, civilization meant "peace, order, the supremacy of law, the prevention of crime, the redress of wrong, the enforcement of contracts, the development and concentration of the military force of the state, the construction of public works, the collection . . . of the revenue required for these objects . . . interfering as little as possible with the comfort or wealth of the inhabitants, and improvement of the people."[5] Stephen's list of responsibilities succinctly encapsulates what we might call the high colonial state. It consciously avoided legislating social or religious change and it focused its efforts on extracting revenue, maintaining an army, and enforcing a kind of "order" over the population.

The order the British imposed was hierarchical and undemocratic. In her Proclamation of 1858, Victoria promised Indians that it was her "will that . . . our subjects, of whatever race or creed, be freely and impartially admitted to office . . . the duties of which they may be qualified by their education, ability, and integrity duly to discharge."[6] Colonial officials very quickly regretted this clause and did all they could to exclude Indians from meaningful and responsible positions. For example, the examinations for entry into the powerful Indian Civil Service were only held in London, which made it extremely difficult for Indians to qualify. To many Indians, therefore, the queen's proclamation was an empty promise: it was their race and religion that disqualified them from responsible posts.

Just as the Rebellion was ending, a prominent Indian Muslim, Syed Ahmed Khan (1817–98; Sayyid Ahmad Khan), published his explanation as to why so many turned against the Company. He noted that Indians had been excluded from the Legislative Council and that therefore

---

5. Quoted in Philips, *Evolution of India and Pakistan*, 59.

6. Keith, 1.383.

the British had little idea of what Indians thought. "The men who have ruled India," he wrote, "should never have forgotten that they were here in the position of foreigners, that they differed from its natives in religion, in customs, in habits of life and thought."[7] The transfer of power to the Crown did not improve matters for Indians. The British belief in their racial superiority and the need for social distance only intensified in the decades after the Rebellion. Indians continued to be alienated from government.

In addition to being undemocratic, colonial "order" was always unstable. Rural unrest continued throughout the second half of the century. Local disturbances were common and were often sparked by frustrations over high revenue demands, endless cycles of debt, and fear of famine. Indeed, a major famine occurred in southern and western India between 1876 and 1878, resulting in many millions of deaths. Opposition to the colonial state, though, was not limited to the peasantry. Educated and prosperous urban Indians, especially in Calcutta and Bombay, also began to see the need for change and questioned the benefits of colonial rule. In 1885 the Indian National Congress was founded and, although it began as a venue for formulating and recommending reforms to colonial officials, it gradually became the locus of more contentious discussion about how to put pressure on the British. At the beginning of the century a major schism in the organization over the most effective tactics to be used pitted the "moderates," such as Dadabhai Naoroji (1825–1917), Surendranath Banerjea (1848–1925), and Gopal Krishna Gokhale (1866–1915), against the "extremists," such as Bal Gangadhar Tilak (1856–1920) and Lala Lajpat Rai (1865–1928). The split was eventually resolved and the 1920s saw new leaders emerge, including Mohandas Karamchand Gandhi (1869–1948; Mahatma Gandhi) and Jawaharlal Nehru (1889–1964). The organization demanded complete independence in 1930, but it took another seventeen years before British rule ended in India.

The rise of Indian nationalism toward the end of the nineteenth century is much debated among historians. What is clear is that there was no single cause; indeed, there was no single nationalism. When the British left in 1947 they handed power over to leaders in two new states, India and Pakistan. What, then, are some of the causes for the emergence of nationalism in India in the decades after the end of the Company? The

---

7. Syed Ahmed Khan, *The Causes of the Indian Revolt* (Karachi: Oxford University Press, 2000), 12.

rapid expansion of railway and telegraph lines, the adoption of steam engines, the proliferation of newspapers, the use of English as a common language among elites, the consolidation of the Company's three armies into a single Indian army, and the existence of a stable British India for more than a generation made it possible for Indians to travel extensively, communicate more easily, and experience increasing economic and military integration. Early nationalist leaders exposed the racism, limitations, and hypocrisy of the colonial state, and some coupled their critiques with a revivalist Hinduism that saw all of India as a sacred homeland. Moreover, Indians were aware of nationalist developments overseas, in Ireland, especially, but also in Italy and Germany.

One of the early nationalists, Bankim Chandra Chatterjee (1838–94; Chatterji), published a veiled critique of colonial rule in 1882. His novel, *Anandamath*, was written in Bengali and set in 1770, at the time of the great Bengal famine. It tells the story of Hindu ascetics who fight a successful battle against the combined forces of the Muslim nawab of Bengal and the Company. In the final chapter a wise man explains to the rebel leader that the victory was over Muslim rule, that the fighting should stop, and that power should now pass to the British. According to his counsel, the time had not yet come for Hindu rule: to revive Hinduism, science must be disseminated, which only the British can do. Moreover, as a practical matter, the Company cannot be defeated: "The English are a friendly power, and no one, in truth, has the power to come off victorious in a fight with the English."[8] Although the concluding chapter suggests support for a Company state, a possible underlying message is that foreign rule is temporary and that a nation, albeit a Hindu nation, will arise. It is left to the reader to decide if, after more than one hundred years, the time has arrived for a new nation to emerge. Chatterjee had to be very careful in how he framed his nationalist narrative because he worked as a government employee and lived in a colonial state. It is perhaps for these reasons that he chose to set the novel in the late eighteenth century, when the nawab and his administrators still had nominal control over Bengal and could safely be depicted as the main enemy.

Chatterjee's ambivalence toward the Company is, in part, a reflection of the fact that he lived in Bengal in the late nineteenth century. Many of

8. Nares Chandra Sen-Gupta, *The Abbey of Bliss: A Translation of Bankim Chandra Chatterjee's Anandamath* (Calcutta: Padmini Mohan Neogi, 1906), 199–200.

his British contemporaries were also ambivalent about the Company, but for very different reasons. These historians tended to see the Company as a prelude to or immature expression of the late Victorian and Edwardian British Empire.[9] It was common then to think that history was the story of progress and that civilizations invariably perfected their forms of governance and increased their scientific knowledge. As a result, the Company was often characterized as much for its failings as for its role in laying the foundations for the empire. Focus was often placed on the corruption and moral failings of the Company's servants but also on the reforms that supposedly led to the development of an incorruptible and duty-bound cadre of civil servants. The Company was therefore seen as occupying a stage of India's development. It was a vehicle for progress but, because it was not itself fully modern, it could not continue to exist and govern India.

In addition to believing in the idea of progress, earlier historians of the Company also saw change happening because of the efforts of a few great men. Men such as Robert Clive and Warren Hastings were described as the builders of empire, while generals and administrators such as Henry Havelock (1795–1857) and the brothers Henry and John Lawrence were seen as its saviors during the Rebellion. Biographers often described them as exemplars, to inspire later generations, and as men who almost single-handedly made Britain great. In some accounts these men were lauded for their courage and love of the British nation, while other narratives praised them for their devotion to duty and sense of moral responsibility.

Earlier Company histories also relied on turning points to explain why and how change happened. The most famous and important is the Battle of Plassey. The 1757 battle pitted the Company's armies, led by Clive, against the forces of the nawab of Bengal. Clive's victory was interpreted as a key event that transformed the Company from a maritime trading venture into a territorial and colonial state. This turning point has been so influential, indeed, that many histories, class syllabi, and courses are still structured around this break. Other turning points include the arrival of Lord Cornwallis as governor general and the Rebellion of 1857.

---

9. For a full discussion of the historiography on the Company, see Philip J. Stern, "History and Historiography of the English East India Company: Past, Present, and Future!" *History Compass* 7, no. 4 (2009): 1146–80.

Historians' view of the Company has changed considerably.[10] One reason for the change is that access to and use of sources has increased and broadened. Scholars now have the ability to read online published material in English for the whole period of the Company's existence, and they have easy access to the Company's records and non-English language sources that are housed in the new British Library. But one of the main reasons assessments of the Company have changed is that, since at least the 1970s, historians have changed their approach to the writing of history.

Historians now tend to argue against the idea that change progresses to a natural end point, or that an individual has extraordinary powers to alter the course of events, or even that there are breaks that can easily and conveniently divide eras. Instead, Company historians often concentrate on explaining change by identifying and examining many causes, some of which are the result of individuals' decisions and actions, but some of which are the result of impersonal trends or even changes in the climate or geography. Moreover, historians commonly notice more evidence of gradual transition than abrupt change. The Battle of Plassey, for example, is given less prominence now than in the past, since scholars see the transition to the Company's territorial and colonial rule as occurring in phases or stages. It took nearly eighty years after the famous battle for the Company to lose all of its trading monopolies, and even as it developed as a colonial state in the late eighteenth century it saw its powers gradually circumscribed by Parliament. Scholars even push the beginnings of colonial rule back to the seventeenth century. Philip Stern, for instance, argues that outlines of "the Company State" appear long before the Battle of Plassey.

Recent studies on the Company suggest that it cannot be characterized in simple ways. In the late seventeenth century it was vilified for being an anti-English monopoly that exported the country's wealth and destroyed the wool industry. One hundred years later it was seen as an extension

---

10. Recent general histories of the Company not referenced in earlier chapters include John Keay, *The Honourable Company: A History of the English East India Company* (New York: Macmillan Publishing Company, 1991); Tirthankar Roy, *The East India Company: The World's Most Powerful Corporation* (New Delhi: Allen Lane, 2012); Niels Steensgaard, *The Asian Trade Revolution of the Seventeenth Century: The East India Companies and the Decline of the Caravan Trade* (Chicago: University of Chicago Press, 1974); Antony Wild, *The East India Company: Trade and Conquest from 1600* (New York: Lyons Press, 2000).

of the nation and a source of much needed revenue. In the 1680s it was derided as a monopoly, but it allowed extensive private trade throughout Asia. In the decades after 1770 the directors argued against war because it would cut into profits, but the Company still became a garrison state and expanded its territories enormously. The Company's contradictions are therefore as much a part of its history as its continuities.

What final conclusion can we make of the Company? Commentators today sometimes compare it to modern corporations, but no company today has an army, issues coins that are current, hangs criminals, or passes laws. Its closest equivalent was the Dutch East India Company, the VOC, but the VOC was abolished in 1799 and never developed the so-called liberal colonial state that emerged in India during the 1820s and 1830s. Yet for all its exceptional aspects, the Company reflected the changes, ideas, and struggles that affected Europe and Southern Asia between 1600 and 1858. Students of the Company can read in its history the rise of global capitalism, the shift of wealth from Asia to Europe, the emergence of the colonial state, and the growth of racial ideologies. In tracing its development we come to understand how and why consumption patterns changed in Britain, why Indian textiles were linked to sugar production in the West Indies, and why the Company became an opium dealer. We see its army turned into an army of occupation and its bureaucracy twisted into a force for control and the collection of revenue. The Company not only reflected the ideas and developments of the early modern era: it helped to shape them.

DOCUMENTS

The documents in this section are selections from primary sources. Most are mentioned in the previous chapters and all provide additional context and depth to many, but not all, of the subjects covered earlier. The majority of the documents are not well known but have been chosen because they are engaging, provocative, and sufficiently complex to sustain a discussion. Most words in this section are written with modern American spellings. Since these documents are selections, not all of the text is always provided.

DOCUMENT 1

The Company's Accusations against the Dutch East India Company (1624)[1]

By the early 1620s the Company found that it could not compete with the Dutch in the spice trade. In 1623 the Dutch arrested a number of Company servants living on the island of Amboyna (Ambon) for conspiring to capture the Dutch fort. They were tortured, and many were executed. This excerpt is from the preface of a book detailing the tortures and executions. It reveals how the Company chose to contrast itself with the Dutch Company. The original spelling is retained.

. . . thou wilt wonder how it commeth to passe, that our Nation, which hath not been wont to receive such disgraces, should now be so weak and unprovided in the Indies, as to suffer such indignities, and to be so grossly overtopped, outraged and vilified there. . . . Herein thou wilt soon

1. Anonymous (John Skinner), Preface, in *A True Relation of the Unjust, Cruell and Barbarous Proceedings against the English at Amboyna* (London: Nathanael Newberry, 1624).

answer thy self, if thou but consider the different end and designe of the English and Dutch Companies trading to the East Indies. . . . The English being subjects of a peaceable Prince, that hath enough of his owne, and is therewith content, without affecting of new acquests; have aymed at nothing in their East-India trade, but a lawfull and competent gaine by commerce and traffick with the people of those parts. And although they have in some places builded Forts, and settled some strength, yet that hath not beene done by force or violence, against the good will of the Magistrates or people of the country; but with their desire, consent and good liking, for the security only of the Trade, and upon the said Magistrate and peoples voluntarie yeelding themselves under the obedience and soverainty of the Crown of England; their owne ancient lawes, customes and priviledges, nevertheless reserved. . . . Upon these grounds, the English Company made their equipages answerable only to a course of comerce and peacable traffick; not expecting any hostility, neither from the Indians, nor especially from the Dutch.

On the other side, the Neatherlanders, from the beginning of their trade in the Indies, not content with the ordinary course of a fair and free commerce, invaded diverse Islands, took some Forts, built others, and laboured nothing more, than the conquests of Countries, and the acquiring of new dominion. By reason whereof, as they were accordingly provided of shipping, souldiers, and all warlike provision, as also of places of Rendevouz upon the shore, and thereby enabled to wrong the English as well as others: so the cost and charges of their shipping, Forts, and souldiers, imployed upon these designes, rose to such an height, as was not to bee maintained by the trade they had in those parts. Wherefore, for a supply, they were forced . . . to fish with dry nets, that is to say, to pick quarrels with the Indians, and so to take their ships, and make prize of their goods. Which yet not answering their charge and adventure, they proceeded also to quarrell with the English, to debarre them of trade to free places; and for attempting such trade, to take their ships and goods . . . thereby to have the whole and sole traffick of the commodities of the Indies in these parts of Europe, in their owne hands; and so they make the price at their pleasure, sufficient to maintain and promote their conquests, and withall to yeeld them an ample benefit of their trade.

DOCUMENT 2

Domestic Opposition to the East India Company (1681)[2]

Almost from its founding, the Company's trading practices and monopoly privileges were controversial in England. In 1681 a rival company, the Levant or Turkey Company, summarized the case against the Company.

The Company of Merchants Trading into the Dominions of the Grand Seignior [The Turkey Company], have for near one hundred years past constantly exported great quantities of the woolen manufactures, and other commodities of the growth of England into Turkey, to the great enriching of this nation . . . in return of which, the goods imported are raw silks . . . and cotton, etc. All of [those exported goods] are manufactured in England, and afford bread to the industrious poor of this nation.

The East India Company, on the other side, export from England immense quantities of gold and silver, with an inconsiderable quantity of cloth, which serves them only to give a color of some benefit to the nation. . . . In return of which their chiefest commodities are callicoes, pepper, wrought silks . . . being an evident damage to the poor of this nation, and . . . an infallible destruction to the Turkey trade.

The Constitution of the Turkey Company being a regulated company, and not driven by a joint stock, is open and comprehensive, admitting any that are bred merchants.

The East India Company on the other side, manage their trade by a joint stock, confined to the narrow compass of some few persons, exclusive to all others, under the penalty of mulcts, fines, seizures, and other extraordinary proceedings. And upon an exact inquiry it will be found . . . that about ten or twelve men have the absolute management of the whole trade . . . so that here is the certain effect of a monopoly to enrich some few, and impoverish many.

---

2. Anonymous, *The Allegations of the Turky Company and Others against the East-India-Company* (no publisher, 1681), 1–3.

Upon consideration of the whole matter, it is humbly hoped, that for relief of the now languishing, though most useful and necessary Turkey trade; His Majesty will be graciously pleased, to permit to the Turkey Company, the exercise of trade in the Red Sea, and all other Dominions of the Grand Seignior . . . and access thereunto, by the most convenient passages; and to forbid the East India Company, to import raw, or wrought silk, into England. And if this doth not seem a reasonable expedient, that then His Majesty would be pleased to . . . end this present joint stock . . . whereby a larger joint stock may be raised . . . so that the Turkey Company, who by the encroachment of the East India Company upon them, have lost or must lose the greatest part of their trade, may have some reparation by partaking of theirs. And that by proviso in the new charter [the Turkey Company], may be defended by a prohibition of raw and wrought silks out of India, which is not only a certain ruin to the Turkey trade, but consequentially a prejudice to the whole nation.

DOCUMENT 3

Criticism of a Company Bigwig and His War against the Mughal Empire (1690)[3]

Sir Josiah Child was the most important figure in the Company's London headquarters during the 1680s. He was one of twenty-four committees (the name given to the directors of the Company) and also rose to be, for a time, the governor. In these roles he managed to force his political enemies out of the management. He also curried favor with the king and his court by distributing large sums as bribes. His most controversial action, however, was a war against the Mughal emperor in India and the king of Siam. He hoped the war would result in better trading privileges for the Company as well as greater control over the actions of independent English traders who were trying to break the Company's

---

3. Anonymous, *Some Remarks upon the State of the East-India Company's Affairs: With Reasons for the Speedy Establishing a New Company, to Regain That Almost Lost Trade, Which Is Computed to Be in Value and Profit One Full Sixth Part of the Trade of the Whole Kingdom* (London: 1690), 3–4.

*monopoly of trade to Asia. The selection below gives us a glimpse
into how one of Sir Josiah's enemies viewed his political schemes
and his decision to go to war. The author mentions the negotia-
tions between the Dutch and English over the pepper port of Bantam on the island of Java, which the Dutch forced the Company
to leave in 1682.*

I shall not here go about to rake into all the miscarriages of the East-India
Company, and consequently misfortunes of the nation, but only touch
upon, and date them, from the time that the stock and Sir Josiah Childe
[Child] were at their greatest height and prosperity, in the year 1682.
When on a sudden he forsook all his old friends that first introduced
him, with great difficulty, into the Committee, and afterwards raised
him to the honor of Governor, throwing them totally out of the management . . . for not yielding and complying with his new projects, which
were foreseen by his said friends and others, to be fatal and destructive:
but he was deaf to their advice, betaking himself to new counselors that
were very ignorant in the trade. And having strengthened himself with
his new party, he proceeded to cast off [those] who had long experience
in that trade . . . and many of them did afterwards fall under his mis-
representation at court as being ill-affected to the government for selling
and lessening their stocks, and not joining in matters that the law would
not justify; so that these gentlemen, or so many of them that stood in
his way, being removed, the great ministers and chief men at Court fell
in with Sir Josiah, not doubting, but to have found a sufficient fund for
carrying on any public design either of war or otherwise: and by his great
annual presents, he could command both at Court and in Westminster
Hall [Parliament] what he pleased; and thereupon a great fleet was prepared with soldiers and all other warlike preparations; sometimes giving
out, "it was against the Dutch", which affair was managed and consulted
by Sir Josiah and a private Committee, although those worthy gentlemen
of the said Committee often declared they knew very little or nothing of
what was transacted: But in the end, the hopeful treaty that was then on
foot in London by Commissioners appointed from Holland for restoring and making satisfaction for Bantam was rejected, and new measures
taken, to the great surprise of the Dutch nation, and the considering men
amongst ourselves, who had any cognizance of the affair: till at last (matters not being yet ripe abroad to fall upon the Protestants) all this warlike

preparations ended in a war with the great and mighty emperor the Mughal and the King of Siam.

This storm thus falling upon the Mughal and the good King of Siam, our ships were employed in India for the taking and seizing of all their, and their subjects, ships and estates, even those in our ports at Bombay, though they had our factors' passes for security, without either declaration of war, or demand first made, which hath occasioned such a confusion and disorder (besides a great diminution of the nation's honor) that all our many beneficial settlements are ruined, the fruit of which we had but yet begun to taste, especially in the Bay of Bengal, which is the greatest and richest province in any known part of the universe.

DOCUMENT 4

English Opposition to Importing Cotton Textiles (1708)[4]

Although the Company began with an eye to the spice trade, it soon discovered that it could make more money buying silks and cotton textiles, known as calicos, in Persia and India and either trading them for spices in Southeast Asia or auctioning them in London. Indian calicos became all the rage in England by the end of the seventeenth century even though the "calico craze" seemed to threaten the domestic wool industry. In response, Parliament passed a series of laws restricting the wearing and use of calico in England. Daniel Defoe was a novelist and political pamphleteer and vigorously opposed the calico trade. One of his arguments was that the Company exported too much silver bullion. In 1720, for instance, he noted that all of Europe, not just England and the Company, were disadvantaged by the export of silver: "Thus, in a word, Europe, like a body in a warm bath, with its veins opened, lies bleeding to death;

---

4. Anonymous (attributed to Daniel Defoe), *Reflections on the Prohibition Act: Wherein the Necessity, Usefulness and Value of That Law, Are Evinced and Demonstrated. In Answer to a Letter on That Subject, from a Gentleman Concern'd in Trade* (London: 1708), 3–8; 13–15.

and her bullion, which is the life and blood of her trade, flows all to India, where 'tis amassed into heaps, for the enriching of the heathen world at the expense of the Christian world."[5] The selection below comes from a pamphlet written in 1708 and argues that the parliamentary ban on certain textiles has helped the economy. As was the custom at the time, the pamphlet is written in the form of a letter.

You require my opinion about the Prohibition Act . . . To which purpose I shall lay down the [following position:] That the Act of Parliament prohibiting the use of the manufactured silks, etc. of India, China, and Persia, in this nation, is one of the happiest and best laws we enjoy, relating to trade.

To prove this, there is nothing further necessary than to consider the circumstances and condition of the English manufactures for the space of six or seven years before and after that law took place, and fairly to compare them together.

As to London, the manufactures were almost lost by the coming in of the East India goods, for divers years before the obtaining of the prohibition; the [trade] generally undone, whole streets uninhabited, many of our best artists left the kingdom; some went to Holland, some to Ireland, others to Scotland. Those that remained were not half employed; the rest reduced to the greatest extremities, of whom many begged their bread, and were forced to be maintained by their parishes.

Let us now take a view of the present state and condition of trade in the places and countries aforementioned, that were thus sunk, deserted and depopulated by these Indian manufactures.

And though it must be owned that the space of eighteen months given by the Act to the dealers of those commodities, to dispose of the vast quantities of them which were then in the nation, together with the influence of the companies, and the bent of all sorts and degrees of people towards these goods, did necessarily suspend for some time the design and influence of this law; yet, God be thanked, the time is now come, when all men that do not shut their eyes, both see and feel the benefit and advantage of it.

---

5. Anonymous (attributed to Daniel Defoe), *Trade to India Critically and Calmly Consider'd, And prov'd to be destructive to the general Trade of Great Britain, as well as to the Woolen and Silk Manufactures in particular* (London: W. Boreham, 1720), 39.

In London, the maker has a market for his goods, artists and workmen are returned from their places of dispersion, and find a full employment for all their hands; the empty streets and houses are again inhabited, and higher rents are paid for them than before. Several new species of manufactures set up, and every day increasing and improving upon our hands; a great part of which are exported to our neighbors, and as much in vogue with them as they are in fashion with us.

Defoe then turns to the prospect that the act will be repealed because of the Company's influence in Parliament.

Even the united Company itself, strong and potent as it is, might, and I hope would miscarry in the attempt. The matter in contest would then be, whether the nation should sink that the Company might rise? Whether the staple manufactures of Great Britain should be once more destroyed, to exalt the tempting excesses of India, China and Persia? Whether our best artists should make a second experiment to instruct our neighbors in our miseries and improvements, that we may starve more luxuriously in Indian habits? Whether we should empty ourselves of our numbers and strength to make more room for prohibited goods? And whether the whole must be impoverished to enrich a few? If these things can be digested, such an attempt might possibly prevail. But in the meantime, I think we are safe enough; and I think we are so, because we are safe in the honor and justice of our legislators . . . by repealing this Act, poverty would come upon them [domestic manufacturers] like an armed man, suddenly, inevitably, and there would be none to help: And what perplexity, what misery, what desolation; nay, what agitations and convulsions all this might occasion, is much fitter for private reflection, than public representation. I love not to mention the beginnings of such woes, and tremble to think how they would end.

DOCUMENT 5

An Early View of Bencoolen, the Company's Pepper Port (1727)[6]

The Dutch ejected the Company from Bantam in Java in 1682, forcing the Company to search for another port from which to export pepper. In 1685 the Company established a fortified settlement at Bencoolen (Bengkulu or here written as Bencolon) on the island of Sumatra. By the end of the seventeenth century the pepper trade was in decline, as the textile trade increased, but it was still important enough to maintain a small garrison and civil administration. Alexander Hamilton, no relation to the later American Founding Father, visited the port at the beginning of the eighteenth century, and his observations indicate that Bencoolen was already developing a reputation as a poorly run and dissolute outpost.

Bencolon is an English colony, but the European inhabitants not very numerous.... The inland Princes are often at variance among themselves, and sometimes are troublesome to the trade of our colony, but as their wars are short, the English are in little danger by them. In the year 1693 there was a great mortality in the colony, the Governor and his Council all died a short time after one another, and one Mr. Sowdon, being the eldest Factor . . . [became the governor] of the colony, but not very fit for that charge, because of his intemperate drinking. [It] fortuned in his short reign, that four princes differed, and rather than run into acts of hostility, referred their differences to the [arbitration] of the English governor, and came to the fort with their plea. Mr. Sowdon soon determined their differences in favor of the two that complained; and because the other seemed dissatisfied with his determination, ordered their heads to be struck off, which ended their disputes effectually, and made them afterwards to make up differences among themselves, without troubling the English....

---

6. Alexander Hamilton, *A New Account of the East Indies* (Edinburgh: John Mosman, 1727), II.114–17.

And ever since that time there has been a succession of moderate Governors, and some have been guilty of as much temerity the other way. For in anno 1719 the then Governor, having some disputes with some of the natives, was somewhat fearful of them. On a festival day, in firing guns, a wad from one of them set fire to a house thatched with reeds, and several others contiguous to it took fire from it, so that it spread through the market place. The Governor believing it to be done maliciously by the natives, left the fort [precipitously], and got on board of a ship ... leaving some chests of money, and all the artillery, arms, ammunition, and other effects of his masters, behind him, and his garrison, following their leader, left their posts and got on board also. ...

The country above Bencolon is mountainous and woody, and I have heard that there are many volcanoes in this island; but whatever may be the cause, the air is full of malignant vapors, and the mountains are continually clothed with thick heavy clouds, that break out in lightning, thunder, rain, and short-lived storms. Their food is not fit for every stomach. Tame buffalo may be had, but no cow-beef. Poultry are scarce and dear, and so is fish, but some sorts of fruits are pretty plentiful; however, the gentlemen there live as merrily, though not so long, as in other places blest with plenty, and so sociable, that they leave their estates to the longest liver.

DOCUMENT 6

Asserting the Company's Power over Defeated Enemies (1765)[7]

After the Company defeated the combined forces of the Mughal emperor and the nawabs of Awadh and Bengal at the Battle of Buxar (October 22, 1764), a treaty was signed at Allahabad in August 1765. The following text is a selection of the eleven articles that formed the treaty between the East India Company, represented by Robert Clive and John Carnac, and the nawab Shuja-ud-daula of Awadh (r. 1754–75) and the newly installed

---

7. Anonymous, *Treaties and Grants from the Country Powers, to the East-India Company* (1774), 142–46, 164–65.

nawab of Bengal, Najm-ud-daula (r. 1765–66). Note how the
Company has already assumed the power to negotiate on behalf
of the nawab of Bengal. This selection retains the original spelling.
One lack (lakh) is 100,000.

Whereas the Right Honourable Robert Lord Clive, Baron Clive, of
Plassey, Knight Companion of the Most Honourable Order of the Bath,
Major General, and Commander of the Forces, President of the Council,
and Governor of Fort William, and of all the settlements belonging to
the United Company of Merchants of England, Trading to the East-
Indies, in the provinces of Bengal, Bahar, and Orissa; and John Carnac,
Esq: Brigadier General, Colonel in the service of the said Company, and
Commanding Officer of their Forces, upon the Bengal establishment, are
invested with full and ample powers, on the behalf of his Excellency, the
Nabob Nudjum ul Dowla, Soubahdar of Bengal, Bahar, and Orissa; and
likewise on the behalf of the United Company of Merchants of England,
Trading to the East-Indies, to negotiate, settle, and finally to conclude a
firm and lasting peace with his Highness, the Nabob Shujah ul Dowla,
Vizier of the Empire: Be it known, to all those to whom it may or shall in
any manner belong, that the above-named Plenipotentiaries have agreed
upon the following Articles with his Highness.

Article I.

A perpetual and universal peace, sincere friendship, and firm union, shall
be established between his Highness, Shujah ul Dowla, and his heirs,
on the one part; and his Excellency, Nudjum ul Dowla, and the English
East-India Company, on the other. . . .

Article II.

In case the dominions of his Highness, Shuja ul Dowla, shall at any time
hereafter be attacked, his Excellency, Nudjum ul Dowla, and the English
Company, shall assist him with a part or the whole of their forces. . . .
In the case the English Company's forces being employed in his Highness's service, the extraordinary expense of the same is to be defrayed by
him.

Article III.

. . . [Shuja-ud-daula] solemnly engages, to deliver up, to the English, whatever Europeans may in future desert from them into his country.

Article VI.

In consideration of the great expense incurred by the English Company, in carrying on the late war, his Highness agrees to pay them (50) fifty lacks of rupees, in the following manner, viz (12) twelve lacks in money, and a deposit of jewels, to the amount of (8) eight lacks, upon the signing of this Treaty (5) five lacks one month after, and the remaining (25) twenty-five lacks by monthly payments. . . .

Article VIII.

His Highness shall allow the English Company to carry on a trade, duty free, throughout the whole of his dominions.

> On November 29, 1768 a second treaty was signed between the Company's representatives and Shuja-ud-daula. Notice how the Company limits the power of its supposed ally.

Whereas unbecoming rumours have been propagated abroad, which tend to the interruption of the firm friendship, union, and confidence, formerly established between his Highness, the Nabob Shuja ul Dowla, Vizier of the empire, on one part; and the Right Honourable Robert, Lord Clive, and General John Carnac, in behalf of the deceased Nabob Nudjum ul Dowla, late Soubahdar of Bengal, Bahar, and Orissa, and the English Company, on the other part; Harry Verelst, Esq. President and Governor of Fort William, and the Council thereof, with a view to the removal of all causes of jealousy and disagreement, and the confirmation of a good disposition on both sides . . . renew and confirm the said Treaty; and moreover, out of a pure desire effectually to eradicate all doubts and jealousies, to establish the present harmony on the most durable basis, and to confirm the former Treaty, doth consent and agree, that the following words shall be inserted as an explanatory clause in the said Treaty: It is . . . agreed, that his Highness shall not entertain a number of forces, exceeding thirty-five thousand men, whether Seapoys, Cavalry, Peons, Artillery Men, Rocket Men, or troops of any denomination whatever, and of this number ten thousand are to be Cavalry, ten battalions of Seapoys . . . not to exceed ten thousand men . . . and his Highness also engages to arm none of his forces, besides the ten thousand mentioned in this Treaty, after the English manner, nor to train them in the discipline of the English troops.

DOCUMENT 7

Exposing the Company's Mismanagement (1772)[8]

The Company's affairs in India and London were badly managed in the late 1760s. Expenditures kept rising while the promise of vast revenues remained unfulfilled. And yet at the same time there was a steady stream of Company employees returning to Britain with such enormous fortunes that they were suddenly among the wealthiest men in Britain. It was not very hard for the public to understand that these "nabobs" had not made their money through their salaries. In 1772 the Company was in a financial and public relations crisis and was forced to turn to Parliament for help. The Company's enemies tried to take advantage of its weakened position by publishing exposés of the Company's maladministration in India, and particularly in Bengal, its most important and wealthy Presidency. One of the Company's most prominent critics was William Bolts, a disaffected trader who had fallen out of favor with the Company. On his return to Europe he published a scathing assessment of the Bengal administration. One of his main points, echoed by others, was that the Company could no longer be allowed to be both a trading company and a government.

It is time the attention of the Legislature [Parliament] of this kingdom should be awakened to the concerns of British subjects in the East Indies, which, notwithstanding all that has been said or written concerning India

---

8. William Bolts, *Considerations on India Affairs; Particularly Respecting the Present State of Bengal and Its Dependencies* (London: J. Almon, 1772), iii–viii.

affairs, seem to have lain neglected, as if those distant individuals were not members of the same body-politic, or did not deserve the care of the mother-country, while this government as yet receives every advantage it chooses from them as subjects.

All the inquiries which have hitherto been made, either by Government or the East India Proprietors, have stopped short at some temporary expedient. No permanent system has been yet adopted for the security of those dominions . . . but if due care be not speedily taken, the nation will not only be soon deprived of the resources at present furnished, but the possession of the very Asiatic territories themselves must be endangered.

In speaking of British subjects, we would be understood to mean his Majesty's newly-acquired Asiatic subjects, as well as the British emigrants residing and established in India. Whatever odium some among the latter may have incurred, they are not all *Nabob-makers*; they are not all *revolutionists*. And notwithstanding the prevailing notions of the ease with which immense fortunes are acquired in those parts . . . there are at this time in Bengal many poor and industrious Britons deprived even of the means of getting an honest livelihood by their best endeavors, who are deserving of a more maternal care from their native country.

Monopolies of all kinds are in their natures unavoidably pernicious; but an absolute government of monopolists, such as at present that of Bengal in fact is, must of all be the most dreadful.

There is in Bengal no freedom in trade, though by that alone it can be made flourishing and importantly beneficial to the British state. All branches of the interior Indian commerce, are, without exception, entirely monopolies of the most cruel and ruinous natures; and so totally corrupted, from every species of abuse, as to be in the last stages towards annihilation. Civil justice is eradicated, and millions are thereby left entirely at the mercy of a few men, who divide the spoils of the public among themselves; while, under such despotism, supported by military violence, the whole interior country, where neither the laws of England reach, or the laws or customs of those countries are permitted to have their course, is no better than in a state of nature.

Let such who place their security in the pretended degeneracy or effeminacy of the natives recollect, that they are those very natives who fight our Indian battles; which they have sometimes done without a single musket being fired by our European troops, to whom they have, on many occasions, shown themselves no way inferior in personal courage. Perhaps it may appear to a considerate man, upon reflection, that it is only the exaggerated fame of what has passed which preserves the possession of things at present, and that the power of the English in India may cease to be formidable as soon as that power becomes well understood. . . . Let those who despise the Asiatics farther reflect, that the most despicable reptiles will turn when trod upon; and that history abounds with instances of nations driven into madness by the cruelty of oppression. It must certainly be best to avoid giving occasion for such extremities. Be it then the more laudable object, as most worthy of this nation, to secure the hearts of the natives by establishing a due administration of justice, and by encouraging manufactories and a free trade in the inland parts of the subjected provinces, without which they can never prosper. Happily for the European invaders of India, there is such an equipoise between Muslims and Hindus, as makes the government of the whole, by a few foreigners, more practicable in Bengal than it would be in any other part of the world; so that if Justice did but hold the scale, that superiority might perhaps be for ages maintained.

DOCUMENT 8

An Erotic Encounter (1789)[9]

The first British novel set in India was written by a woman, but published anonymously in 1789. As was conventional at the time, it was written in the form of letters, in this case from Sophia Goldborne, who has just arrived in Calcutta, to her great friend in England, Arabella. The plot is wafer-thin—will Sophia find a husband?—but the novel reveals what daily life was like in Calcutta during the 1780s. Toward the end of the story Sophia and her soon-to-be husband, Doyly, witness a grand procession by the nawab (or nabob) of Bengal. By the 1780s the nawab had lost all power but was still an object of curiosity to the British.

[The nawab's] guards, on the occasion, were no less in number than his whole battalion of black troops, fine-looking fellows—and their

---

9. Anonymous, *Hartly House, Calcutta . . . Reprinted from the Edition of 1789* (Calcutta: Thacker, Spink and Co., 1908), 270–73.

complexions gave a grandeur to the scene. Their uniform and their turbans were new, and their fire-arms glittering bright; and I would have
given the world on the instant to have been a Nabobess, and entitled to
so magnificent a train.

Seven elephants of the first magnitude were led by their keepers, in
like manner as our sumpter-horses; seated on the back of one of which,
on a throne of indescribable splendor, was his Nabobship, with a man
behind him, holding a superb fan, in the very act of collecting the breezes
in his service.

The throne was composed of gold, pearls, and brilliants, and the
Nabob's dress worth a sovereignty; nor was ever animal more grandly
caparisoned than the no less honored than exalted elephant on which
he rode.

His state-palanquin followed, and was by much the most desirable
object my eyes ever encountered, and differently built to those used by
the Europeans....

I was stationed nearly on a level with the throne as it passed along;—
and judge, Arabella, if you can, of the ambitious throbs my heart experienced, when I saw the Nabob's eyes, sparkling with admiration, fixed
on my face! Doyly turned pale, and the procession advanced—yet were
my charms unforgotten by him; for he twice or thrice looked back, and
constituted me the envy of the women, and the torture of the men; in a
word, my conquest was as evident as the noon-day sun: and who would
dream of a mortal female's refusing an enthroned adorer, with the wealth
of the Indies at his feet?

Down knelt the half-reasoning animal, at the entrance of the Governor's house, for his illustrious master to alight;—so powerful, yet so
docile!—so gentle, yet so terrific in appearance! I am dying, Arabella, to
have one of these very elephants at my command.

I thought of Lady Wortley Montague's account of her being noticed
by the Grand Seignior, when spectator of a Turkish procession, on the
Nabob's observation of me;—but there was this difference between the
circumstances—namely, that the attention the Sultan paid that Lady was
merely *en passant*; whereas this Nabob of Nabobs proved, in the face of
all the people, how long he bore me in mind—that is, how deeply he was
wounded—and I hold myself in expectance of hearing more of him.

DOCUMENT 9

The Spectacle of Tipu Sultan's Death (1799)[10]

Tipu Sultan, the ruler of Mysore in Southern India, loomed large in the British imagination. His wealth, power, and aggressive opposition to the Company made him the quintessential "Oriental despot." The last Anglo-Mysore war began in early 1799 and on May 4 British and allied troops stormed his fortress in his capital, Seringapatam (Srirangapatna), defeated his army, and killed him. His death removed a potent threat to Company-controlled territory and allowed the Company to continue its expansion. Even after his death, the British public continued to be fascinated by him. The following selection is an advertisement for a performance of the storming of Tipu's fortress that was placed in the London Times only a few months after news of his death arrived in England.

EXTRAORDINARY NOVELTY
MISS SMITH'S BENEFIT
ROYAL AMPHITHEATRE, ASTLEY'S,
WESTMINTER-BRIDGE

THIS EVENING will be presented (never performed), an entirely New, Grand, Historical Spectacle of Action, founded on the recent Occurrences in India, called The STORMING of SERINGAPATAM; or, The DEATH OF TIPPOO SAIB. The Songs, Duets, and Choruses, written by Mr. Upton, and the whole of the Spectacle invented, composed, arranged, and got up by Mr. ASTLEY, jun. with entire new and superb Dresses, new and extensive Scenery and Machinery, new Music, etc. In the course of the Piece, the following most striking Scenery will be displayed: 1. An Indian Sea-Port; 2. A View near the River Cavery; 3. The Banqueting Garden of Tippoo Sultaun; 4. The Commander in Chief General Harris's Marque; 5. A Correct View of the City of Seringapatam, with the whole of Tippoo's Army, Elephants, Camels, etc. in Motion; together with the Mysore Army, consisting of Peadars,

---

10. *The Times* (London), Monday, September 30, 1799, 1.

Bungaries, Serdars forming a Camp near Fort Periapatam; 6. A British Battery opening a brisk Fire on Tippoo's Picquet Guard, particularly the Blowing up of a Powder Mill; 7. A View of the British and Company's Army crossing the River Cavery, with Pontoons, and a Portable Bridge of Boats; 8. The fortification of Seringapatam, with the Springing of a Mint; 9. External View of Tippoo's Palace, with his Two Sons firing from the Window; and 10th, The Zenana and City on Fire, with a Variety of Circumstances that attended this important Conquest. Preceding the above, at Half past Six o'clock precisely, 1st Time these 3 Years, and for this Night only, a Serio, Comic, Nautical Ballet of Action by Mr. Astley, jun. called TRUE BLUE; or, BRITISH BULL DOGS. Principal Characters Miss Smith, and Mr. Astley, jun. (being most assuredly his last appearance this Season). By particular Desire, and also for this Night only, the Operational Ballet of HONI SOIT QUI MAL Y PENSE. . . . In the intervals of the above three capital Amusements, the Performances of the VENTRILOQUIST, various Comic Songs, Equestrian Exercises, Slack Rope Vaulting, Troop of Jumpers, etc. To conclude with a New, Superb, Comic Pantomime, by Mr. Astley, jun. called The DAEMONS TRIBUNAL. Doors to be opened at Half past 5 o'clock.

DOCUMENT 10

Arguments for Opening India to Missionaries (1805)[11]

By the beginning of the nineteenth century, pressure was building on the Company and Parliament to allow missionaries into India. The standard argument made by those who opposed opening India to missionaries was that proselytization would likely cause such resentment among Indians, and especially within the army, that it might set off a mutiny or general rebellion. Others, such as the Reverend Claudius Buchanan, one of the Company's

---

11. Claudius Buchanan, *Memoir of the Expediency of an Ecclesiastical Establishment for British India; Both as the Means of Perpetuating the Christian Religion among Our Own Countrymen; and as a Foundation for the Ultimate Civilization of the Natives* (London: T. Cadell and W. Davies, 1805), 12–13, 30–32, 39.

*chaplains in Calcutta, argued that the Company had a moral obli-
gation to "civilize" Hindus and Muslims (or Hindoos and Mahometans) and that, moreover, doing so would actually strengthen
and protect Company rule.*

This is the only country in the world, civilized or barbarous, where no
tenth is paid; where no twentieth, no hundredth, no thousandth part of
its revenues is given by government, for the support of the religion of that
government; and it is the only instance in the annals of our country where
church and state have been dismembered. We seem at present to be trying the question, "Whether religion be necessary for a state;" whether a
remote commercial empire having no sign of the Deity, no temple, no
type of anything heavenly, may not yet maintain its Christian purity, and
its political strength amidst Pagan superstition, and a voluptuous and
unprincipled people?

The Mahometans profess a religion, which has ever been characterised
by political bigotry and intemperate zeal. In this country that religion still
retains the character of its bloody origin; particularly among the higher
classes. Whenever the Mahometan feels his religion touched, he grasps
his dagger. . . . We have consolidated our Indian empire by our power;
and it is now impregnable; but will the Mahometan ever bend humbly to
Christian domination? Never, while he is a Mahometan.

Is it then good policy to cherish a vindictive religion in the bosom of
the empire for ever? Would it not accord with the dictates of the soundest
wisdom to allow Christian schools to be established, where the children
of poor Mahometans might learn another temper. . . . The adult Hindoo
will hardly depart from his idol, or the Mahometan from his prophet,
in his old age; but their children, when left destitute, may be brought up
Christians, if the British parliament please.

. . . Is there not more danger of losing this country, in the revolution
of ages, (for an empire without a religious establishment cannot stand
for ever,) by leaving the dispositions and prejudices of the people in
their present state, than by any change that Christian knowledge and an
improved state of civil society, would produce in them? . . . At present,
there is no natural bond of union between us and them. There is nothing
common in laws, language or religion, in interest, color or country. And
what is chiefly worthy of notice, we can approach them in no other way
than by the means of our religion.

The moral state of the Hindoos is represented as being still worse than that of the Mahometans. . . . neither truth, nor honesty, gratitude, nor charity, is to be found in the breast of a Hindoo. How can it be otherwise? The Hindoo children have no moral *instruction*. If the inhabitants of the British isles had no moral instruction, would they be moral? The Hindoos have no moral *books*. What branch of their mythology has not more of falsehood and vice in it, than of truth and virtue? They have no moral *gods*. The robber and the prostitute lift up their hands with the infant and the priest, before an horrible idol of clay painted red, deformed and disgusting as the vices which are practiced before it.

No Christian nation ever possessed such an *extensive* field for the propagation of the Christian faith, as that afforded to us by our influence over the hundred million natives of Hindoostan. No other nation ever possessed such *facilities* for the extension of its faith as we now have in the government of a passive people; who yield submissively to our mild sway, reverence our principles, and acknowledge our dominion to be a blessing. Why should it be thought incredible that Providence hath been pleased . . . to subjugate this Eastern empire to the most civilized nation in the world, *for this very purpose?*

DOCUMENT 11

An Anti-Missionary Perspective (1808)[12]

Three years after Claudius Buchanan published his plea for the establishment of an official church of India, an anonymous Company military officer, thought to be Charles Stuart, published his own book refuting Buchanan's arguments point by point. Stuart argued that the 1806 mutiny at Vellore, in Southern India, proved that proselytism would undermine the Company's control over its Indian subjects. More remarkably, he also "vindicated" Hindus by assembling textual and personal evidence to show that Hindus were moral individuals and that Hinduism was nothing

---

12. A Bengal Officer (attributed to Charles Stuart), *Vindication of the Hindoos from the Aspersions of the Reverend Claudius Buchanan, M.A. with a Refutation of the Arguments Exhibited in His Memoir* ... (London: R. and J. Rodwell, 1808), 74, 77, 81–85.

*like Buchanan's caricature. Perhaps most astonishingly, Stuart
rebuffed Buchanan's claim that Hindus have too many holidays
and should be content with only the (Christian) Sunday holiday
by pointing out that menial labor is extremely hard. By the early
nineteenth century we find few accounts of Indians by the British
that are both sympathetic and aware that daily life was grueling.
The perspective in the selection below is therefore noteworthy
for being more the exception than the rule.*

"Another obstacle," says Mr. Buchanan, "to the improvement of the
natives, is the great number of their holydays." . . . Mr. Buchanan asks,
"in what other country would it be considered a means of promoting the
happiness of the common people, to *grant them* so great a portion of the
year, to spend in idleness and dissipation?"

Is this, the dignified language of an European Clergyman, to a free
people? or, is it not rather, the language of a master to his servants; of a
despot to his slaves; of a pedagogue to his scholars; or, of a West-Indian
planter to the wretched sons of Africa, whom fortune hath doomed to
unlimited subserviency in his household?

Averse, however, to the official recognition of any Hindoo holydays;
Mr. Buchanan observes, that, "to those natives employed in the public service,
the fifty-two Sundays are sufficient for rest from bodily labor:" and he sub-
joins, in a note, that "no people require fewer days of rest, than the Hindoos;
for they know nothing of that corporal exertion, and fatigue, from labor,
which, in other countries, render regular repose so grateful to the body and
spirits."

We must hence conclude, that this gentleman has never proceeded up
the river Ganges, and witnessed the exertions of the boatmen, in tracking
against the stream, for three months successively, up to the frontier stations.

Does he conceive that there is no fatigue attendant on the labor of thus
daily contending with a strong current, for eight or ten hours together,
exposed to the fervid rays of an Indian sun, in the months of April, May,
and June; the hottest season of the year?—or, does he not think it labo-
rious, in the rainy season, when the river has overflowed its banks, to
see men under the necessity of tracking, more than half the day perhaps,
through the water; commonly breast-high; and often more? Does not
such labor imply corporeal exertion, and consequent fatigue? . . .

Has Mr. Buchanan never stepped into the country, to view the hus-
bandman at his plough, or the farmer irrigating his field, in the sultry

season of the year, when there is scarcely a breath of air in the heavens; while the lord of the soil sits basking in the comforts of a good habitation; though scarcely able to respire under the oppressive weight of a light calico Banian [cotton clothing]?

Has he never witnessed, at this season, the labor of excavating tanks; of sinking wells; of embanking rivers; of cutting down the corn, in the hot months of March and April; of individuals carrying burdens on their heads, of forty pounds weight, on a journey or a march, for fifteen or twenty miles in a forenoon? Or has he not even looked about him at the Presidency; and cast an eye to the dock-yards, the Custom-house, and the store-rooms of the merchants? He would there discover, that the London porter has vastly the advantage of the Indian; his labor being comparatively limited, in loading his cart or wagon; while, masts and yards of ships, the largest timbers, and all the paraphernalia of the merchant, in the East, are commonly transported, a considerable distance, on men's shoulders.

Has he not seen women, constantly throughout the day, carrying large jars of water, on their heads, or their hips, for domestic purpose? or seen them act as laborers, in carrying brick, mortar, clay, etc. in baskets, on their heads? ...

To people so employed, would he deny the recreation of a holyday; were it even a holyday, for the mere purpose of recreation. . . . Would it then be reasonable thus to deprive the Hindoos of their calendar, and compel them to substitute our own? This would strike at the very root of their religion.

DOCUMENT 12

A British Prisoner of War Returns Home from India (1824)[13]

In the second half of the eighteenth century, the Company fought four wars against the southern Indian state of Mysore. Although the Company was eventually able to defeat Mysore, a large number of British soldiers and sailors were captured or held captive

---

13. James Scurry, *The Captivity, Sufferings, and Escape, of James Scurry, Who Was Detained a Prisoner during Ten Years, in the Dominions of Hyder Ali and Tippoo Saib. Written by Himself* (London: Henry Fisher, 1824), 252–55.

by Mysore. Some of these men died in captivity, but others were given new lives as infantrymen in Mysore's army. James Scurry was one of those men. He had been a sailor in the British navy and had been captured by a French ship, whose captain eventually transferred him, and others, to Haider Ali, the ruler of Mysore. Scurry lived for ten years in Mysore but eventually managed to escape. When he returned to England he wrote a narrative of his time as a captive, but it was not published until after his death. In his narrative, Scurry goes to great length to depict Haider Ali and his son, Tipu Sultan, as tyrants—he is forcibly converted to Islam by being circumcised—but he also reveals that Mysore's rulers offered him a new life as a Muslim soldier with a wife and two children. The selection below is from his book's final chapter. It was written by his editor and describes Scurry's life once he returned home.

From his long confinement in India, and his involuntary conformity to Asiatic manners, he had nearly forgotten the customs of his early years, and the delicate refinements of his native land. To the wearing of English clothes he felt the greatest aversion; nor could he even sit, except according to the manner to which he had been so long accustomed. Of a knife and fork he had almost lost the use, nor could he eat anything with comfort, only in the style to which stern necessity had compelled him to submit. His language was broken and confused, having lost nearly all its vernacular idiom. His body was disfigured with scars; and his skin was likewise so deeply tinged with the heat of the climate in which he had so long resided, and by the rays of the sun, to which he had been so much exposed, that it was only a few shades removed from black. It so nearly resembled the swarthy complexion of the negroes, that he might have passed through Africa without being at all noted for the singularity of his color. These combined peculiarities exposed him to several inconveniences, and brought upon him many an eager gaze, and many a curious inquiry, and pointed observation.

On leaving London, he travelled by coach to Exeter, to visit his friends, but stopping at an inn on the road to dine, instead of conforming to the customs of his fellow-travellers, he followed those which he had been obliged to adopt in Asia, to the no small amusement of his companions, and the equal astonishment of the people belonging to the house. His bones, offal, and rejected food, without ceremony were thrown on the floor, no regard being paid either to company or carpets; and when admonished of the impropriety of his conduct, his inattention to the hints which were given, and perseverance in domestic irregularity, only served to confirm those who witnessed his singularities, that he was either deranged, or some foreigner totally unacquainted with the refinements of civilized life.

DOCUMENT 13

Advice to a Young Company Employee Traveling to India for the First Time (1827)[14]

By the early nineteenth century the Company's British employees were routinely expressing racist attitudes toward Indians. The following passages were written by a middle-aged soldier as advice to a young cadet or writer preparing to leave for India.

On first landing . . . I regret to say that, among the luxuries of the East, sensual pleasures stand preeminent, and cannot be too severely reprobated, or too carefully guarded against . . . it becomes a matter of lounge for a young man first to resort to drinking-houses, and thence to repair to scenes of profligacy, which I cannot describe, where, at noon-day, he indulges his before uncorrupted passions, until at last he becomes an habitual debauchee, and sinks into the grave an early victim to sensuality, perhaps without a friend to soothe his sad pillow of disease, or to close his dying eyes.

A young man, on joining his regiment, which happens to be stationed in some remote part of the country . . . finds every officer of the regiment living separate, and *keeping native women*. With these women they spend the greater part of their time, to the entire neglect of the more intellectual and rational pursuits of men. With such examples before his eyes; at a

---

14. John Shipp, *Memoirs of the Extraordinary Military Career of John Shipp, Late a Lieutenant in His Majesty's 87th Regiment. Written by Himself* (London: Hurst, Chance, and Co, 1827), 1.281–87.

solitary place, far from any large station, where good society is to be met with; deprived of the company of his brother officers, and doomed to a life of unvaried monotony; the inexperienced youth who joins the regiment is but too often induced to fall in with the prevailing folly; and, at length, instigated by others, and seduced by the amorous professions of a mercenary fair (or rather black) one, he consents to keep her and her numerous attendants. This connection being formed, he may, probably, ask himself this question: "Who is it that I have thus selected to be my companion, the sharer of my fortunes, the participator of my cares, the solace of my woes, and the partner of my bed?" If he does not know, I will tell him, in plain terms, but without the least exaggeration. She is a black woman, laboring under the influence of dark idolatry; so ignorant as to be wholly unfit for your companion; so immodest and lascivious as to be disgusting; jealous in her disposition; cruel in her nature; despotic to your household; extravagant in her expenditure; and her sole object in connecting herself with you, is the mercenary prospect of having herself, and those whom she may please to call her relations, kept at your expense. This, young man, is a true character of the object you have selected to spend your days with.

To a consciousness of the consequences of this illicit and vicious connection, a man is first awakened by the inharmonious jabber of half a dozen black bantlings surrounding his table, which groans under huge dishes of curry and rice. When each little darkling is ushered into the world, gold bangles are expected for the mother, silver ones for the nurses, new dresses for all the lady's relations, and a grand dinner to her whole circle of acquaintance,—at least fifty persons.

Thus goes on the life of a man who has once formed a connection of the kind I speak, till at last he awakens to reflection and remorse, and distractedly asks himself—"What have I been doing?" . . . Has he love?—No. Has he peace of mind? No. Are the children which he is supporting his own?—Very doubtful, even this . . . In short, he has nothing but the gratification of a sensual appetite to set against all the misery which must inevitably be entailed on him by its indulgence. His moral principles become vitiated; his prospects for the future cannot fail to be blighted; and he has little but wretchedness to look forward to. I have myself known officers intimately who have formed these sad connections, and who, although they certainly did not absolutely become Muslims or Hindus, yet have been so infatuated as to lose, to all appearance, every thought for the present, and all regard for the future.

DOCUMENT 14

Missionary Sentiments (1830)[15]

The poem below concerns a sati, or woman who is burnt to death on her husband's funeral pyre. The practice of sati was not common but it became an easy way for evangelicals to caricature Hinduism as barbaric.

Sonnet—The Suttee
David Lester Richardson

Her last fond wishes breathed, a farewell smile
    Is lingering on the calm unclouded brow
    Of yon deluded victim. Firmly now
She mounts, with dauntless mien, the funeral Pile
Where lies her earthly lord. The Brahmin's guile
    Hath wrought its will—fraternal hands bestow
    The quick death-flame—the crackling embers glow—
And flakes of hideous smoke the skies defile!
    The ruthless throng their ready aid supply,
And pour the kindling oil. The stunning sound
    Of dissonant drums—the priest's exulting cry—
The failing martyr's pleading voice have drowned;
While fiercely-burning rafters fall around,
    And shroud her frame from horror's straining eye!

---

15. David Lester Richardson, *Literary Leaves or Prose and Verse, Chiefly Written in India* (London: W. H. Allan & Co. Leadenhall Street, 1840), 1.303. For biographical information and the text of the poem, see Mary Ellen Gibson, *Anglophone Poetry in Colonial India, 1780–1913: A Critical Anthology* (Athens: Ohio University Press, 2011), 137–39.

DOCUMENT 15

A Lady's Arrival in Calcutta (1820s; 1850)[16]

Fanny Parkes lived in India during the first half of the nineteenth century and wrote a lively, entertaining, and revealing account of her stay. Unlike other narratives written around the same time, she displays an exuberance for life in India and a fondness for Indians, although we must remember that, as the wife of a mid-level colonial official, she enjoyed privileges that were available to few Indians. The following selection is from the beginning of her book, when she first arrives in Calcutta in the early 1820s. It gives us her initial impressions of India, but it also shows what kinds of things and people were most important to the newly arrived.

Calcutta has been styled the City of Palaces, and it well deserves the name. The Government House stands on the Maidan, near the river; the city, and St. Andrew's Church, lie behind it; to the left is that part called Chowringhee, filled with beautiful detached houses, surrounded by gardens. . . .

The houses are all stuccoed on the outside, and seem as if built of stone. The rent of unfurnished houses in Chowringhee is very high; we gave 325 rupees a month for ours, the larger ones are from 4 to 500 per month.

The style of an Indian house differs altogether from that of one in England.

The floors are entirely covered with Indian matting, than which nothing can be cooler or more agreeable. For a few weeks, in the cold season, fine Persian carpets, or carpets from Mirzapore are used. . . . The most beautiful French furniture was to be bought in Calcutta of M. de Bast, at whose shop marble tables, fine mirrors, and luxurious couches were in abundance. Very excellent furniture was also to be had at the Europe shops, made by native workmen under the superintendence of European

---

16. Fanny Parkes, *Wanderings of a Pilgrim, in Search of the Picturesque, during Four-and-Twenty Years in the East; with Revelations of Life in the Zenana* (London: Pelham Richardson, 1850), 20–23.

cabinet and furniture makers; and furniture of an inferior description in the native bazaars.

. . . The number of servants necessary to an establishment in India, is most surprising to a person fresh from Europe: it appeared the commencement of ruin. Their wages are not high, and they find themselves in food; nevertheless, from their number, the expense is very great.

A very useful but expensive person in an establishment is a sircar; the man attends every morning early to receive orders, he then proceeds to the bazaars, or to the Europe shops, and brings back for inspection and approval, furniture, books, dresses, or whatever may have been ordered: his profit is a heavy percentage on all the purchases for the family.

One morning our sircar, in answer to my having observed that the articles were highly priced, said, "You are my father and my mother, and I am your poor little child: I have only taken two annas in the rupee, dustoorie."[17]

This man's language was a strong specimen of Eastern hyperbole: one day he said to me, "You are my mother, and my father, and *my God!*" With great disgust, I reproved him severely for using such terms, when he explained, "you are my protector and my support, therefore you are to me as my God." The offence was never repeated. . . . they dress themselves with the utmost care and most scrupulous neatness in white muslin . . . the turban often consists of twenty-one yards of fine Indian muslin, by fourteen inches in breadth, most carefully folded and arranged in small plaits; his reed pen is behind his ear, and the roll of paper in his hand is in readiness for the orders of the sahib. . . .

Dustoorie is an absolute tax.[18] The durwan will turn from the gate the boxwallas, people who bring articles for sale in boxes, unless he gets dustoorie for admittance. If the sahib buy any article, his sirdar-bearer will demand dustoorie. If the mem sahiba purchase finery, the ayha must have her dustoorie—which, of course, is added to the price the gentleman is compelled to pay. . . . It appeared curious to be surrounded by servants who, with the exception of the tailor, could not speak one word of English; and I was forced to learn to speak Hindostanee.

---

17. There are sixteen annas to the rupee.

18. Parkes mentions a doorman (durwan), traveling salesmen (boxwallas, or boxwallahs), British man (sahib), British woman (mem sahiba or memsahib) and nursemaid (ayha, or ayah).

To a griffin, as a new comer is called for the first year, India is a most interest-ing country; every thing appears on so vast a scale, and the novelty is so great.

In *December*, the climate was so delightful, it rendered the country preferable to any place under the sun; could it always have continued the same, I should have advised all people to flee unto the East.

My husband gave me a beautiful Arab [horse], Azor by name, but as the Sa'is [groom] always persisted in calling him Aurora, or a Roarer, we were obliged to change his name to Rajah. I felt very happy cantering my beautiful high-caste Arab on the race-course at 6 a.m., or, in the evening, on the well-watered drive in front of the Government House....

The arrival of the 16th Lancers, and the approaching departure of the Governor-general, rendered Calcutta extremely gay. Dinner parties and fancy balls were numerous; at the latter, the costumes were excellent and superb.

DOCUMENT 16

Touring India (1837; 1866)[19]

Emily Eden was a contemporary of Fanny Parkes, but their writ-ing styles and attitudes toward India and Indians were starkly different. Eden was the sister of the governor general, Lord Auck-land (George Eden), and accompanied him on a long tour across northern India in 1837. The following passages are taken from the beginning of her book, published in 1866 in the form of letters to her sister, and give us a taste of how she lived in India as the sister of the Company's most powerful man. As was the custom, she abbreviates names, so that her brother, for example, is written simply as G., for George.

The first selection describes the scene when the governor general's troupe arrived at Patna.

It was a Hindu holiday. I must do the Hindus the justice to say that they make as many holidays out of one year as most people do out of ten;

---

19. Emily Eden, *"Up the Country": Letters Written to Her Sister from the Upper Provinces of India* (London: Richard Bentley, 1866), 1.15–17, 18–20, 27–28.

and I am not at all sure whether a small importation of Hindus would not be acceptable to you, to accompany your boys to school as regulators of their school-days. It would be a safeguard against their being over-worked. The whole bank [of the river] was lined with natives bringing immense baskets of fruit for "the Ganges to look at," as the Nazir (the head of the governor general's native servants) expressed it; and they were dipping their baskets into the river with their graceful salaams and then bowing their heads down to the water. They are much more clothed here than in Bengal, and the women wear bright crimson veils, or yellow with crimson borders, and sometimes purple dresses with crimson borders, and have generally a little brown baby, with a scarlet cap on, perched on their hips. I wish you would have one little brown baby for a change; they are so much prettier than white children. Behind these crowds of people, there were old mosques and temples and natives' houses, and the boats of rich natives in front with gilded sterns, and painted peacocks at the prow. In short, just what people say of India; you know it all, but it is pretty to see and I mean the "moral" of my Indian experience to be, that it is the most picturesque population, with the ugliest scenery, that was ever put together.

The second selection describes the governor general's durbar (darbar), or assembly.

Then there was company at luncheon; and, at half-past three, G. held a durbar. Some of the rajahs came in great state—one with a gold howdah on his elephant; another had a crimson velvet covering to his carriage, embroidered with gold, and they all had a great many retainers. To some of them G. gave gold dresses and turbans, and we went behind a screen to see Mr. T. and the other gentlemen help the rajahs into their gold coats. The instant the durbar was over we set off, an immense party, to see Patna, and we saw the Durgah, one of the largest Mussulman temples there is, and then went to part of the town where the streets are too narrow for a carriage, and where they provided . . . elephants for us, and we poked along, through herds of natives, to a curious Sikh temple, which is kept up by contributions from Runjeet Singh. The priest read us a little bit of their Bible (not the Koran), very much to our edification, and he brought out a sword in a red scabbard, which they worship, and they gave George some petitions, and then we went home to another great dinner.

The final selection is from her description of an event that occurred at Ghazipur, to the west of Patna. At the end of the selection she mentions Kent, a county in southern England.

There were two women on the landing-place with a petition. They were Hindu *ladies*, and were carried down in covered palanquins, and very much enveloped in veils. They flung themselves on the ground, and laid hold of G., and screamed and sobbed in a horrid way, but without showing their faces, and absolutely howled at last, before they could be carried off. They wanted a pardon for the husband of one of them, who, with his followers, is said to have murdered about half a village full of Mussulmans, and these women say he did not do it, but that the Nazir of that village was his enemy, and did the murders, and then laid it on their party. These little traits are to give you an insight into the manners and customs of the East, and to open and improve your mind, etc. After we had made our way through all of these impediments, we rested for a time, and then went to see the cantonments, and to evening service, which was read by two of the gentlemen remarkably well. Then we came back to a great dinner, and one of the longest I ever assisted at. . . . The dinners are certainly endless, and I do not wonder they think us very rapid at Government House. There is sometimes half an hour between the courses. A Mr. S., the judge, sat on one side of me, and after some discourse the man seemed to know his Kent! . . . Visions of country balls and cricket matches came back. He knew Eden Farm and Penge Common; in short, I liked him very much, and I think he too was refreshed with the reminiscences of his youth.

DOCUMENT 17

The Beginning of a Disastrous War (1838)[20]

In the late 1830s the Company became increasingly alarmed by the expansion of the Russian Empire into Central Asia, Russian influence over Iran, and Russian efforts to influence the ruler of

---

20. *The Oriental Herald and Colonial Intelligencer: Containing a Digest of Interesting and Useful Information from the Indian Presidencies and the Eastern Nations* (London: Madden & Co., 1839), Vol. III (January to June), 100–102.

Afghanistan, Dost Mohammad. To counter Russian and Iranian encroachment, the governor general, Lord Auckland, decided to establish his own puppet in Afghanistan. In 1838 he joined forces with the Sikh leader Ranjit Singh and the former ruler of Afghanistan Shah Shuja and sent a large Company army into Afghanistan to depose Dost Mohammad and install Shah Shuja. In October of that year Lord Auckland issued a document, known as the Simla Manifesto, spelling out the reasons for the invasion. The final paragraphs are reproduced below and give a rosy picture of what was expected to happen. Dost Mohammad was indeed defeated and deposed, but the Company's army was eventually forced to withdraw in January 1842. As the army, composed of more than 16,000 soldiers and camp followers, left Kabul it was attacked repeatedly, and almost every person was killed or died of exposure. It was a humiliating defeat. Shah Shuja was assassinated shortly after the British left Kabul. The foreign power referred to in this manifesto is Iran.

The Right Hon. the Governor-General of India having with the concurrence of the Supreme Council, directed the assemblage of a British force for the service across the Indus, his Lordship deems it proper to publish the following exposition of reasons which have led to this important measure. . . .

The welfare of our possessions in the East requires that we should have on our western frontier an ally who is interested in resisting aggression and establishing tranquility, in the place of chiefs ranging themselves in subservience to a hostile power, and seeking to promote schemes of conquest and aggrandizement.

After a serious and mature deliberation, the Governor-General was satisfied that pressing necessity, as well as every consideration of policy and justice, warranted us in espousing the cause of Shah Sooja-ool-Moolk, whose popularity throughout Afghanistan had been proved to his Lordship by the strong and unanimous testimony of the best authorities. Having arrived at this determination, the Governor-General was further of opinion that it was just and proper, no less from the position of Maharaja Runjeet Singh, than from his undeviating friendship towards the British Govt., that his Highness should have the offer of becoming a party to the contemplated operations. Mr. Macnaghten was accordingly deputed in June last to the Court of his Highness, and the result of his mission has been the conclusion of a tripartite treaty by the British Government, the Maharaja, and Schah [sic] Sooja-ool-Moolk, whereby his Highness is guaranteed in his present possessions, and has bound himself to co-operate for the restoration of the Schah to the throne of his ancestors. . . . by the measures completed or in progress it may reasonably be hoped that the general freedom and security of commerce will be promoted; that the name and just influence of the British Government will gain their proper footing among the nations of Central Asia; that tranquility will be established upon the most important frontier of India, and that a lasting barrier will be raised against hostile intrigue and encroachment.

His Majesty Schah Soojah-ool-Moolk will enter Afghanistan surrounded by his own troops, and will be supported against foreign interference and factious opposition by a British army. The Governor-General confidently hopes that the Schah will be speedily replaced on his throne by his own subjects and adherents, and when once he shall be secured in power, and the independence and integrity of Afghanistan established, the British army will be withdrawn. The Governor-General has been led to these measures by the duty which is imposed upon him of providing for the security of the British crown; but he rejoices that in the discharge of his duty he will be enabled to assist in restoring the union and prosperity of the Afghan people. Throughout the approaching operations British influence will be sedulously employed to further every measure of general benefit, to reconcile differences, to secure oblivion of injuries, and to put an end to the distractions by which for so many years the welfare and happiness of the Afghans have been impaired. Even to the chiefs whose hostile proceedings have given just cause of offence to the British Government it will seek to secure liberal and honorable treatment, on their tendering early submission, and ceasing from opposition to that course of measures which may be judged the most suitable for the general advantage of their country.

DOCUMENT 18

First Reactions in Britain to the News of the Rebellion (1857)[21]

The Company came to an end because of a rebellion that began in May 1857 and quickly spread throughout much of northern India. In Britain, the news of the Rebellion, or Mutiny as it was generally called at the time, prompted heated debate about the causes and the most appropriate course of action to remedy the situation. The following excerpts are from the Illustrated London News *and show the level of anxiety and anger in Britain. The author incorrectly suggests that Russia may have played a role in the Rebellion.*

The state of affairs in India may well excite the alarm of the nation; but it will do more: it will excite its courage and its wisdom.... Our house in India is on fire. We are not insured. To lose that house would be to lose power, prestige, and character—to descend in the rank of nations, and take a position more in accordance with our size on the map of Europe than with the greatness of our past glory and present ambition. The fire must be extinguished at any cost. All ordinary considerations give way before the greatness and suddenness of such a danger. Fortunately the Indian Government has vigour enough for the emergency, and if it have not means will be supported by all the wealth, power, energy, and resources of Great Britain. In this case there will be no grudging. The nation knows its work, and woe betide the statesman who shall stand between it and the consummation!

By the next mail we shall in all probability hear that the Mutiny has been confined to the one Presidency in which it originated; that it has been quenched in the blood of the mutineers; that every native regiment that took part in it has been annihilated; that the murderers of Englishmen, women, and children in Delhi and Meerut have been signally avenged; and that such an example has been made as will strike Terror into the minds of the native population, and keep it there for a century to come. Whether it were desirable that we should win India by the sword is no

---

21. *Illustrated London News*, XXXI.867, Saturday, July 4, 1857, 1–2.

longer a question. Having won it we must keep it. The sword procured it, and the sword must guard it. We rule both by the dread of our present power, and by the remembrance of our past invincibility. The dread and remembrance must be maintained at all costs and hazards, or the day will but too speedily come when British dominion in the East will be of as little account as the might of Sesostris or the throne of Nebuchadnezzar, or any thing else that has passed away for ever.

[The author then discusses possible causes of the Rebellion and ends with the suggestion "that Russian emissaries are, and have long been, at work, not only at the outposts and frontiers of our Indian Empire, but in the very heart of the country."]

There are many persons in England who laugh at this idea, who treat it as a monomania or a Russophobia, and think that the alleged intrigues of Russia in the East are idle bugbears, engendered only in the diseased brains of bigoted politicians. But those who know Russia best, and India most, do not treat this supposition with scorn; but, on the contrary, find too many reasons for believing that every act of hostility against us— whether it springs from Cabul, Burmah, or Persia, or whether it arises within the circle of our own frontier—is more or less connected with Russian intrigues and Russian money. . . . All these things, and many others, must be taken into account. . . .

What the nation has now to do is to punish. After punishment will come inquiry as to the best and most available means of prevention for the future. And among these means two of the most essential are—a large increase of the European force, both of officers and men, and an extension of railway throughout the length and breadth of India . . . so that these forces may be easily moved at the shortest notice from one extremity of India to the other. . . . We owe the people of India much. We owe them peace, we owe them security, we owe them good government; and if we pay them these debts many blessings will follow. By these means we may be enabled to make amends for the arbitrariness of our rule by its justice and beneficence. Let us not make the mistake of thinking we owe them Christianity, and of endeavouring to force it upon them before they are ripe to receive it. Christianity was never yet successfully inculcated by the sword, and never will be. Soldiers and railroads are what are needed in India; and if the savage outbreak of Meerut and Delhi prove the means of providing both, that Mutiny, distressing as it is, will have, in all probability, the great merit of being the last, and of preparing the way for the permanent pacification and real prosperity of India.

SELECT BIBLIOGRAPHY

The list below represents the principal histories of the East India Company that are referenced in this book. All other secondary and primary sources may be found in the footnotes.

Alavi, Seema. *The Sepoys and the Company: Tradition and Transition in Northern India 1770–1830*. Delhi: Oxford University Press, 1995.

Bayly, C. A. *Indian Society and the Making of the British Empire*. Hyderabad: Orient Longman, 1990.

Bowen, H. V. *Revenue and Reform: The Indian Problem in British Politics 1757–1773*. Cambridge: Cambridge University Press, 1991.

———. *The Business of Empire: The East India Company and Imperial Britain, 1756–1833*. Cambridge: Cambridge University Press, 2008.

Carson, Penelope. *The East India Company and Religion, 1698–1858*. Woodbridge: Boydell Press, 2012.

Chaudhuri, K. N. *The English East India Company: The Study of an Early Joint-Stock Company 1600–1640*. London: Frank Cass & Co LTD, 1965.

———. *The Trading World of Asia and the East India Company, 1600–1760*. Cambridge: Cambridge University Press, 1978.

Dirks, Nicholas B. *The Scandal of Empire: India and the Creation of Imperial Britain*. Cambridge, MA: Harvard University Press, 2006.

Erikson, Emily. *Between Monopoly and Free Trade: The English East India Company, 1600–1757*. Princeton: Princeton University Press, 2014.

Farrington, Anthony. *Trading Places: The East India Company and Asia 1600–1834*. London: British Library, 2002.

Furber, Holden. *Rival Empires of Trade in the Orient, 1600–1800*. Minneapolis: University of Minnesota Press, 1976.

Guha, Ranajit. *A Rule of Property for Bengal: An Essay on the Idea of Permanent Settlement*. New Delhi: Orient Longman LTD, 1982.

Keay, John. *The Honourable Company: A History of the English East India Company*. New York: Macmillan Publishing Company, 1991.

Lawson, Philip. *The East India Company: A History*. London: Longman, 1987.

Marshall, P. J. *The Impeachment of Warren Hastings*. London: Oxford University Press, 1965.

———. *Bengal: The British Bridgehead, Eastern India 1740–1828*. Hyderabad: Orient Longman, 1990.

Ogborn, Miles. *Indian Ink: Script and Print in the Making of the English East India Company*. Chicago: University of Chicago, 2007.

Pearson, Michael. *The Indian Ocean*. London: Routledge, 2006.

Philips, C. H. *The East India Company 1784–1834*. Manchester: Manchester University Press, 1961 [1940].

Prakash, Om. *European Commercial Enterprise in Pre-Colonial India*. Cambridge: Cambridge University Press, 1998.

Robins, Nick. *The Corporation That Changed the World: How the East India Company Shaped the Modern Multinational*. London: Pluto Press, 2006.

Roy, Tirthankar. *The East India Company: The World's Most Powerful Corporation*. New Delhi: Allen Lane, 2012.

Stern, Philip J. *The Company State: Corporate Sovereignty and the Early Modern Foundations of the British Empire in India*. New York: Oxford University Press, 2011.

Sutherland, Lucy S. *The East India Company in Eighteenth-Century Politics*. Oxford: Oxford University Press, 1952.

Teltscher, Kate. *India Inscribed: European and British Writing on India, 1600–1800*. Delhi: Oxford University Press, 1995.

Travers, Robert. *Ideology and Empire in Eighteenth-Century India: The British in Bengal*. Cambridge: Cambridge University Press, 2007.

Turnbull, C. M. *The Straits Settlements, 1826–67: Indian Presidency to Crown Colony*. London: Athlone Press, 1972.

Wild, Antony. *The East India Company: Trade and Conquest from 1600*. New York: Lyons Press, 2000.

INDEX

Index